HEAVILY
BUTLER
RIVER
ISLAND
Generals Cut
Butler's Rice Mill Chimney 1858
GENERALS
RIVER
ISLAND
MIDDLE
RABBIT I.
ALTAMAHA
CHAMPNEY
Wood Cut
ISLAND
BROUGHTON
SOUTH
ALTAMAHA
Dents Creek
WOODED
EVELYN 448
GRANTLY 345
ELIZAFIELD 724
Shell Road
WOODED
Broadfield
HEAVILY WOODED

# Planter Management and Capitalism in Ante-Bellum Georgia

COLUMBIA UNIVERSITY STUDIES IN THE HISTORY OF AMERICAN AGRICULTURE

*Number 13*

# Planter Management and Capitalism in Ante-Bellum Georgia

*The Journal of Hugh Fraser Grant Ricegrower*

EDITED WITH
INTRODUCTORY CHAPTERS BY
ALBERT VIRGIL HOUSE

---

*1954*

COLUMBIA UNIVERSITY PRESS

NEW YORK

*Library of Congress Catalog Card Number: 53–8756*

PUBLISHED IN GREAT BRITAIN, CANADA, INDIA, AND PAKISTAN
BY GEOFFREY CUMBERLEGE, OXFORD UNIVERSITY PRESS,
LONDON, TORONTO, BOMBAY, AND KARACHI.

MANUFACTURED IN THE UNITED STATES OF AMERICA

# Columbia University Studies in the History of American Agriculture

EDITED BY

# Foreword

EVERY PERSON interested in the history of the South and especially in gaining a better understanding of the capitalistic agricultural economy of the Southern plantation has reason to be grateful to Mr. Albert V. House for this highly informing book. In 1938 Mr. House had the good fortune to acquire the Journal and Account Book of Elizafield, a Georgia rice plantation. So replete is this document with details and insights of plantation life in the pre-Civil War South that Mr. House resolved to make its contents available to the general public and particularly to students of Southern ante-bellum history. Everyone, including the late Everett E. Edwards, long the fountain head of research in agricultural history in this country, from whom Mr. House sought advice as to the wisdom of the proposed undertaking gave enthusiastic encouragement. Unfortunately, World War II and a long span of military service delayed publication.

In the pages which follow Mr. House not only provides us with the Elizafield Journal and Account Book covering the years 1839–60 but, in chapter form, with an interpretative analysis. These chapters—"Elizafield and Its Owners," "The Culture of Rice in Georgia," "Finance, Supply, and Management Practices," and "The Milling and Marketing of Georgia Rice, 1830–60"—add greatly to the value of the Journal itself, enhanced as it is by careful editorial comment in the form of footnote citations. Only when one reads the account of the source material examined by Mr. House in checking the reliability of the Journal and Account Book and interpreting the contents thereof can he fully appreciate the extent of his contribution.

It is natural that this book should appear as one of the volumes in the Columbia University Studies in the History of American Agriculture. The series was instituted for the double purpose of lending encouragement to those who would enrich American historiography by adding to it worthwhile material; and secondly, by making available illuminating historical documents which otherwise might not be of service. This book, in full measure, contributes to these ends.

H. J. C.
R. G. T.

*Columbia University*
*September, 1953*

# Preface

At the mid-point of the twentieth century, touring motorists driving south from historic Savannah on U.S. Route 17 usually speed through the entire length of coastal Georgia in a few short hours. Their route provides glimpses of wild semi-tropical undergrowth, drainage canals, and run-down shacks of wayside, marginal farmers. Here and there the momentary sight of the sea or a glistening inlet or bay relieves the monotony of the trip. At Midway, about twenty-seven miles southwest of Savannah, they come upon a perfect New England-type church, which was planted in this part of the South over 150 years ago, with Puritan-style tower, white fences, etc. The highway also proceeds through Riceboro, the old Liberty County seat, whose name was derived from the plentiful production of that staple in the area. As the journey continues through miles of swampy, tangled undergrowth, the presence of a group of live oaks and a few chimney bricks in small clearings suggest the life that existed along this route a century or more ago. Eventually the motorists enter the turpentine country with its "stripped" slash-pine trees, each with a metal trough to catch the drippings of resinous gum from the wounded trees. The small coastal town of Darien, with its library, courthouse, filling stations, and farm-supply establishments, soon comes into view. This metropolis on the banks of the river bearing its name was a distributing center and seaport more than a century ago, when its population was a mere 500 souls.

After passing through this small commercial mart, the route once again enters a long stretch of swampland. Along built-up causeways and new modern bridges the road hops from island to island in the estuary of the Altamaha River system. Halfway across this maze of creeks, branches, and streams lies the old Butler Plantation which was the scene of Fanny Kemble's uncritical observations on Southern life, based on her brief and unhappy exile from the stage due to her marriage to a Georgia planter in 1834. Her husband's establishment was one of the largest and best-equipped rice plantations along the Georgia rice coast. Today it specializes in satisfying the curiosity of tourists and producing market garden products.

As our tourists finally complete the crossing of the Altamaha River swamplands and reach dry land at a slight rise near a bend in the road, they are confronted with a large roadside sign announcing the location nearby of the Boys' Estate Orphanage, the supposed site of some early Spanish missions. Unless our motorists are determined to sleep that night in Florida, they may be tempted to visit the estate and examine the supposed ruins. Since they are not specialists on local history, they will not know that recent scholarship has established quite definitely that the ruins are the remnants of an old plantation sugarhouse. A short journey of a few rods down a dirt road leads them to the entrance to the orphanage. The winding drive through slash-pine, scrub oak, and wild bush growth leads to a modern building which is the headquarters of Boys' Estate. Here they may learn that this entire area is the location of Elizafield Plantation, one of the oldest and most productive of rice plantations on the Georgia rice coast.

In the early decades of the nineteenth century, Elizafield's owners and the proprietors of neighboring plantations grew sugar cane on their upland acres and extracted the juice at mills housed in tabby sugarhouses. In the 1830's rice became the favorite crop produced on the lowlands of Elizafield and those of Hopeton, Altama, Evelyn, Grantley, Broadfield, Hofwyl, and New Hope plantations located near-by on the south side of the south branch of the Altamaha River. The volume and value of the rice produced on these plantations a century ago was surpassed in ante-bellum Georgia only by the planters in the Savannah River region. One of these Altamaha plantations today is a truck farm, and the others are shooting preserves or public and private show places. Brunswick, with its famous Marshes of Glynn, is located thirteen miles farther south, and both St. Simons Island and Sea Island, with their charming blend of modern resort atmosphere and the remains of colonial life, lie just offshore. However, the plantations on the banks of the Altamaha have unique significance because they represent a chapter in the history of the economic life of coastal Georgia which did not reach its peak until the eve of the Civil War.

Some of the records of the capitalistic agricultural economy practiced on these river plantations have been preserved. Those dealing with Hopeton, the largest of these plantations, are in the Southern Historical Collection at the University of North Carolina Library at Chapel Hill; the plantation journal and account book of Elizafield (hereinafter referred to as the Elizafield Journal) covering the years 1839-60 is, however, in the possession of the writer. While less extensive than the Hopeton records, the Elizafield Journal, which is reproduced in this volume, contains considerable evidence of the complicated nature of the production, financial, and marketing problems faced by its owner during those years. The Elizafield Journal was acquired by the writer in 1938, and its contents were summarized in a brief article in *Agricultural History*, XIII (October, 1939), 208-17. In the summer of 1941 a Grant-in-Aid from the Social Science Research Council made possible a field trip to search through various depositories of Southern history, to visit the scene of the life here portrayed, and to talk with various descendants of the owners of these plantations as well as with local historical scholars in Savannah, Darien, and in Glynn County.

The completion of this project was interrupted by four and one-half years of military service, but the many friends and helpful critics who assisted in the early stages of the research have urged and contributed to its completion. They all have provided stimulation, guidance, and assistance to the writer. Foremost in this group is the late Everett E. Edwards of the United States Department of Agriculture, who first introduced the writer to research in the field of agricultural history. His many bibliographical and editorial suggestions, as well as his continuing friendly encouragement, were of assistance at every stage and have made possible the completion of this study. Dr. J. G. De Roulhac Hamilton, formerly Director of the Southern Historical Collection at the University of North Carolina Library, made available all pertinent manuscripts in that unusual depository. He also, with infinite charm and wisdom, provided a framework of fact and interpretation of the Old South which could not help but be enlightening to this student of northern ancestry who was about to enter upon a study of the plantation system. Still another great interpreter of American life and institutions who has influenced this endeavour was the late Charles A. Beard. Personal association with this grand old scholar as a colleague at the Johns Hopkins University in 1940-41, when the project was in the planning stages, affected the perspective and scope of the investigation. Mrs. Margaret Davis Cate of Brunswick and Sea Island, Georgia, gave generously of her extensive knowledge of the history of persons, places, and practices in Glynn County, Georgia, the locale of this study. She also served as guide and advance agent in arranging visits to various plantations and the homes of descendants of the planters mentioned in the Elizafield Journal of Hugh Fraser Grant.

Others who provided leads and suggestions are Professor E. Merton Coulter of the University of Georgia, Professor Fletcher M. Green of the University of North Carolina, Dr. Herbert A. Kellar of the McCormick Historical Association, Madison, Wisconsin, and E. E. Carter of the United States Forestry Service, Washington, D.C. Likewise, the following Georgia residents and specialists in the history of the coastal area of that state were helpful: Miss Bessie Lewis of Pine Harbor, Miss Miriam and Miss Ophelia Dent of Hofwyl plantation, the late Cator Woolfolk of Altama plantation, Mrs. F. D. Aiken (a descendant of Hugh Fraser Grant) of St. Simons Island, Georgia, and Mr. R. J. Wood and the late Marmaduke Floyd of Savannah. The staffs of the following university and college libraries extended every courtesy: University of Georgia, Duke University, University of North Carolina, Yale University, Harvard Business School, and Clemson Agricultural College, Clemson, South Carolina. Comparable consideration and assistance was received from the staff personnel of the Georgia State Department of Archives and History at Atlanta; Chatham County Court House, Savannah; and Glynn County Court House in Brunswick, Georgia. By far the richest source on the local history of the Georgia coast consulted was the valuable collection of newspapers and local documents of every sort maintained at Hodgson Hall, Savannah, the headquarters for the Georgia Historical Society, where Mrs. Marmaduke Floyd presided for many years.

Thanks are also due to Dean Louis M. Hacker and Dean Harry J. Carman, both of Columbia University, for guidance and stimulation at various stages in the accomplishment of the project.

Finally, I find myself in the not unusual position of academic researchers in that I am indebted to my wife, who typed the documentary portion of the manuscript and encouraged the study continuously.

Albert V. House

*Endicott, New York*

# Contents

## Part I: The Production and Marketing of Rice in Ante-Bellum Georgia



## Part II: The Journal and Account Book 1834–61 of Hugh Fraser Grant of Elizafield Plantation Glynn County, Georgia

## Part III: Directory, Notes on Sources and Index

# *Illustrations*

# PART I

## The Production and Marketing of Rice in Ante-Bellum Georgia

# Chapter One

## ELIZAFIELD AND ITS OWNERS

A COASTAL PLAIN averaging about twenty miles in width extends along the entire hundred-odd-mile coast line of Georgia. It includes salt marshes, tide swamps, sea islands, and flat areas on the mainland. The soil varies from swamp muck to clay loam; from sand to clay to sandy loam. A variety of trees including pines, cabbage palmettos, and live oaks thrive on these soils, although the undergrowth occasionally is of smothering thickness.[1] Numerous creeks, inlets, bays, and rivers cut the coast line as it wanders out to sea and back into the pine barrens. The Savannah River, which serves as the boundary with South Carolina on the north, and the St. Marys River, performing a similar function as to Florida on the south, are the waterways most widely known to "alien" population from outside the state. However, the Altamaha River system is the more extensive and drains the hills and valleys of north and central Georgia, emptying into the Atlantic at a point approximately midway down the shore line from north to south. This river, fed by its tributaries, breaks into several branches as it approaches salt water. Its usually slow-moving waters continuously deposit a rich alluvial soil over a wide area along its banks.[2] A plentiful supply of both rainfall and sunshine, plus the long growing season of a semitropical climate, make this a desirable agricultural district for staple crops.

During colonial times some indigo and sea-island cotton were raised along this estuary and on the myriad islands composing

[1] R. M. Harper, "Agriculture in Lower Georgia, 1850-1880," *Georgia Historical Quarterly*, VI (June, 1922), 107.

[2] William S. Irvine, *Brunswick and Glynn County, Georgia* (Brunswick, 1902), p. 34.

the river delta, but these crops were supplanted by sugar cane in the second decade of the nineteenth century. The dominance of sugar was short-lived since by the 1830's the planters of the region were shifting over to rice as their main crop. The presence of a usually gentle tide which flowed for some eight or more miles up the various branches of the river, as well as the availability of fertile swampland, encouraged this move. The impetus for this change came largely from the Carolinas where the old rice kings were faced with declining profits due to rising costs, soil deterioration, exhaustion of protecting timber in the uplands, and the disastrous erosion which resulted from the introduction of clean culture crops such as cotton in the piedmont. They extended their activities to the Savannah River region by the 1820's and to the Altamaha area by the 1830's, where the crops produced rivaled those of the older regions both in quality and quantity. These new rice lands, which were built up from the frontier, jungle-like swamps of Georgia, often functioned as outpost plantations for the parent establishments to the north. The wealthy planters of the Charleston and Georgetown areas often established their sons or other relatives as managers of these newly cleared areas and even turned over title to them to their offspring when the Georgia plantations were going concerns.[3]

The Carolina rice growers, however, were not the only planters to sense the potential returns from large-scale rice production in the tide-flow region of Georgia. Native Georgians had been raising some rice on St. Simons Island and in the Savannah River basin since before the American Revolution. In the early decades of the nineteenth century, they too turned to large-scale rice production. Dr. Robert Grant, a native of Leith, Scotland, was one of the earliest of the island planters to expand his activities to the mainland. He had arrived in South Carolina during the closing years of the American Revolution and soon married Sarah Foxworth, a member of one of the leading families of that state. Sometime before 1800 he established residence on St. Simons and began securing title to tide swampland on the south bank of the Altamaha River, some six to eight miles inland from its mouth. By June, 1809, he had purchased a substantial parcel

[3] Manigault Plantation Records, 1833-37, 5 volumes, Southern Historical Collection, University of North Carolina Library. See also Albert V. House, Jr., ed., "Charles Manigault's Essay on the Open Planting of Rice," *Agricultural History* XVI (October, 1942), 184-93.

of land on Six-Mile Creek, a very small tributary of the Altamaha, from William Mien and Robert Mackey.[4] Five hundred adjoining acres were added on October 9, 1817, and three hundred more on November 3, 1818, by purchase and grant. Several hundred acres of highland and pineland adjoining to the south were secured by 1825.[5] The combined acreage, totaling upwards of fifteen hundred acres, was known as Elizafield Plantation.

Dr. Grant's plantation was excellently located. He had a reasonable balance of tide swampland for staple crops, pinelands for living quarters for his family and slaves, and uplands for the production of food crops of corn, peas, turnips, and yams for his labor force. His neighbors constituted a distinguished band of successful planters, many of whom were active in the political and economic life of the state. Included in this group were members of the Troup, Dent, Huger, and Butler families.[6] Upstream a few miles James Hamilton Couper presided over Hopeton as manager of one of the largest and most successful of ante-bellum sugar and rice plantations.[7] Although the Grant property extended to the South Altamaha River, the clearings on the highlands which contained the plantation buildings, garden, mills, barns, and burial ground were on "a small fresh water creek which was dug open for use as a part of the Brunswick-Altamaha Canal, cut about a century ago. The distance from . . . the river is the better part of a mile by the present straight canal, and was farther by the small winding creek."[8]

Definite evidence that the Grant family was in residence at Elizafield by 1813 is found at the family burial ground, both on the earliest headstone of a son who died in that year, and in the bricks of a corner block of the graveyard wall.[9] In the years immediately following, Dr. Grant constructed a sugarworks on

[4] Glynn County Records, Brunswick, Georgia, Deed Book G, reproducing indenture transferring Elizafield from Robert and Sarah Grant to Hugh Fraser Grant. Paper by Marmaduke Floyd, in *Georgia's Disputed Ruins*, E. M. Coulter, ed. (Chapel Hill, 1937), p. 132, reports having studied other Glynn County Records which indicate that Dr. Robert Grant secured title to some of this land in the 1790's.

[5] Glynn County Records, Deed Book G, p. 353, and Deed Book H, p. 341.

[6] U.S. Census Office, Seventh Census, 1850, MSS, volume on Glynn County, Georgia, p. 5.

[7] James Hamilton Couper Papers, Southern Historical Collection, University of North Carolina Library.

[8] Floyd, *Georgia's Disputed Ruins*, p. 40.

[9] *Ibid.*, p. 134.

a high piece of land, which may once have been the south bank of the Altamaha River before it changed its course.[10] This site was near a high-tide landing place on Six-Mile Creek. Somewhat later the creek was dug out for use by rice flats and other small craft. When the ill-fated Brunswick-Altamaha Canal was dug through the Grant property in 1833, the water supply for the creek leading to the sugarworks was severely depleted. Both the sugarworks and the landing place were soon abandoned. A new landing place was constructed on the canal itself with a causeway connecting with the high ground. This was contemporaneous with the shift to large-scale rice culture and the building of a rice mill near the new outlet to the river.[11]

Late in 1833 Dr. Robert Grant decided to retire from the life of an active planter and return with his wife to a quiet existence on St. Simons Island. His children had grown to maturity, and all, with the possible exception of Charles, had left the family home. One daughter, Elizabeth, had been married to Robert Hogan at Elizafield in January, 1827, and was living in the North. A son, Dr. H. Allen Grant, had married wealth in New York City. Still another son, Hugh Fraser Grant, had settled as a rice planter in South Carolina after marrying Mary Elizabeth Fraser of Georgetown. His father-in-law was the Reverend Hugh Fraser for whom he had been named, while his mother-in-law had been a Buford before her marriage.[12]

[10] The ruins of these tabby (oystershell stucco) buildings have been identified erroneously as those of the Spanish Mission of Santo Domingo de Talaje. This was the result of amateur historical research, a regional effort to attract and intrigue tourists, and the well-developed publicity sense and unyielding conviction of a recent owner of Elizafield, who gave the property to the state as an historical shrine. These myths were exploded definitely by a study of Marmaduke Floyd of Savannah and an archaeological report on the Elizafield ruins by James A. Ford. These two documents were combined with the observations of Thomas Spaulding of Sapelo Island on sugar culture and published in 1937 by the University of North Carolina Press under the title of *Georgia's Disputed Ruins*, E. M. Coulter, editor. Needless to say, the scars left on the participants by the disputes and disappointments in this entire controversy have not yet wholly disappeared.

[11] Floyd, *Georgia's Disputed Ruins*, p. 136. Many of the details here taken from the study by Floyd were confirmed later by the writer in the course of his personal inspection of the plantation area in the summer of 1941.

[12] Many of the details of the history of the Grant family were obtained during an interview with Mrs. F. D. Aiken of St. Simons Island, a great-great-granddaughter of Dr. Robert Grant. She received much of her information from the lips of her grandmother, who lived at Elizafield before 1860 and was well versed on various items of family history.

In disposing of his Altamaha lands Dr. Robert Grant drew up extensive plans for his future welfare and that of various members of his family. He divided Elizafield into two nearly equal parts, one of which was to retain the name Elizafield and the other to be known as Evelyn. On December 21, 1833, he executed two indentures with somewhat similar financial provisions.[13] The portion that was to be called Elizafield was transferred to his son, Hugh Fraser Grant, then living in South Carolina, while the Evelyn acres were assigned to his son Charles. Each indenture called for the payment of annuities of $500 each to Dr. Robert Grant and his wife, Sarah, during their lifetimes, while a comparable lifetime annuity of thirty-five pounds sterling was to be paid to Helen Grant of Scotland, a relative of Dr. Grant. In addition a lump sum payment of $12,500 was required of each son. Hugh Fraser Grant received title to 105 slaves for Elizafield, while Charles Grant acquired 113 slaves for Evelyn. As added insurance for his future, Dr. Grant also required his son, Charles, to sign a mortgage to guarantee fulfillment of the provisions of the agreement.[14] The records do not show that any such mortgage was arranged between Hugh Fraser Grant and his father. This may indicate merely that this son had other financial resources and was able to make the cash payment or that the father had faith in this son's intention and capacity to provide for the annuities. On the other hand, this significant omission may reveal that Dr. Grant was painfully aware of the comparative managerial and financial abilities and habits of his two sons and felt called upon to exercise some pressure on Charles.

The later history of the operation of the two plantations under his sons' management shows that the father was wise to take this precaution. Hugh Fraser Grant went on to build up his ricelands, both in area and productiveness, and become one of the leading planters and citizens of the region. Charles, on the other hand, was continually in financial trouble. As early as April, 1837, he had removed to Savannah, and his father had taken back all the land and the slaves whom the son had not yet sold off to keep his head above water. This, however, did not include twenty-seven acres of choice Evelyn swampland adjoining Elizafield which Hugh Fraser Grant had purchased from

[13] Glynn County Records, Deed Book G, p. 353, and Deed Book H, p. 341.
[14] *Ibid.*, Deed Book K, pp. 346-49.

Charles for $2,500 on July 20, 1834.[15] Charles tried his hand twice again as a planter at Evelyn, but each time he sank so deeply in debt that his brother had to redeem the plantation for him. Various other planters, including J. C. Tunno and T. P. Huger, purchased the plantation after Dr. Grant's death but without great success. Each time that these acres reverted to the estate, Hugh Fraser Grant operated them during the interim as part of his own enterprise. Entries describing these operations were made in his Elizafield Journal. In some years they were incorporated with the notations on Elizafield activities; in other years they were maintained separately. In the course of the years during which Evelyn was being passed back and forth between owners, the narrow strip containing the 345 easternmost acres and running parallel to present U.S. Route 17 came to be known as Grantly and was operated separately. In the 1850's Hugh Fraser Grant planted these lands, which were sometimes referred to as Grubby Neck, and kept the record of their crops in his Elizafield Journal reproduced in this volume.

By the time of his father's death in 1843, Hugh Fraser Grant was well established as one of the leading plantation entrepreneurs of the Georgia coast. He served as executor of his father's estate in conjunction with his mother. In this capacity by March, 1844, he secured a settlement with his brother Charles of the Evelyn mortgage held by his parents.[16] Hugh Fraser Grant had been planting these acres himself for two years previous, but in December, 1844, he advertized the entire Evelyn property for sale in a Savannah newspaper.[17] Meanwhile, having weathered several rough years, he launched a program of expansion and opened up new lands for cultivation. These efforts included the partial clearing of Champney's Island, which he later sold to J. C. Tunno. The island was a natural extension of his property, since it lay just across the narrow South Altamaha River from Elizafield. He also purchased considerable acreage at Carteret's Point for the sum of $6,000. These lands were located a few miles down the river and were planted to provisions crops for his slaves and to sea-island cotton. His annual tax returns for the decade 1840-50 showed that he claimed ownership at one time to approximately 1,790 acres. These included three hundred

[15] *Ibid.*, p. 515.
[16] *Ibid.*, p. 341.
[17] Savannah *Daily Georgian*, December 23, 1844.

acres of riceland, fourteen hundred acres of pineland (some of which were located some distance inland at the site of his summer home), and ninety acres of second-quality hammock lands. According to the manuscript census returns for 1850 he reported $40,000 worth of real estate and upwards of $60,000 in personal property, including slaves.[18] These figures were raised to $50,000 and $73,000 respectively by the census of 1860.[19] This wealth was attained despite disastrous real estate losses due to fire and a succession of severe blows to his prosperity, including a deadly epidemic of measles among his slaves and the ruinous flooding of his lands on various occasions due to sudden freshets and high tides.

The Elizafield Journal also shows that Hugh Fraser Grant acquired the stature of a substantial and leading citizen in the county. His family grew with the arrival of numerous children; he himself was confirmed in the neighboring Episcopal Church and later became the financial bulwark of the congregation. He accepted the captaincy of the local militia known as the Glynn County Rangers. Finally, he found himself continuously named as administrator, trustee, or coexecutor of the estates of his neighbors upon their departure from this world. His business sense and integrity were such that he was somewhat overburdened with duties of this sort. His tribulations in settling these estates often extended over a period of years for each estate and illustrate the peculiar nature of property under the plantation system.

As a going concern the plantation with its slaves and debts to factors could not be broken up into parcels of land and human flesh for sale. However, buyers with adequate financial resources to enable them to take over the entire plantation were not readily available. Occasionally sons or close relatives with adequate training in plantation management who possessed the confidence of the factors with claims against the estate or new sources of financial assistance were at hand. Even in such an eventuality, the remaining heirs could not be satisfied promptly, since even a successful plantation entrepreneur probably would require several good years to accumulate sufficient profits to enable him to pay

[18] U.S. Census Office, Seventh Census, 1850, MSS, volume on Glynn County, Georgia, p. 5.

[19] *Ibid.*, Eighth Census, 1860, MSS, volume on Glynn County, Georgia, pp. 221-29.

off the heirs. However, disasters and setbacks continually were the lot of planters in the two decades before the Civil War, owing to the whims of nature, the competition of new land, and the fluctuations of world prices for cotton, rice, and other staples. In these circumstances it is little wonder that the myriad duties of executors extended over many years before final settlement. The routine often followed on the Georgia rice coast was as follows: first, let a son or relative of the deceased have a try at it, usually because the will had suggested the same; second, if he failed, a neighbor or neighbor's son took a flyer at running the acreage; third, the executor or trustee might plant the acres himself; and finally, as a last resort, the property might be sold at auction.[20] The last was the fruit of desperation and pressure from the heirs and the factors who had advanced money to run the plantation during the life of the deceased. Such drastic action often was the only recourse for the executor of even the finest properties if he wished to wipe out the debts which accumulated rapidly during the trial-and-error search for a capable operator or purchaser of the plantation.

While the property and community responsibilities of Hugh Fraser Grant were expanding in the 1840's a pattern of family life developed at Elizafield which illustrated many of the finer points of plantation living. One son and five daughters participated in the routine which was followed at the plantation from November to April each year. In keeping with the usual custom of the Georgia coast, the family was removed each summer to a camp or summer house "far enough back from the coast so that the smell of salt water was no longer in the air." This reflected the contemporary belief that some sort of miasma or disease-breeding fog was given off by the marshes after sundown, which spelled fever and possible death to white men. Modern science has shown that this "fog" was malaria-bearing mosquitoes. The black slave population had a large degree of immunity from the bite of the Anopheles species of mosquitoes and thus could remain in the area at all times. During the late spring and early fall months the plantation owners such as Mr. Grant commuted

[20] Savannah *Daily Georgian*, November 18, 1839, Sales Notice of New Hope Plantation; *ibid.*, December 31, 1839; *ibid.*, December 12, 1840, Estate of B. F. Cater; *ibid.*, December 11, 1841, Estate of John G. Bell; *ibid.*, December 23, 1844, Sales Notice of Evelyn; *ibid.*, December 31, 1844. See also Journal No. 2, May 31, 1841, J. H. Couper MSS, Southern Historical Collection, University of North Carolina Library.

each day to their holdings to check on the progress of the crop and other management problems. Late each afternoon, however, they hitched up their horse-drawn carriages and headed for the summer home or camp, usually eight to ten miles distant. Some old accounts tell of the sight of certain planters laying on the whip rather heavily in a race to reach the acknowledged dividing line between safe and dangerous territory before the declining sun completed its downward course and disappeared over the western horizon. Some years the entire Grant family spent the summer in the interior of the state and on one occasion passed the hottest months at Catoosa Springs, a resort in northern Georgia. As the daughters grew up, some were sent to the North for the summer and even to Europe for extended periods. The happiest and fullest months, however, seem to have been spent at Elizafield when the entire family could be present at the spot where their roots were deepest.

There are practically no physical remains still standing of the numerous buildings of the plantation as they existed in the mid-nineteenth century. The brick chimney of the old mill still remains, heavily covered with climbing vines. The walls of the sugarhouse, which have been mistaken by some for an old Spanish mission, are fairly intact and show the outlines of the structure. A compilation of data on Georgia plantations, prepared in connection with the bicentenary of Georgia in 1933, contains considerable information on the buildings, gardens, and life at Elizafield.[21] While subject to the usual reservations as to accuracy on specific details found in all such anniversary publications prepared by local writers, the sketch of Elizafield gives much of the atmosphere of the milieu in which the Grants lived from 1840 to 1860. A "large two-story frame dwelling graced by Corinthian columned porticos" is mentioned. A school house, a formal garden, a Bermuda grass lawn, an oystershell walk, and the various slave quarters and outbuildings are also listed.[22] A visit to the scene confirms the grace and beauty of the site with its large live oaks, many of which are still standing.

Hugh Fraser Grant presided over the daily routine of the up-

[21] Loraine M. Cooney, comp., and Hattie C. Rainwater, ed., *Garden History of Georgia*, 1733-1933 (Atlanta, 1933), pp. 50-51. The sketch of Elizafield was prepared by Florence Marye. The map of Elizafield garden was drawn by P. Thornton Marye.

[22] *Ibid.*

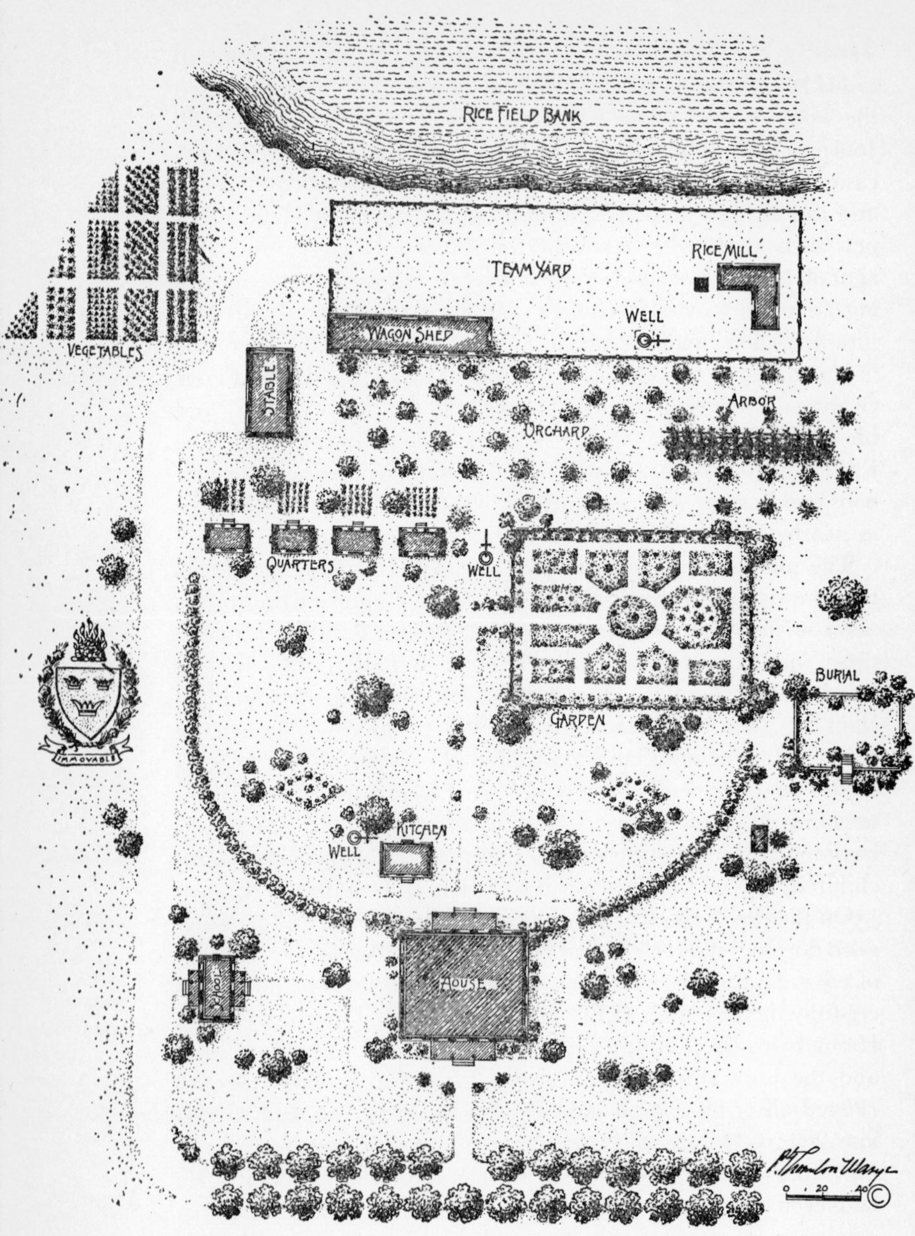


GARDEN AND GROUNDS OF ELIZAFIELD PLANTATION

A reconstructed sketch by P. Thornton Marye which appeared in Loraine M. Cooney, compiler, and Hattie C. Rainwater, editor, *Garden History of Georgia, 1733–1933* (Atlanta, 1933), pp. 50–51. Reproduced by permission of the copyright owner, The Peachtree Garden Club of Atlanta, Georgia.

wards of 125 souls who lived at Elizafield. He usually referred to his labor force as "the people" or "the hands." He never used the word "slaves" when mentioning his chattels in the Elizafield Journal. The usual holidays at Christmas and other special occasions were granted to the Negroes. Shoes, blankets, osnabergs, and rations were dispensed at appropriate intervals. Hand products such as shingles, made by the slaves in their leisure time, actually were purchased by their master. Their diseases, including "the itch," measles, cholera, and gonorrhea, were treated by sure-fire, homemade remedies, listed conveniently near the index sheets of the Elizafield Journal. Meanwhile, Hugh Fraser Grant enjoyed his "seegars," purchased by the hundreds, and his casks of Madeira and port wines, which he imported. The Elizafield Journal also lists various feminine purchases of ribbons and hats, as well as numerous bills from doctors and dentists in nearby Brunswick and more distant Savannah.

The plantation society in which the Grant family moved carried the names of many of the citizens of Georgia who are famous in the history of the ante-bellum South. Prominent among these were the Hugers, Kings, Troups, Butlers, Dents, Bryans, Bonds, and Coupers. The plantations of these distinguished clans lay mostly in the Altamaha River estuary, although by blood ties, proximity, and association they were also usually included in the general category of "Sea Island Society." Social intercourse and intermarriage within this closely knit group was common and were illustrated by the marital history of the Grant children, one of whom married a Troup and another a King.

On the eve of the Civil War the economic wealth and personal good fortune of Hugh Fraser Grant and his family were worthy of envy. During the preceding decade he had been planting successfully the rice lands of Elizafield, Grantly, and much of Evelyn. He had weathered a series of setbacks due to disease, fire, floods, and the uncertain price of rice on the world market. He had cleared all of his capital indebtedness to his parents and to various factors. He was, of course, indebted to his factors for operating expenses each year, but such a situation was customary. He had even accumulated enough surplus cash to try his hand at owning some stock of the Marine Bank of Savannah. His only son, who bore his name, reached manhood's estate in 1859 and was ready to assume his rightful place in society as a planter. Arrangements to this end were completed on April 8, 1861, by the sale of forty-one slaves and the 345 acres of Grantly to the son for $60,000. The terms were generous and allowed Hugh Fraser Grant, Jr., considerable leeway. He paid his father only $3,000 as a down payment on the sale contract which called for $60,000 to be paid sometime or $30,000 paid in ten yearly installments beginning with March 1, 1862, plus interest."[23] The war and military duty prevented fulfillment of the terms of the sale contract, and on August 26, 1867, Hugh Fraser, Jr., signed over title to the Grantly acres to his mother, with his father and himself as trustees for the mother.[24]

The story of the effect of the war years on Elizafield, its owners, and its people cannot be pieced together from the Elizafield Journal reproduced in this volume. With the exception of a scathing reference to the "Vandal Yankeys" in 1861 and the draft of a letter criticizing the graft and inefficiency in the construction of seacoast fortifications, there is no mention of the great struggle. From other sources, such as the Georgia State Archives and the collection of documents dealing with the estate of Hugh Fraser Grant on file at the Chatham County Courthouse in Savannah, a partial account of the sad fate which overtook the Grant family and their property can be reconstructed.

In the 1840's the elder Hugh Fraser Grant became associated with the Glynn County Rangers, a volunteer company of cavalry. By 1848 he had been elected Captain of the company, which had thirty-seven of the adventuresome younger men of the county on its rolls. They were described by their Captain as "entirely without arms . . . all handsomely uniformed and well mounted."[25] Sometime later the unit was partially equipped with sabers, pistols, holsters, and cartridge boxes, but in 1855 the remnants of this equipment were turned over to the state militia in Savannah.[26] The flowery address of their Captain on the occasion of the presentation of their colors is recorded in the Elizafield Journal (see page 290). The service record of the Grant family filed in the Georgia State Archives reveals that Hugh Fraser Grant was enrolled in the Glynn County Reserve during the years 1863-65, but there is no mention of Hugh Fraser, Jr.[27]

[23] Glynn County Records, Deed Book N, p. 265. [24] *Ibid.*, p. 503.

[25] Annual Report of Glynn Rangers, 1848, in the Glynn County Folio, Georgia State Archives.

[26] Memorandum of Cavalry Arms Received by Major P. H. Behn from Capt. Hugh F. Grant, 1855, in the H. F. Grant MSS, Georgia State Archives.

[27] Alphabetical Service Record of Citizens of Glynn County, Georgia State Archives.

However, a letter dated September 26, 1861, from Hugh Fraser Grant to Governor J. E. Brown contains evidence that the younger Grant was then serving with the Glynn Guards stationed at St. Simons Island. After sweetening up Governor Brown with some laudatory phrases, the elder Grant asked that his son be appointed an aide-de-camp on the governor's staff. This request was justified by the claim that

> my health is such that I am unable to attend to my own business, & he being my only Son & a family of daughters, that if you will give him that appointment it would relieve him from camp life and enable him to assist me & at the same time will be ready whenever you require his services to aid in defense of his Country.[28]

Since the only action on this plea for special treatment is the notation "file" on the letter, it may be assumed that the younger Grant was not exempted from the arduous and boring experience of camp life and patrol duty on St. Simons as the result of the intervention of his father.

The majority of the Grant family and some of the Negroes passed the war years at Waresboro, Ware County, in the interior of Georgia. The elder Grant recorded a two-day visit to Savannah in October, 1862, but the Elizafield Journal throws no light on the question as to whether the plantation was abandoned temporarily or operated on a reduced scale. Immediately after the war, the elder Grant was forced to mortgage Sedgmoor, his summer home, for the sum of $1,426.87.[29]

The next quarter century witnessed the steady decline in the fortunes of the Grant family and the productivity of their property. By the time of the death of Hugh Fraser Grant the elder in 1873, he had lost the title to Elizafield to four creditors but still retained the right of redemption. In 1867, after conveying title to Grantly to his mother, Hugh Fraser, Jr., moved to Savannah and attempted to make a living in the commercial life of that city as a bookkeeper and later as a commission merchant. He attained creditable success and eventually was elected president of the Savannah Board of Trade in 1884.[30] Meanwhile, he attempted to run Grantly and, after his father's death, Elizafield in absentia.

[28] Hugh Fraser Grant to Governor J. E. Brown, September 26, 1861, in the H. F. Grant MSS, Georgia State Archives. In the record of the transfer of Grantly to Hugh Fraser Grant, Jr., on April 6, 1861, cited in note 23 above, the elder Grant is referred to as Major Grant.

[29] Glynn County Records, Deed Book N, p. 373 (September 29, 1865).

[30] *Directory for the City of Savannah*, 1884.

His success in this endeavor was limited, to say the least. All of the financial claims against Elizafield eventually were consolidated in the hands of a Savannah factor named George J. Mills.[31] The younger Grant borrowed a total of $8,553.60 from Mills but spent only $5,898.18 of that sum on the estate. The debt to Mills was reduced to $3,069.60 by 1880 and, with an operational profit of $5,280.86 for the year 1882, Hugh Fraser, Jr., expected soon to extinguish the last trace of debt on the family plantation. In 1885, however, he left Georgia and took up permanent residence in Asheville, North Carolina, possibly for seasons of health. He carried along a memento of the past glory of his family in the form of his father's Elizafield Journal. This document was discovered by a purchaser of his Asheville residence in the 1920's and through him came into the hands of the writer.

The elder Grant died at Winchester, Virginia, on March 17, 1873, where he had been visiting a daughter. He was buried in Bonaventure Cemetery, Savannah. His wife lived a few more years, but she was buried beside him in May, 1881, in that hauntingly beautiful cemetery, with its white drives and walks lined with live oaks which in turn are covered with heavy and luxuriant hanging moss.[32] The will of the elder Grant (dated August 1, 1871) took notice of the fact that his widow held two $5,000 insurance policies on his life, plus property of her own (Grantly). His executors were instructed to sell Elizafield and divide the proceeds among four of the children. In the event the property could not be sold, the executors were advised to rent or manage the plantation.[33] Under this mandate, his son, who was now calling himself H. Fraser Grant, struggled for twelve years attempting to redeem the title to the family lands but gave up in 1885, when he left the state. His brother-in-law, Mallery P. King, was then prevailed upon to accept appointment as administrator of the estate. The appraisal of the property incidental to its transfer revealed that the once glorious and thriving example of ante-

[31] All information concerning the management and financial status of Elizafield in the postwar years is based on a study of numerous petitions, reports, and exhibits filed in Chatham County Courthouse, Savannah, Georgia, by H. Fraser Grant and Mallery P. King as executors and administrators of the estate of Hugh Fraser Grant.

[32] Chatham County Records, Savannah, Georgia, and data on headstones in Bonaventure cemetery.

[33] Last Will and Testament of Hugh Fraser Grant, in Chatham County Records, Savannah, Georgia.

bellum planter capitalism had been reduced in market value to a mere $7,644.15. Of course, emancipation of the slaves was responsible for about $75,000 of this depreciation. But absentee management, the general difficulties which afflicted agricultural production in the postwar South, the loss of the West Indies market for rice, and the competition of new ricelands and techniques in other parts of the United States and the world sounded the death knell of the tide-flow ricelands of Georgia.

Mallery P. King supervised the planting of Elizafield lands for four more years; then he too gave up the fight against debts, compound interest, and low rice prices. During these four years he operated on a complete crop-lien basis and paid Mills $27,080.82 on a series of notes which with interest amounted to $29,479.79. He even used the $2,059.29 received from the liquidation sale of horses and tools at Grantly in 1888 as a part payment on the debt. In spite of his rather strenuous efforts and intelligent management, the estate still owed Mills $2,399.57 after Elizafield had been sold at public auction in 1889 and passed into other hands.

Three years later Sarah A. Benedict, King's sister-in-law and one of the daughters of Hugh Fraser Grant the elder, demanded an accounting from King in a law suit heard in Chatham County Court, Savannah. The exhibits submitted by King tell in detail the sad story of the final days of Elizafield as a rice-growing agricultural unit. They provide a documented account which reveals the inability of this once proud and productive model of planter capitalism to survive a succession of blows which included the loss of its labor force by emancipation, the stress of the turbulence of the Reconstruction years, and the competition of the commercial production of rice by new methods on new lands. Incidentally, the demise of Elizafield was not unique, since all of the neighboring rice plantations along the Altamaha suffered the same fate, although a few lasted into the present century before they were driven into the wall. With the final liquidation of the estate of Hugh Fraser Grant the elder at public auction, a case history illustrating certain phases of the social and economic life of the Old South was brought to a close. The impossibility of its resurrection in a pattern even faintly resembling its ante-bellum operation was further dramatized by the scattering of the Grant children to various parts of a nation which was on the threshold of the twentieth century.

# Chapter Two

## THE CULTURE OF RICE IN GEORGIA

THE LITERATURE on the rice-growing industry in the antebellum South has been concerned largely with the techniques, procedures, and problems of the coastal planters of the Carolinas, especially South Carolina. Old Charleston, Georgetown, and the Cooper and Edisto rivers have come to be synonymous with rice plantation society. This unique society grew to maturity before the American Revolution, and, until the decade before the Civil War, dominated the political thinking and social customs of the Palmetto State and also much of the coastal and sea-island population from Albermarle Sound to Florida. It was a proud society and a cultured one, with many facets. It was highly literate and produced men with an experimental, even scientific, turn of mind. Since the greater portion of the Carolina rice crop eventually was consumed in the world market, the political and economic thinking of the area was influenced by European culture. All of these characteristics combined to produce a flood of printed words dealing with rice-growing methods and life on the rice plantations of the Carolinas. The pages of the *Southern Agriculturist, Affleck's Southern Rural Almanac,* and *DeBow's Review* were filled with the reports of various Carolina planters which described those plantation routines and agricultural experiments that had proven most advantageous. Many of these brochures were penned by Robert F. W. Allston, the distinguished planter, scientist, and governor of South Carolina.[1] In the mid-nineteenth century such northern agricultural reporters and observers as Frederick Law Olmsted and Solon Robinson echoed the concept

[1] *BeBow's Review,* I (April, 1846), 320-56; IV (December, 1847), 502-11; XVI (June, 1854), 589-615.

that the Carolinas were the last word on rice growing. Yet their inspections coincided with the period when the Carolina rice plantations had passed their period of greatest productivity and were on the downgrade.[2]

Twentieth-century writers of historical fiction, romantic family memoirs, and specialty articles have rediscovered the Carolina coast as a rewarding literary theme.[3] Many of these authors have become sentimental victims of their source materials, and have mistaken for truth the propaganda retorts answering northern charges against the plantation system. They have kept the traditions of coastal society alive with little or no critical revision and re-evaluation of the records left by its members. Historical scholars of the present century have, however, made a real beginning at the task of rescuing the story of the rice-growing industry from the clutches of the propagandist and novelist. The finest and most complete of these to date is the recently published volume of the papers of Governor Robert F. W. Allston, edited by J. H. Easterby.[4] Such general reviews of Southern agricultural life as the works of L. C. Gray[5] and U. B. Phillips[6] contain brief but good sections on ante-bellum rice culture. David Doar and D. C. Heyward, whose family roots were in the rice-growing regions, have produced fine monographs on the subject.[7] Finally, annotated bibliographies, which serve as excellent guides to the

[2] F. L. Olmsted, *A Journey in the Seaboard Slave States* (New York, 1859), pp. 462-88; H. A. Kellar, ed., *Solon Robinson, Pioneer and Agriculturist* (Indianapolis, 1936), II, 349-55, 364-68.

[3] The list includes Ravenal Sass, Archibald Rutledge, and Elizabeth Page.

[4] J. H. Easterby, ed., *The South Carolina Rice Plantation, as Revealed in the Papers of Robert F. W. Allston* (Chicago, 1945). These papers are largely personal correspondence of the Allston family, with some additional overseer's reports, slave documents, financial reports, and letters from factors. They do not provide a continuous record of the culture of separate fields or even plantations in contrast with the Elizafield Journal and Account Book. Also they do not contain complete and continuous records of financial transactions with factors over a period of years. This volume provides excellent background material and a multitude of details on many phases of rice-plantation life but lacks sufficient continuous data to serve as the basis for a case study of rice-planter capitalism over a period of years.

[5] L. C. Gray, *History of Agriculture in Southern United States to 1860* (Washington, 1933), pp. 277-90, 721-31.

[6] U. B. Phillips, ed., *Plantation and Frontier*, Vols. I and II of *A Documentary History of American Industrial Society* (Cleveland, 1910), I, 134-66; U. B. Phillips, *American Negro Slavery* (New York, 1918), pp. 247-59.

[7] David Doar, *Rice and Rice Planting in the South Carolina Low Country* (Charleston, 1936); Duncan C. Heyward, *Seed from Madagascar* (Chapel Hill, 1937).

literature on rice growing, have been produced by A. S. Salley[8] and by E. E. Edwards in his extensive *Bibliography of the History of Agriculture in the United States.*[9]

By contrast the published record of the production, management, and marketing methods of Georgia rice growers is small in quantity and limited in scope.[10] Why has this region, which grew to challenge the pre-eminence and productivity per acre of the Carolinas by 1850, been comparatively neglected by students of American agriculture? Various answers to this query may be made, but the following are the most plausible: (1) the Georgia rice plantations were considered to be a mere extension of the Carolinas; (2) their period of great productivity was brief (1850-60) and was ended by the advent of war; and (3) adequate and extensive documentary material on Georgia rice plantations has not found its way into print or even into depositories. A hurried survey of the descriptive and documentary accounts on Georgia rice culture will partially confirm the last reason. The roll is short, since only Fanny Kemble,[11] L. C. Gray, and U. B. Phillips mentioned the Georgia rice fields as distinctive entities. Even they seem to have regarded these as mere outposts of the parent enterprises in the Carolinas.

It must be admitted that the 1830's and 1840's witnessed the considerable extension of the activities of many Carolina planters down along the coast of Georgia and even as far as northern Florida. They were forced to this expansion by the disastrous change in their economic and political fortunes during those decades. The successful expansion of cotton culture in the piedmont and uplands of the Carolinas played havoc with the political and economic monopoly of the coastal region. Exhaustion of readily available timber along the streams and the excessive planting of such clean culture crops as cotton and corn in the interior completely upset the established water-flow pattern and accentuated

[8] A. S. Salley, "Bibliography of Rice Industry in South Carolina," in David Doar, *Rice and Rice Planting in the South Carolina Low Country*, pp. 54-68.

[9] E. E. Edwards, "A Bibliography of the History of Agriculture in the United States," U.S. Department of Agriculture, *Miscellaneous Publication 84* (Washington, 1930), pp. 75-76, 113, 151-52.

[10] For a review of the literature on this subject consult Albert V. House, Jr., "The Management of a Rice Plantation in Georgia, 1834-1861, as Revealed in the Journal of Hugh Fraser Grant," *Agricultural History*, XIII (October, 1939), 208-17.

[11] Francis A. Kemble, *Journal of a Residence on a Georgia Plantation in 1838-39* (New York, 1863).

the disastrous effects of the depositing of eroded and somewhat sterile soil from the interior on the coastal lowlands. In addition, the supply of light timber products such as shingles, scantlings, and lathes which were usually shipped along with rice to the West Indian markets was exhausted. Thus, the captains of smaller coastal ships began to look elsewhere for ports where they might pick up both rice for the hold and lumber for the deck cargo. The Georgia coast with its many rivers lined with timber and its largely unworked soil seemed to be an answer to the problem of the Carolina planters.[12] Before 1840 many of the Georgia rice plantations were part of the economic life of the Carolinas since Charleston served as their factorage and marketing center. It should be noted, however, that the majority of these "Carolina plantations" were located in the Savannah River basin. Yet, by 1860 the crops from over three-fifths of the acreage in this region even were sent to Savannah. On the near-by Ogeechee River, nearly the entire crop was marketed in that fast-growing mercantile center of coastal Georgia.[13]

Rice had been grown in Georgia since the middle of the eighteenth century, albeit on a small scale. With the opening up of the tide-flow swamps of the five great rivers of Georgia to large-scale rice production, Sea-Island and coastal Georgia families provided most of the leadership for the new effort. They gradually shifted from reliance on sea-island cotton and sugar and began to clear more swamplands and plant more rice. Although much of the seed and techniques of rice culture were imported from the old masters in the Carolinas, Georgia planters eventually learned that their production, financing, and marketing problems differed somewhat from those of the older rice-growing regions to the north. Any student, well grounded in the Carolina story, will discover these variations by a careful study of the Elizafield Journal reproduced in this volume. He will still further sense the diversity if he consults the manuscript collections on ante-bellum Georgia agricultural life to be found in the Southern Historical Collection at the University of North Carolina Li-

[12] See editorial introduction in Albert V. House, Jr., ed., "Charles Manigault's Essay on the Open Planting of Rice," *Agricultural History*, XVI (October, 1942), 184-93, for a more extended summary of this dilemma of the Carolina planters.

[13] Louis Manigault, Analysis of Savannah River Plantations in 1860, Louis Manigault MSS Diary, Southern Historical Collection, University of North Carolina Library.

brary and other Georgia records in the possession of the Duke University Library. Taken altogether these source materials, especially the Elizafield Journal, the J. H. Couper account books, and both Manigault collections provide the raw data for a detailed study of the functioning of Georgia rice-planter capitalism in the first half of the nineteenth century.[14]

The differences between the problems and practices of the Georgia planters and those in Carolina may seem minor to the casual observer. They are largely questions of degree and result from seemingly slight variations in soil, climate, rainfall, tides, transportation, and marketing and credit facilities, and even include the arrival dates of such plantation pests as bobolinks, sometimes referred to as ricebirds or Maybirds. But all farmers know that very minor differences in these basic factors in agricultural production can spell success in one region and comparative failure in areas near-by. One legendary Midwestern farmer is reported to have expressed this truth succinctly with the somewhat blasphemous observation that "he was going to quit farming and get into some business that God had less to do with."

In the nineteenth century rice was grown along the banks and on the islands of all five of the larger rivers emptying into the Atlantic Ocean along the Georgia coast, namely: the Savannah, Ogeechee, Altamaha, Satilla, and St. Marys rivers. In addition, some of the small streams and inlets had their rice fields. Chatham County, the northernmost region on the banks of the Savannah, was the heaviest producer, reporting 25,934,000 pounds for the crop of 1859.[15] In Camden, the southernmost county, the crop yield was two-fifths that of the Savannah area, with 10,330,000 pounds in the same year. McIntosh and Glynn counties on opposite shores of the Altamaha produced 6,421,000 and 4,842,000 pounds, respectively, toward the over-all total of 52,507,652 pounds for the state.[16] Using a conservative estimate of forty-five pounds per bushel and forty-five bushels per acre, it becomes

[14] In passing it should be pointed out that the coastal region of Georgia was a stronghold of the Whig Party in the South in contrast to the Calhoun followers of the Carolinas. This may reflect subtle but decisive variations in the economic outlook of the regions.

[15] C. Mildred Thompson, *Reconstruction in Georgia, Economic, Social and Political, 1865-1872* (New York, 1915), p. 304, quoting the 1860 U.S. census reports.

[16] *Ibid.* The total figure includes 2,548,000 pounds from Liberty and 1,609,000 pounds from Bryan counties.

apparent that the total acreage planted in the state was in excess of 26,000 acres—possibly as high as 30,000 acres. Louis Manigault, the proprietor of Gowrie Plantation in the Savannah region, made his own estimate of rice plantings and crop yield along the Savannah and Ogeechee rivers in 1859. Including 11,800 acres on the South Carolina shore, he estimated that about 17,587 acres of the Savannah River basin were planted to rice, with 6,550 acres devoted to the same crop on the banks of the near-by Ogeechee River.[17] According to the 1840 census Georgia had, in 1839, produced over 13,000,000 pounds of rice which was equal to 20 percent of the South Carolina crop. This earned her second place among all rice-producing states in the United States.[18] By 1859 Georgia had quadrupled its output, with the result that its crop was approximately 45 percent of that of the older state. This effort enabled Georgia to retain her position as second among rice-growing states, with a total which placed her far ahead of all areas except the Palmetto State.[19]

The comparatively small number of acres (about 30,000) planted to rice in Georgia was owing to the unusual soil requirements for growing rice by the tide-flow method. As suggested by the term, tides were employed to flood and drain the rice fields. This meant that all ricelands had to be located above the salt-water-line on fresh-water rivers, but where the fresh-water level was definitely raised by each high tide at the mouth of the stream. On the usually sluggish rivers of Georgia this rice-growing zone began about five to ten miles from the open ocean and continued for another six to ten miles inland. All islands, shores, and river swamps which were somewhat flat and not too high above the river were eligible for consideration as ricelands. Medium to heavy surface soil such as clay and swamp muck was the best for growing a good crop. While some sandy loam might be tolerated as part of the surface soil, the subsoil had to be largely clay so that the fields would retain water well when flooded and not lose an appreciable amount through seepage or absorption.[20] These conditions were met by the fertile and largely untouched

[17] Louis Manigault MSS, Southern Historical Collection, University of North Carolina Library.

[18] Quoted by Robert F. W. Allston in *DeBow's Review* I (April, 1846), 332.

[19] U.S. Department of Agriculture, *Yearbook*, 1922, p. 516.

[20] MSS Diary, Louis Manigault MSS, Southern Historical Collection, University of North Carolina Library, containing memo dated 1844 by C. Manigault.

lands along the rivers of coastal Georgia. Passing through the rich alluvial lands of the interiors of the state with their clay foundations, the Georgia rivers had for years been depositing rich soils on the sandy loam of the coastal belt.[21] The rate of flow of these rivers usually was so slow that this depositing of upland soils did not take place except as the result of unusually heavy rain storms, often referred to as freshets. The Elizafield Journal reveals that such floodings occurred with sufficient frequency to provide a continuing supply of new soil from the interior for the ricelands.[22] It is plain, however, that the supply of lands fit for rice culture was strictly limited by the unusual requirements of location and soil consistency. In summary, it may be concluded that the lands available to the Georgia planters in the nineteenth century were comparable roughly in extent and characteristics to those exploited by South Carolina planters in the preceding century. As of 1840-50 South Carolina lands were not expected to average more than forty bushels of rice per acre while in the same period Georgia lands produced upwards of fifty bushels per acre.

In Georgia old sugar lands appropriately located could be adapted to rice culture with some changes due to the need for a plentiful supply of water. But a large portion of the rice acreage of Georgia, as of 1850, resulted from the clearing of new lands. The process of preparing new lands for rice culture has been ably described by Ulrich B. Phillips and need not be repeated in detail.[23] The only point which that pioneer historian of Southern life neglected to stress was the unconscionable amount of labor that was required to build a new rice field. Most such fields were made from tangled swamps filled with undergrowth and jungle timber. Working solely with hand tools slave gangs had to root out all such growth, level the field nearly as smooth as a pool table, and construct a complicated system of banks (levees or dikes), canals, ditches, drains, and quarter-drains to protect

[21] W. S. Irvine, *Brunswick and Glynn County, Georgia* (Brunswick, 1902), p. 34; H. W. Reed, ed., *Brunswick and Glynn County* (Brunswick, 1895), p. 13; R. M. Harper, "Agriculture in Lower Georgia, 1850-1880," *Georgia Historical Quarterly*, VI (1922), 107.

[22] The beneficial effects from new soil deposits "from last year's gale" were confirmed by Charles Manigault in a letter to his son Louis who was in Paris at the time. C. to L. Manigault, August 29, 1855, in the Louis Manigault MSS, Duke University Library.

[23] U. B. Phillips, *Life and Labor in the Old South* (Boston, 1929), pp. 116-17.

the field against the river current and facilitate their flooding and drainage. Trunks, which were really large wooden culverts were buried in the main bank nearest the river at a level slightly above the usual low-tide mark. These trunks, which were sometimes referred to as floodgates, had doors or gates at both ends which were so attached that they could either be pulled up or merely loosened and allowed to swing. Weighted with stones at the bottom, the swinging inner door would open in response to the pressure of the river as it flowed in through the raised outer door and culvert at high tide, thus flooding the field. When the tidal pressure lessened owing to the receding waters of the river, the inner door would automatically close tightly and be held in place by the weight of the stones and the pressure of water in the field. Draining the field called for reversing the arrangement of the trunk gates with the inner door raised and the outer door allowed to swing. At low tide the swinging outer door would then be forced open by the pressure of the water in the field, and the water would drain out of the planted area. Since the field might not drain in the short period of time before the next high tide, the swinging outer door would promptly close tightly when it felt outside pressure from the incoming new high tide. Thus, no additional water would be allowed to enter the draining field.

This system was so efficient that unless water animals, driftwood, or other bulky refuse interfered with their operations, the floodgates could be set and left comparatively unattended. On occasion, hurricane waters blowing in from the ocean or freshet waters pouring down from upcountry were known to create such pressure on these trunks that they would "blow up." This was particularly true when the culvert had been installed on a sandy loam foundation which might erode rapidly under the pressure of surging waters. Regardless of whether the trunk blew up despite the heavy load of earth over it or blew out into the river or field, a bad break in the main bank would be opened which promptly inundated the entire field. If the flood were fresh water, the crop suffered some damage; if salt water, the crop was ruined and the field was unusable for several years until it had been leeched by the passage of time.[24] Experienced plantation managers braced open both doors of the trunk when a storm of such proportions was in the offing. By so doing the crop might

[24] Louis to Charles Manigault, March 10, 1854, in Louis Manigault MSS, Duke University Library.

suffer somewhat from too much or too salt water, but they preserved the trunk and prevented a bad break which would surely ruin the crop and require endless hours to repair the bank.[25]

One Georgia planter set down the specifications for "a good sized trunk for a 20 acre square" as follows: "4 ft. 4 inches by 1 ft. 9 inches in the clear inside & as near 40 feet long as possible —the sides 5 or 6 inches thick & if each of one piece the better. The top & bottom plank 3 to 5 inches as convenient."[26] Another Georgia planter, who also owned several successful rice plantations in South Carolina, recorded the total footage of lumber which he purchased in 1833 for the construction of two flood gates as follows:[27]

*Cost of Flood Gate*

| | | | |
|---|---|---|---|
| Bill of lumber got | 24 logs — | 30 ft long by | 12 inches |
| by Mr. Oliver for | 8 | 40 | 13 |
| my two Flood Gates | 4 | 20 | 10 |
| built in 1833 | 2 | 32 | 18 |
| | 7 | 25 | 16 to be sawd in four for Studs to flood gates. |

248 Best 2 in plank 20 ft long for floor to flood gates.

The construction of these trunks and the remainder of the extensive irrigation and drainage system called for some understanding of the rudiments of practical engineering. Owners, managers, and overseers, profiting by Carolina experience and using their own knowledge of soil and tides on Georgia rivers, worked out the details and dimensions for the most efficient layout for the water systems of their rice fields. Their lands were divided by natural or artificial barriers into fields or squares usually of 18 to 20 acres. A main canal about 6 feet wide at the top, 4 feet wide at the bottom, and 5 feet deep was dug directly behind and parallel to the main river levee. Branches of this canal extended down both sides of the field. These sometimes had alternate outlets into adjoining fields and could be controlled by gates. However, in general, one field or square only was flowed or drained at any one time. The canal waters were also used as transportation routes by plantation "flats" (long, narrow, shal-

[25] *Ibid.*, Charles to Louis Manigault, February 28, 1854.

[26] Slave List and Plantation Notes, 1814-47, in the Mackey-Stiles MSS, Southern Historical Collection, University of North Carolina Library.

[27] Slave Record Book (Gowrie), in the C. Manigault MSS, Southern Historical Collection, University of North Carolina Library.

low-draft flatboats) which were loaded with the harvested rice from the fields in the fall. Each field or square was cut up into plots of about one acre each by drains (or face ditches) which opened off the canal. Likewise, each drain had various shorter outlets, called quarter-drains. The center ditch or drain in each acre was usually four feet wide at the top, two feet wide at the bottom, and four feet deep. The quarter-drains were 16 to 24 inches wide at the top, 1 foot wide at the bottom, and about 3 feet deep. These dimensions were taken into consideration in figuring the daily tasks of 600 cubic feet per day required of all prime hands engaged in excavation work.[28] This water system reduced to a surprising degree the acreage of arable land which could be planted. James Hamilton Couper, the meticulous and scientific administrator of Hopeton on the Altamaha, concluded after careful survey and calculations that, of a potential 736 acres, his planting area on his cotton, cane, and rice lands was reduced to 635 acres by margins, roads, ditches, and banks. The last two, which he classified as "improvements," required 31 and 25 acres, respectively, for a total of fifty-six acres which were devoted to the water system.[29]

After the rice field had been built and the water system was ready to operate, the actual preparation of the topsoil for planting was undertaken. Surprisingly, this task was performed largely by hand labor and tools with only limited use of plows and harrows. While Carolina practice called for annual plowing and harrowing, using mules for draft power, Georgia practice (with the exception of some "Carolina" planters in the Savannah River basin) seems to have limited such "machine work" to every third year. There are a variety of possible explanations for this routine. First and foremost was the fact that in the nineteenth century Georgia's firm clay soils had not been exhausted by excessive use and oxidation. Thus, there was no *need* from the standpoint of soil fertility to plow deeply each year. Next, with

[28] These details were compiled from the following sources: Phillips, *Life and Labor in the Old South*, pp. 116-17; Slave Record Book (Gowrie), C. Manigault MSS, and Slave List and Plantation Notes, 1814-47, Mackey-Stiles MSS, both in Southern Historical Collection, University of North Carolina Library; Louis to Charles Manigault, January 6, 1854, Louis Manigault MSS, Duke University Library; and Agricultural Notes, 33, J. H. Couper MSS, Southern Historical Collection, University of North Carolina Library.

[29] Crop Record Book, 1831, J. H. Couper MSS, Southern Historical Collection, University of North Carolina Library.

subsoil plows costing $16[30] and mules both scarce and high-priced, Georgia planters seemingly preferred to rely on their labor force. The slaves had to be kept busy anyway, and the winter months were usually slack, so why not use this portion of the capital investment in the plantation to "turn the soil" with seven-inch rice hoes costing about 85 cents each.[31]

Such plowing, harrowing, and turning of the soil as was necessary was accomplished usually in January, February, and early March. At that point the planter or manager drew up a tentative planting schedule which was determined largely by the dates forecast for the appearance of the new and full moons for both March and April.[32] He desired to stagger his planting so that successive fields would be ready for the water to be turned on at the same time that a plentiful supply of water would be available in the river owing to the high run of tides with the new and full moons. As a result he usually planned his program with three plantings: one in March and two in April, with an additional late planting possible during the last days of May or early June. A few planters on the southernmost rivers of Georgia planted early enough to catch the first run of high tides in March, but this was risky owing to the possibility of cold weather which would retard the sprouting of the new seedlings. The late planting was a better gamble because the long growing season in southern Georgia did not come to an end until late October or early November. But harvesting such a late crop might develop into a real problem if it were sufficiently far advanced to be tempting to the ricebirds as they swung back south to their winter resort habitat in the Caribbean area. Experience had taught the planters that unless the seeds were covered with water promptly after sowing, a variety of disasters might occur. These included failure to sprout, withering of the seedling under a hot sun or dry ground, or being devoured by rats or birds. The schedule for the usual dry culture of rice called for a series of short flowings and

[30] Journal No. 2, January 25, 1845, J. H. Couper MSS, Southern Historical Collection, University of North Carolina Library.

[31] *Ibid.*, January 25, 1839.

[32] In describing the routine of rice planting, great reliance has been placed on the descriptions of the process in C. Manigault MSS, Mackey-Stiles MSS, Kollock MSS, Agricultural Notes in J. H. Couper MSS—all in the Southern Historical Collection, University of North Carolina Library; Louis Manigault MSS, Duke University Library; the Elizafield Journal of Hugh Fraser Grant; and the extensive articles on the general subject scattered through the *Southern Agriculturist*.

hoeings during the first half of the growing season. The duration of each operation was just enough so that if the original planting had been accomplished at a time of high tides, similar high tides would always recur as each operation was completed and a need for more water apparent.

A procedure known as "trenching" was completed immediately before the actual sowing of the seed. Using hand labor or a draft animal hitched to a light marking drag the level field was laid off in parallel drills or shallow trenches about 3 inches wide and 15 inches from center to center. The seed was sown by hand in these trenches at the rate of three bushels per acre for new land and from two to two and one-half bushels per acre for other fields. When the traditional "covered planting" was employed, field hands, dragging light wooden bats behind them, covered the seed lightly with about 2 inches of soil. Care had to be exercised to prevent the trenching gang from getting too far ahead of the sowers and wielders of the bats, since a shower or windstorm might cake the soil, harden the walls of the trenches, or level them entirely if they were allowed to stand open for even two days before the seed was sown.[33]

Georgia planters produced their own seed, bought it from neighboring planters who specialized in its production, or ordered high quality Carolina seed through their factors in Savannah or Charleston. The most popular type was common white rice which generally was available at reasonable prices. Hugh Fraser Grant referred to seed which he purchased from a neighbor, J. C. Tunno, while James Hamilton Couper of Hopeton listed in his journal for 1843 the purchase of 500 bushels of seed rice from the same man at 75 cents per bushel.[34] By contrast the Hopeton journals show that Couper had to pay $1.25 per bushel for 206 bushels of seed rice purchased from his factor in Charleston in 1839.[35] Gold Seed rice, a strain which was highly developed in the Carolinas, may be the type referred to by Charles Manigault in his essay on the open planting of rice.[36] In that composition he revealed that he customarily bought thirty to forty bushels of seed

[33] C. Manigault to Louis Manigault, February 21, 1856, Louis Manigault MSS, Duke University Library.

[34] Journal No. 2, December 31, 1843, J. H. Couper MSS, Southern Historical Collection, University of North Carolina Library.

[35] *Ibid.*, February 21, 1839.

[36] Albert V. House, Jr., ed., "Charles Manigault's Essay on the Open Planting of Rice," *Agricultural History*, XVI (October, 1942), 190.

rice each year, which he planted for seed for the following year. By this method he acquired annually about 1,000 bushels of high quality seed at minimum cost. Some white bearded rice, which was often called Siberian barley, was raised in Georgia in small quantities. It was unusual in that it could be grown on highland with a minimum of water. This strain was not highly considered as a commercial crop but was raised primarily as food for Negroes.[37]

According to current standards seed could contain no more than one kernel per hundred of volunteer rice, that outlaw off-brand grain which sprouted from fallen rice in the field. After the first year this grain was reddish in appearance; and although its food value was approximately equal to that of pure strains, buyers and the consuming public would not purchase it, hence a desire to stamp it out. Seed rice also had to be handled carefully during threshing so that its shell or core would not be cracked. In 1856 Charles Manigault instructed his son Louis in the art of threshing seed rice as follows:

> Let me call your attention to *Seed Rice.* To pass it through a steam thresher you well know is out of the question— & the flail stick breaks much of it also. —Many a grain which looks well has received a blow which has split the shell & when planted, & swollen, the water oozes through the split, rots the grain & it never sprouts, &c. The best way to do this is, when you have a Load of market rice all ready in the mill awaiting a vessell, then turn too & thresh your 1500 barrells of seed in this way. Get Six empty Rice barrells with two hands to each, who in the barnyard close to the stack of seed rice rake a sheef each, & beat it *Carefully* on the edge of the barrell until all good size ripe grain falls *therein.* The straw with the rest of the grains, on it must then be passed through the thresher as soon as convenient. You will thus have first rate seed.[38]

Most laymen or casual students of American economic history are unaware of the myriad functions of water in rice growing. They have seen pictures of Orientals and poor farmers in the Mediterranean area working in water-filled rice paddies. They also have heard that rice has been grown in United States only in those areas where a plentiful supply of water was available

[37] Robert F. W. Allston, *DeBow's Review*, I, 320-56; *Southern Agriculturist*, III (April 20, 1830), 356-57.

[38] C. Manigault to Louis Manigault, January 10, 1856, Louis Manigault MSS, Duke University Library.

either by pumping or by the action of the tides. So they conclude that rice needs unusual amounts of water for nourishment and will not grow on dry land. This judgment is incorrect and shows a lack of understanding of the services performed by the great volume of water usually associated with ricelands during the growing season. Rice can be raised in small quantities on highlands with no more water than is required for corn or cotton. However, such a crop will not prosper, and the yield will be small. Wherever large quantities of water can be turned onto fields and drained out periodically, the water *assists* in the culture of rice and both *expands* and *facilitates* production in the following ways:

1. The initial flow of water swells and bursts the seed rapidly.
2. The second and third flows stretch the plants rapidly and help keep down the growth of grass, weeds, and volunteer rice, since healthy rice grows more rapidly in deep water than these unwanted outlaws.
3. The last flow, known as the harvest flow, supports the stalks bearing the ripening grain, which otherwise would become top-heavy as the grain reached maturity and topple to the ground.

In actual practice each rice planter was his own "rice doctor" as one authority on the subject has said.[39] The traditional method of dry culture or covered planting for the growing of rice has been described previously in rough outline. Planters in the Carolinas and Georgia agreed on two phases only of the flowing procedure connected with this type of culture. First, they both put on water for five to eight days immediately after sowing and covering with soil. This application of water was known as the sprout flow and started the rapid germination of the seed. Second, at the other end of the growing process, all planters put on water for a six-to-eight weeks harvest or joint flow. During this period the level of the water was continuously raised so that it remained "just below a white streak which is always seen on the stalks of rice just below the ear."[40] In between the sprout and harvest flows the frequency, type, and duration of water flowings, drying periods, and hoeings varied from area to area, from plantation to plantation, and even from year to year on some fields. The experienced planter or overseer watched the progress of the

[39] E. B. Copeland, *Rice* (London, 1924), p. 54.

[40] J. D. Legare, "Synopsis of the Culture of Rice—on Black River," *Southern Agriculturist*, 2d Series, I (February, 1841), 80-81.

rice very closely and ordered the appropriate remedy of more, less, or no water at all as his knowledge and observations dictated. However, a usual pattern was developed which called for the following routine:

1. After the sprout flow the fields were allowed to dry for about ten days. In this interval the rice first appeared above ground, and a light hoeing and some picking of grass were accomplished.

2. Then the point flow was put on for eight to ten days, which stretched the rice plants up rapidly to about 6 or 8 inches in height.

3. The water was then drained off for two weeks, which period usually saw another light hoeing after the plants had recovered somewhat from the sudden disappearance of the supporting water.

4. The next flowing was known as the stretch flow and lasted nearly three weeks, with water continuously topping the rice by 10 inches.

5. The water was then drawn off slowly and the fields allowed to dry. The fields were hoed once or even twice during a period of upwards of thirty days.

6. The harvest flow was then put on, and the necessity for manual care of the field was ended until it was time for the sickle.[41]

The water culture of rice was nearly the complete antithesis of the covered-planting process just described. It called for extreme dependence on water throughout the growing season. It was used to a limited extent in Carolina, but no evidence of its use in Georgia has been found in the course of a considerable search of the source materials. The actual planting was in the traditional pattern, but the first water was kept on for sixty days. After thirty days of dry culture with one or two hoeings, the water was turned back on for ninety more days.[42] This required a grow-

[41] This description of the intermediate flowings is a synthesis of planting practice as described in various articles in the *Southern Agriculturist* and the MSS records of five Georgia planters. However, it follows most closely the description set forth by Charles Manigault in his essay on "The Open Planting of Rice" (see note 36 above) and in his letter of February 21, 1855, to his son Louis, Louis Manigault MSS, Duke University Library.

[42] "Report of Committee on Cultivation of Rice," read before State Agricultural Society of South Carolina in December, 1842, and published in *Southern Agriculturist*, 2d Series, III (July, 1843), 241-46.

ing season of nearly six months as well as very firm soil. It did, however, reduce the necessity for a large labor force to perform the usual four or five hoeings. There were even a few planters who never drained off the water from planting to harvest time. Slave gangs, wading in the water, picked out the worst of the grass and weeds and let the rest go at that.

A third method of rice culture was originated (probably) in South Carolina in the 1820's in an attempt to solve the problem of declining crop yields from the largely worn-out soil of the ricelands of that state. It stands in an intermediate position between the two methods previously described in the matter of frequency and volume of water flowings. It was variously called open planting, open-trench planting, and planting with clayed-seed. A few writers and planters incorrectly referred to it as "water culture." It was distinctly a gamble but, if successful, paid off with larger crops grown in two or three weeks less time with less field labor necessary at all stages except harvest time when more was often needed because of the size of the crop. Charles Manigault described this method learnedly, in meticulous detail, and with a thorough analysis of the pros and cons of the technique in his essay on the subject.[43] Ulrich B. Phillips also gave a brief outline of the process in his *Life and Labor in the Old South.*[44] J. D. Legare, the editor of the *Southern Agriculturist,* also described it in his publication as did the South Carolina Committee on the Cultivation of Rice in its 1842 *Report.*[45]

In open planting the land was prepared in exactly the same fashion as for covered planting, and seed was sown in the same amounts. The seed, however, had been clayed before planting. This was accomplished by spreading seed very thinly on a very large flat seed board. Powdered clay was then sprinkled over the seed and a small quantity of water added. This mixture was then stirred and agitated gently by hand until each kernel of seed had become wrapped in a thin covering blanket of wet clay. The seed was then allowed to dry somewhat and planted. Some planters liked this technique especially because the slaves were not tempted to make away with the clayed seed for their personal cooking pots. As a result a given supply of seed rice seemed to plant more acres than the pure seed used in covered planting.

[43] See notes 12, 36, and 41 above.

[44] *Life and Labor in the Old South,* p. 115.

[45] See notes 40 and 42 above.

After sowing in the open trenches 1½ feet of water was let on slowly without any covering with soil. This flow remained on the field for twenty-one days. It was then drawn off gradually and the field allowed to dry for fifteen days. During this time the field was hoed once lightly to destroy volunteer rice, and the young plants grew to a height of 2 to 3 inches. Also in this dry interval they turned green and put down good roots. Strong rich clay soil was required for the plants to survive their treatment to this point. These first five to six weeks were anxious ones for the planters since a great gamble was involved. At any time during the early weeks a windstorm, with or without rain, would tear out the plants which had not yet put down firm roots and pile them all in a matted heap up against the banks of the field, thus ruining the planting. After the first light hoeing, the field was flowed again for twenty days, then dried again in preparation for a vigorous second hoeing and possibly a third hoeing during a forty-day dry period. The harvest flow was then put on, and the crop left to mature.

The advantages of this system were many: labor was saved; crop yields were increased; the growing season shortened; and the fields kept noticeably cleaner of volunteer rice and grass. Yet few Georgia planters used this method on a large scale. They were not pushed to it by declining yields due to soil exhaustion. Also they seemed content with traditional methods and did not cotton to the new-fangled ideas. Their labor forces were adequate to perform the usual five hoeings so there was no point in cutting the number of hoeings to three and having the problem of keeping the Negroes busy. Hugh Fraser Grant tried this open planting once on one of his smaller fields, but there is no record in the Elizafield Journal of its subsequent use. Some Carolina planters in the Savannah River basin used it successfully, notably the Manigaults, but there were too many variables in the method to interest any but the most adventuresome, experienced, and scientific-minded planters, not the least of which was the need for extra labor at harvest time. This was a definite difference as compared with Carolina practice since, by 1852, the elder Manigault recorded the fact that *all* the planters in the Georgetown area planted their second and third plantings by the open method.[46] Cold weather evidently made it unwise to leave the seed uncovered during the first planting.

[46] C. Manigault's Essay, House, ed., *Agricultural History*, XVI, 191.

With perfect growing conditions, expert use of water, and efficient performance by an adequate labor force, rice could be grown in Georgia in 125 days. Such an ideal combination of factors, however, seldom occurred. Dry spells when water was not plentiful or when freshets poured too much over the fields tended to extend the growing season. The return of chilly weather in late March or early April sometimes retarded the growth of the newly planted seedlings. Certain pests, notably ricebirds and rats, often destroyed entire fields in the early planting stages, when the grain was vulnerable to their forays. Such disasters forced replantings which prolonged the growing season into the fall months. The ricebirds, which arrived in quantity on the Altamaha by mid-April, hit the Savannah River basin by April 25. They hovered around for four or five weeks before continuing their leisurely flight north. Occasionally, they appeared an entire month early as in 1843, when they interfered with the first planting at Elizafield on March 9. These pests consumed the seed as it was dropped and even scratched it out of the lightly covered trenches. They were frustrated largely when the fields were covered with water and spurned the grain when the seedling had grown sufficiently to exhaust the core or meat of the kernel of seed rice. The rats were a startling and serious menace the year round. They attacked rice stacks in the field and in the yard. They also did a thorough job of tearing up a newly planted field if left unmolested. On the Savannah River these rodents were killed by the thousands by specially trained "rice curs," and old slaves were rewarded with one pound of tobacco for every 100 rats brought in. One old man killed 4,000 alone during the winter and another reported 30 to 40 killed daily for a three month's total of 2,700.[47]

A study of the planting and harvesting dates in the Elizafield Journal of Hugh Fraser Grant shows that his shortest growing season required 148 days, his longest 183, with an average of 165 days. He used the older covered planting method almost exclusively, so it is fair to assume that planters who won their gamble with open planting may have reduced the average for such fields to 145 days. According to the U.S. Department of Agriculture *Yearbook* for 1922, the following conditions are necessary for the successful growing of rice:

[47] MSS Diary, 1844, Louis Manigault MSS, Southern Historical Collection, University of North Carolina Library.

1. A depth of approximately 6 inches of water during a period of at least seventy-five days
2. Relatively high humidity
3. A mean temperature of 70 degrees Fahrenheit during a growing season of four to six months
4. Precipitation of between 50 and 60 inches, well distributed throughout the year within the rice area and upon the watershed of its streams
5. Medium to rather heavy soil in level tracts and a subsoil impervious to water[48]

All of these requirements were met by the best Georgia rice-lands. The planters whose first planting caught the early March tides put the harvest flow on before July 1, watched the ears "shooting out" before August 1, and began cutting around August 20. This was the routine followed by Hugh Fraser Grant as shown in the Elizafield Journal. Successive plantings followed at two-week intervals, although occasionally the later plantings, maturing more rapidly, were ready for harvesting before the previous planting had been cut.

Harvesting of rice in Georgia required five distinct steps. The first was cutting off the "ear-bearing" upper portion of the stalks with hand sickles. This was a two-handed operation in which the field hand grasped a handful of stalks with his left hand and swung the sickle with his right, leaving a generous stubble. As all wielders of the sickle or scythe know this task was easier to perform when done with a high degree of rhythm. With the completion of the rhythmic stroke the hand turned and gently deposited the sheaves of grain on the stubble, there as the second step it was allowed to dry for twenty-four hours at least. The third step was a dual operation in which the dried sheaves were tied together and stacked in the field. As hands were available these stacks were loaded onto flats for transportation to the barnyard as the fourth step. Finally, when all the grain had been gathered in from the fields the entire crop was restacked in the yard, after careful examination and separation of wet stacks which might spoil the remainder while awaiting preparation for the market.[49] These wet stacks were taken apart and slowly dried

[48] Department of Agriculture *Yearbook*, 1922, p. 518.

[49] This description is based on the brief sketch provided by Professor Phillips in his *Life and Labor in the Old South*, p. 115, and a study of both the Elizafield Journal and the Manigault MSS, in the Southern Historical Col-

before restacking. If they had been badly injured by water, they were set aside for separate mill handling.[50]

It is obvious that a long stretch of cloudless days was necessary for a successful season. Heavy rain could delay harvesting and knock much of the grain off the sheaves after they were cut and before being transported to the barnyard. The reports of overseers and planters express their deep thankfulness to the powers that be when harvest weather held clear. Harvesting was usually finished by the last of September in Georgia, but an unusual late planting in June was not ready for the sickle until October. With the successful completion of all field tasks connected with the growing of rice, the primary crop of the plantation, managers and labor force were free to turn their attention to other crops and tasks in preparation for life on the plantation during the oncoming winter.

---

lection, University of North Carolina Library, and in the Duke University Library.

[50] C. Manigault to Louis Manigault, January 3, 1856, Louis Manigault MSS, Duke University Library.

# Chapter Three

## FINANCE, SUPPLY, AND MANAGEMENT PRACTICES

THE DAY has long since passed when serious scholars continue to refer to the Southern plantation system as an example of feudal economy. That faulty concept, which held sway in the nineteenth and early twentieth centuries, reflected a double error. It was based on shadowy knowledge of medieval feudalism and on a false evaluation of the plantation system by bitterly partisan abolitionists and the clerical and political orators who echoed their mistaken judgments. Historical scholarship in recent years has added greatly to our knowledge of both feudalism and plantations. We now know that feudalism, which was concerned with political control and military defense among noblemen, was a distinct and separate system of relationships from manorialism, which was concerned with man's relation to land and primarily with the economics of production in the medieval economy. We have come to sense that the idea of a blooded aristocracy with distinct social, economic, and political privileges is not limited to the Middle Ages alone. This type of control of society by a privileged class existed before the Fall of Rome and survived somewhat the breakdown of medieval life. It retained much of its vigor in England where traces of its power can still be found in law, custom, society, and land-ownership. It was transplanted to the new world in the seventeenth century and thrived in the Southern and some Middle colonies until well into the nineteenth century.

It is true that control by privileged families, closely bound together by blood ties, reached a peak of power during medieval times. It is also true that a similar aristocracy whose economic base was tobacco, rice, or cotton dominated life in Virginia, the Carolinas, and other parts of the South for many years. But although they lived in a species of "feudal splendor," the relationship of the leaders of Southern life to each other was not feudal, and their economic wealth was not based on the manorial system of production. Rather, this system was generally referred to as the "plantation system." In the past half-century a growing list of students of Southern life, following the lead of Ulrich B. Phillips,[1] have come to see that the plantation system was really a species of capitalistic production. The phrase "planter capitalism" has been coined to describe the economic basis of ante-bellum society in the South.[2] In justifying this term it was pointed out that the owner-managers of Southern plantations who lived in old Virginny and Magnolialand really were comparable to those owner-managers of New England who lived in the big white house on the hill and supervised the production of textiles, tools, and gadgets in the factory located down by the falls of the river. True the plantation entrepreneurs operated with a rather static labor force and secured their credit and supplies from factors, while the factory owners had a fluid labor force and borrowed from banks; but in many respects their production problems were quite similar. They both produced for a distant market over which they had no control. Thus, they both were at the mercy of "price" and the middlemen who supplied transportation and marketing services. They both made an earnest attempt to use the newest machinery and scientific methods of production. Each had a heavy capital investment, one in slaves and land, the other in buildings and machines. Each had a trace of the gambler in his makeup and was willing to take a chance that his energy and wits would be handsomely rewarded in terms of economic wealth, political power, and social leadership.

This analogy has not been accepted too cheerfully by the descendants of these early exponents of the "American Way" now living on both sides of the Mason-Dixon line. They are repelled

[1] In addition to the works of Professor Phillips previously cited, see also his "On the Economics of Slavery, 1815-60," in the *Annual Report* of the American Historical Association (1912), pp. 150-51, and "The Economics of the Plantation," *South Atlantic Quarterly*, II (1904), 231-36.

[2] Louis Hacker, *The Triumph of American Capitalism* (New York, 1940), pp. 280-321, contains an extended discussion of planter capitalism. See also Francis B. Simkins, *The South, Old and New, a History 1820-1947* (New York, 1947), pp. 33-54.

by the idea that the civilizations of their respective ancestors, which they have been clothing with romantic idealism, should be associated with each other in any way. They hasten to point out a multitude of differences in human values and economic practices. It is obvious that there were many differences, but the fact remains that after the American colonies escaped from both the benefits and the crippling regimentation of the British imperial system by the War of Independence in 1776, "His Majesties' Plantations" ceased to be. Thenceforth, agricultural production in southern United States no longer conformed to the classical definition of plantations. This term had been used previously to refer to a system of production of scarce staple crops and raw materials in frontier areas, by native or forced labor, for the benefit of absentee owners who reflected the over-all economic needs of an empire. Price and profits were secondary in importance to the volume of production, since goods and scarce raw materials needed to complete the economic and military strength of the empire were the primary consideration. Remnants of this concept survived until recent years saw the eclipse of the German, Italian, Japanese, British, French, and Dutch empires. Some traces of it may be found in the current Soviet program for national self-sufficiency through control of the economies of satellite states.

It may be maintained that the coastal agricultural lands which produced tobacco, indigo, sea-island cotton, rice, and some sugar were plantations in the colonial days. Yet the advent of economic freedom and the disappearance of guaranteed markets and subsidies produced a somewhat new economic situation. New sources of credit had to be found, and their crops were sold in a world-wide market under competitive conditions. The centers of tobacco production moved inland, and much of the crop was raised by smaller independent farmers. Sugar production soon disappeared from the Atlantic coast and moved into Louisiana. Indigo production ceased and sea-island cotton was largely replaced by the extensive growing of short-staple cotton in the piedmont and uplands of the South. However, rice production remained tied to the coastal regions because of its dependence on tides. Rice plantations alone were in a position to nurture the economic and social traditions of the old coastal society. They specialized in production and the improvement of their lands and techniques. They were not free to move on to new lands at will. With the exception of the new Georgia and Florida ricelands, no new areas were available for their highly specialized type of agricultural production. Thus, in a way, they remained apart from the main stream of Southern life as it developed after 1820. The opening up of new tobacco and cotton lands in the piedmont and black belt and the expansion of the sugar-growing fields of the lower Mississippi region were accomplished chiefly by men with less education, culture, and political training than the leaders of *the old coastal society.* These newer entrepreneurs reflected a strong economic drive, and were concerned with profits and speculation in lands and slaves. They exhausted the fertile surface soil by production techniques which might better be called land-butchery and then moved on. Meanwhile the coastal rice planters were tied to their tide-flow swamps. They could not run away to new fields but had to sink or swim economically by means of efficient production. They had to face the problems of credit, land use, price, and management with the hope that nature, the weather, and the Good Lord would not add to their vicissitudes.

Georgia rice plantations were not cash-and-carry economic institutions. Like all capitalistic enterprises they operated through credit advances from various sources. Again, following the usual pattern, their credit was for two purposes: first to provide the capital goods (slaves, lands, buildings, and heavy tools) for the undertaking; and second, to meet the seasonal operating needs of the plantation (food, clothing, seed, repair supplies, and the usual out-of-pocket expenses from planting to harvest time). These operating requirements are comparable to the pay rolls and expenses for raw materials and power disbursed by a factory manager.

The sources of credit available to planters were more varied than is generally known. References to plantation finance are limited in number and quality.[3] Most writers have disposed of the problem by brief and somewhat vague references to the factors or factorage house to whom the planter consigned his crop. After listing a breath-taking series of functions performed by the factor for the planter, the reader is left with the impression that the factorage house provided planters with unlimited drawing accounts and a fat check book which could be used to cover any and all expenses of the plantation and the planter's family.[4] While

[3] Easterby, ed., *The South Carolina Rice Plantation*, pp. 43-49, is an exception to this statement since he discusses capital credit rather adequately.

[4] Phillips, *Life and Labor in the Old South*, pp. 140-42, illustrates this judgment.

this picture of the planter-factor relationship is not basically incorrect, it is incomplete and fails to provide a clear picture of the sources, uses, and limitations of plantation credit.

Alfred H. Stone, one of the few scholars who have written authoritatively on the factorage system in the Southern States, published his brief masterpiece over three decades ago.[5] After describing the historical origins of the system in the West Indies, where the factor was the home agent of the colonial planter, he showed the additional functions of the agent as merchant, banker, and purchasing principal for his clients. He gave a detailed and accurate sketch of the factorage system in the growing of cotton but had one sentence only devoted to rice factors. Thus, it seems desirable in the course of this study to re-examine the relationships existing between factors and rice planters in Georgia on matters pertaining to credit, supplies, and marketing.

From $50,000 to $100,000 was required for a planter to enter the field of rice production in Georgia in the 1830's and 1840's. Slaves were priced at $300 to $500, uncleared rice swamp at around $40 an acre and fully cleared rice swampland as high as $80 an acre.[6] How then did a new rice planter get his start? New planters came from four general sources as follows:

1. Sons, sons-in-law, or other relatives of established planters
2. Intelligent overseers who wanted to try their hands at being planters in their own right
3. Managers designated by factors or creditors who found themselves in possession of plantation lands as the result of the failure of planters to whom they had extended credit.[7]
4. Wealthy outsiders who were intrigued with plantation life and wanted to become members of planter society

A study of many rice plantations in the Savannah and Altamaha river basins suggests that a large number of the new rice planters of those areas received their initial start through family

[5] Alfred H. Stone, "The Cotton Factorage System of the Southern States," *American Historical Review*, XX (April, 1915), 557-65.

[6] Memos by C. Manigault dated 1844 and January 1, 1845, MSS Diary, Louis Manigault MSS, Southern Historical Collection, University of North Carolina Library.

[7] James H. Couper of Hopeton Plantation is an excellent example of this type, since he was installed as manager of Hopeton and other plantations by his father's chief creditor, when his father lost his lands. John Couper to James Couper, May 24, 1828, John Couper MSS, Southern Historical Collection, University of North Carolina Library.

support from successful planters. In such cases the parents, through gift, loan, or inheritance, provided the new planter with the largest portion of his capital goods. True, the elder planter often called on his own factor to extend long-term credit to the beginner, but there was a considerable number of instances where the parent sold slaves, land, and even buildings to his son on credit.[8] This amoeba-type of reproduction by which one plantation became two was possibly more common among rice plantations than in tobacco, cotton, or sugar lands. In some instances, parents or relatives bid in property of neighboring estates at auction and turned over the operation of the additional lands to the younger generation, with the added incentive of an option to buy at a later date.

All of the other types of new planters listed above had to lean very heavily on factors to supply long-term credit to finance their capital investment. The wealthy outsiders may have been a possible exception to this generalization, since their resources possibly were adequate. However, even they acquired their new property through the services of a factor, since he alone had an acquaintance with plantations or undeveloped lands which were available for purchase.[9] He alone had current and expert knowledge of the condition of various plantations and their productive potentialities. Likewise, the new planter needed a factorage contact for supplies and the marketing of his future crops.

When long-term credit was secured from a factor, the indebtedness was usually recognized by a note. Interest charges were at least 8 per cent, with the possibility of an additional brokerage charge of one-half of one per cent if the factor had to rediscount the note. If through bad luck, poor management, or unwise heavy expenses the planter did not extinguish the debt incurred by his seasonal drawing account before the next planting, he signed a note for the balance due and paid the usual interest of 8 per cent.[10] Planters with established reputations could sometimes secure large credit advances by the simple expedient of issuing their

[8] Hugh Fraser Grant was established at Elizafield by this method, as described in Chapter 1 above. The Manigault MSS; collections at the University of North Carolina Library and the Duke University Library show that Louis Manigault was installed at Gowrie by his father Charles in a similar manner.

[9] Stone, "The Cotton Factorage System of the Southern States," *American Historical Review*, XX (1915), 558.

[10] *Ibid.*, p. 561; also factors' accounts in the Elizafield Journal and letter of John Couper to James Couper cited in note 7 above.

own bonds, which were discounted at regional banks or any other local source with surplus cash to invest.[11] This bond technique was used to purchase the slaves and transport them from one plantation to another and even for the purchase of real estate. The bonds might be worded somewhat like modern chattel mortgage bonds or carry no guarantee but the good name of the issuer.

Operating credit to provide the seasonal supply and service needs of the plantation and the planter's family was extended by the factorage house which received the harvested crop. In general, planters did not deal with more than one factor at a time, but when they operated more than one plantation, they often sent the crop of various plantations to different factors. There developed a custom whereby a factor acquired pre-emptive rights to the crop of particular plantations, possibly because he held evidences of long-term indebtedness on the property, through relations with previous owners.[12]

Planters used their operating drawing accounts as the modern businessman uses his checking account with a commercial bank. They paid for plantation supplies and services secured from sources other than the factor by drawing a draft on him for the needed amount, payable to the person from whom the planters had secured these supplies or services. The planters cashed drafts on the factors for personal pocket money. Supplies and services provided by the factor were handled as mere bookkeeping entries on their accounts with the planter and a statement sent to him on each transaction. If planters were in danger of overdrawing their account with one factor they deposited a draft drawn on some other factor who served as their agent for additional plantations which they might be operating.[13] The total drawing account was usually the factor's estimate of the expected value of the current crop, plus any surplus which might have remained from the transactions of the preceding year. Occasionally factors charged interest for the entire drawing account regardless of whether it was used up, but they usually secured their return by a multitude of charges on each service performed for the planter.

There was still another type of operating credit which is

[11] Easterby, ed., *The South Carolina Rice Plantation*, pp. 43-45.

[12] This is illustrated by the Elizafield Journal, which shows that the crops of Elizafield were sent to one factor while that of Evelyn was sent to another.

[13] All items in this paragraph are illustrated by the Elizafield Journal.

GEORGIA RICE COAST IN THE 1850'S

A reproduction of a portion of *Map of the State of Georgia*, compiled by J. R. Butts in 1859 and revised by A. G. Butts in 1870.

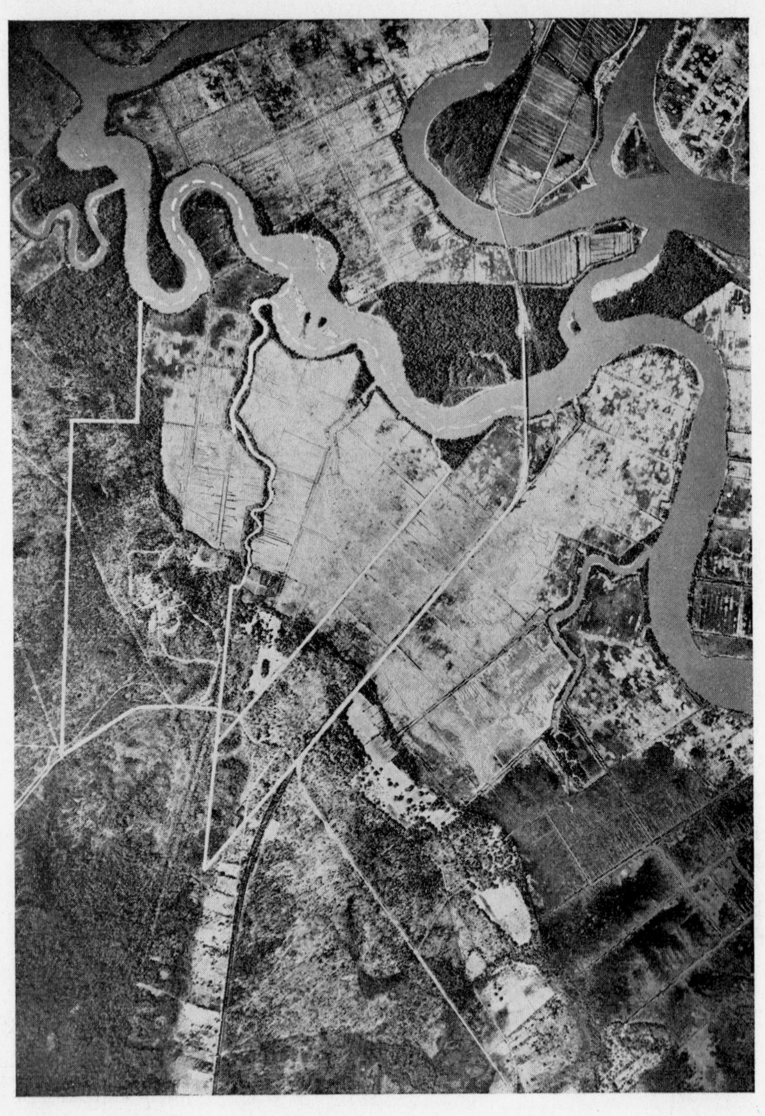

Air Photo of Altamaha Rice Plantation Area Today

A section of an air photo taken by the Geological Survey of the U.S. Department of the Interior in 1948.

seldom mentioned in discussions of plantation finance. This resulted from planters having a variety of economic relationships with their trusted neighbors. The volume of this community exchange of goods and services was quite large, at least in the Altamaha River region. In addition to hiring out their slaves for short periods to neighbors, planters traded simple building materials, salt, livestock, food, and other plantation supplies with one another. True, they eventually paid for these by drafts on their factors, but the credit was actually extended by the neighboring planter who delivered the goods and awaited payment. Some planters had such extensive economic relations with their neighbors that they did not provide payment after each transaction but had a seasonal settlement instead. This type of credit is common in rural communities today.[14]

The question of how or why planters shifted factors is a thorny one, and nothing definitive can be claimed. Most of the Georgia planters dealt with factorage houses in Charleston until 1830. In the years thereafter, Savannah grew as a commercial center and was capable of meeting the supply, marketing, and credit needs of the majority of the rice planters of the Georgia coast.[15] As a result they slowly ended their Charleston connections and operated through Savannah factors. The process by which this transfer was effected is not entirely clear. The planters who were fortunate enough to be clear of debt could merely shift allegiance, but their number was very, very few. Others may have suffered foreclosure by Charleston factors and, when they re-entered the picture on a new tract, they operated through Savannah credit. However, the greater portion made the change by the simple expedient of securing sufficient credit from their new Savannah agents to enable them to satisfy their accounts in Charleston. The development of commercial banking in Savannah provided additional resources to enable the factors and commission houses of that city to extend considerable new credit.

[14] Journals in J. H. Couper MSS, Southern Historical Collection, University of North Carolina Library, illustrate this practice, especially when supplemented by various entries in the Elizafield Journal.

[15] The following sources tell the story of the growth of Savannah 1830-60: Charles H. Olmsted, "Savannah in the '40s," *Georgia Historical Quarterly*, I (September, 1917), 243-52; Roland M. Harper, "Some Savannah Vital Statistics of a Century Ago," *ibid.*, XV (September, 1931), 252-71; C. S. H. Hardee, "Recollections of Old Savannah," *ibid.*, XII (June, 1928), 353-88; Godfrey Barnesley MSS, Duke University Library; and C. F. Mills MSS, Southern Historical Collection, University of North Carolina Library.

Survey accounts of ante-bellum plantation economy stress the one-crop character of agricultural production in the Southern States. They point out the questionable economic wisdom of the planters' practice of placing all their eggs in one basket by concentrating on a single cash crop, which was subject to wild variations in price on the world market. By implication or explicit statements they chide the entire South for its lazy and expensive practice of buying food and other supply materials at ruinous prices from outside the area. They point out that land, materials, and human resources were available to enable the South to produce a large portion of the supplies consumed on the plantations and wonder why this was not done. It can only be said that the writers of such accounts have not examined the source materials on plantation economy with sufficient care or they would not make such sweeping misstatements. Recent research has shown that large quantities of the grain and meat consumed in the ante-bellum South was produced in the area. True, a large portion of this was offered for sale by yeomen white farmers and was purchased by the planters, largely through factors. Yet many planters made an earnest attempt to cut down on their supply bills by producing a great variety of foods and products on their own lands.[16] They also engaged in a continuous exchange of such

[16] Various phases of these observations on plantation provision problems and practices are illustrated by Journal No. 2, December 31, 1839, and Agricultural Notes, p. 51, in J. H. Couper MSS, Southern Historical Collection, University of North Carolina Library. See also Ossaban Island Plantation Book, 1857, in George Kollock MSS, also in Southern Historical Collection, and H. A. Kellar, ed., *Solon Robinson, Pioneer and Agriculturist* (Indianapolis, 1936), II, 349-55. Phillips, ed., *Plantation and Frontier*, pp. 134-66, passim, reproduces various documentary items showing considerable acreage and effort devoted to raising provisions crops. *The Southern Agriculturist* contains numerous articles summarizing studies of the problem, i.e., an article by a rice planter entitled "On the Culture of Corn, Sweet Potatoes and Oats, and the Management of Cattle," 2d Series, IV (January 25, 1831), 172-76. There are occasional references in the Port of Savannah Records, Duke University Library, to shipments of corn *from* Savannah to Havana and European ports, such as the manifest of the Schooner Torrente of June 8, 1833, which showed 295 bushels of corn carried to Havana. Table LV of *The Seventh Census of the United States: 1850* (Washington, 1853), p. lxxxii, indicates that Georgia was seventh in the production of indian corn in that year, with a total crop of about 30,000,000 bushels. She was closely followed by Alabama with 28,000,000 bushels and North Carolina with 27,000,000 bushels. Three of the four leaders were states in the Old Northwest, namely, Ohio with 59,000,000 bushels, Illinois with 57,000,000 bushels, and Indiana with nearly 53,000,000 bushels. Surprisingly, Kentucky ranked second in the nation with 58,000,000 bushels. Fifth place was held down by Tennessee with 52,000,000 bushels, and Virginia ranked sixth with 35,-

goods with their neighbors as has been pointed out.

While the potentially high cash profits of cotton and some other plantation crops may have tempted the planters to neglect the production of provisions, a study of the practices of rice planters in Georgia shows that they, at least, gave considerable attention to the problem of the production of plantation supplies and partially solved it. As the manager of an enterprise the planter had to consider all the factors involved, including the current and predicted price of rice and the availability of labor and suitable land for the production of supply crops. He then made the decision as to just what portion of his supplies he would attempt to produce in any given year. In general, it was more profitable to use ricelands for the growing of rice, unless the soil needed to lie fallow for a year or so. Thus, rice planters did not attempt to raise food crops unless they possessed highlands, hammock lands, or some other acres which were not adapted to the growing of rice.[17] Like modern industrial concerns, they saw no ultimate profit in sacrificing the benefits of specialization by the *diversion* of their resources to the production of other goods. When such auxiliary production could be engaged in without interference with the growth of the main cash crop, a variety of provisions was raised.

Food for the family, the overseer, the labor force, and the plantation animals was potentially the most expensive supply item. The diet for the slaves was mainly slips (small sweet potatoes), roots (larger potatoes and turnips), peas (probably black-eyed), corn meal, salt pork or bacon, and whatever rice flour or third-quality rice was not worth sending to market, and salt. At holiday times they received fresh pork and other surprises. The family consumed whichever of the above items were suited to their more educated appetites, together with such luxuries as ham, sugar, wine, and beef. The overseer usually had his pick of the provisions produced by the plantation (except beef) but had to purchase any fancy foods out of his salary, which ran

000,000 bushels. Pennsylvania and New York, the great grain growing areas of the previous generation, were far down the list with rankings of eleventh and twelfth and production of 19,000,000 and 17,000,000 bushels, respectively.

[17] Hammock lands is a name given to fertile areas where the soil has a limestone base with a surface of sandy loam which has been enriched by the vegetation deposits of large numbers of magnolia, beech, spruce pine, sweet gum, evergreen oak, and dogwood. See R. M. Harper, "Agriculture in Lower Georgia, 1850-1880," *Georgia Historical Quarterly*, VI (1922), 105.

from $400 to $1,000 a year. The oxen and small herd of livestock which was kept for the family subsisted on a diet of rice-straw, pasturage, and possibly some cowpeas, while the horses and ponies received both grain and hay purchased from the outside.[18]

The acreage devoted to raising provisions varied from year to year. Hugh Fraser Grant had a limited amount of land that could be used for the purpose. Therefore, he purchased additional acres at Carteret's Point near-by and attempted unsuccessfully to meet his entire food requirements by their cultivation.[19] His neighbor, James Hamilton Couper, planted less than 100 of his 700 acres to food crops during the first decade (1820-30) of his operation of Hopeton. But the succeeding years saw an even larger acreage devoted to such crops. In 1841 he planted over 200 acres with corn, potatoes, and peas of a total acreage which had by then been expanded to 850 acres.[20] This ratio of approximately one-fifth of his land planted to provisions was exceeded by Hugh Fraser Grant who, in 1844, planted 100 acres to supply crops and 280 to rice.

Available evidence suggests that Altamaha River rice planters raised the major portion of the slips, roots, and peas consumed on their plantations. Despite their best efforts they usually were forced to buy large quantities of corn from Florida or through factors in Savannah or Charleston at prices ranging from 50 to 90 cents a bushel.[21] They seemed to have made little or no effort to produce pork products of any kind and so had to order them through factors. As long as sugar was produced in the region, cane products were purchased from neighbors.[22] Occasionally considerable quantities of rice were exchanged with neighbors for corn.[23] Luxury items including "seegars," wine, and whiskey were ordered in bulk quantities from factors. Salt was procured

[18] This survey of dietary items is drawn largely from the Elizafield Journal, somewhat supplemented by information found in the MSS collections of other plantations previously cited.

[19] See the Elizafield Journal for confirmation.

[20] Crops Record Book, 1818-30, and Summary of Crops at Hopeton, 1827-41, J. H. Couper MSS, Southern Historical Collection, University of North Carolina Library.

[21] Prices quoted from the Elizafield Journal, and Journal No. 2 of J. H. Couper MSS, Southern Historical Collection, University of North Carolina Library.

[22] Journal No. 2, June 4, 1839, of J. H. Couper MSS, Southern Historical Collection, University of North Carolina Library.

[23] *Ibid.*, December 31, 1839.

from factors who shared in shipload consignments to Savannah from England.[24]

Simple building materials, such as bricks, lumber, and shingles were sometimes produced on the plantation by semiskilled slaves. More frequently they were ordered from near-by suppliers of such items, some of whom were marginal yeomen who scraped a meager living from some poor quality land and the forest. These items were paid for by drafts on factors or by plantation provision crops. Lathes, nails, white lead, paint oil, tar, and lime usually had to be ordered through the factor. However, Altamaha River planters sometimes patronized ship chandlery firms in the near-by small seaport of Darien, who carried many of these goods. Heavier tools such as steam engines (and repair parts for the same), plows, and other bulky hardware were ordered from the factors, although Hugh Fraser Grant developed the practice of ordering many of such items direct from dealers in Savannah.[25]

Clothing, blankets, and shoes priced at about $1.00 a pair,[26] were ordered from factors for the slaves. Family clothing was purchased by special order or through personal selection during trips to Savannah from dealers in that city. The Elizafield Journal is filled with reference to payments to merchants for hats, ribbons, and fine cloth. Factors made all arrangements for trips of the planter's families to New York, Europe, and other resorts. Medical care for the family was similar to arrangements for private medical attention today. However, the planter usually provided for the care of his slave population by a contract with a neighboring physician at around $1.50 per slave per year. The doctor agreed to be available on call whenever serious sickness occurred among the slaves, with no extra compensation for travel expenses.[27] Dentistry for the family was performed during visits to Savannah as shown in the Elizafield Journal.

[24] Sales and Invoice Book, July 16, 1840, and October 30, 1841, C. F. Mills MSS, Southern Historical Collection, University of North Carolina Library.

[25] All data on building materials obtained from the Elizafield Journal, supplemented by entries from the C. Manigault MSS and the J. H. Couper MSS, both in the Southern Historical Collection, University of North Carolina Library.

[26] Journal No. 2, December 31, 1841, and November 15, 1842, J. H. Couper MSS, Southern Historical Collection, University of North Carolina Library.

[27] MSS Diary, Memo by C. Manigault dated April 15, 1845, Louis Manigault MSS, Southern Historical Collection, University of North Carolina Library.

In these days of modern industrial production the public press is full of references to the role of management in contemporary economic strife and in disagreements with labor, the consuming public, and government. The general public, academicians, and business experts have learned of the existence of a highly specialized corps of men known as management engineers. These specialists are continually making a series of time, cost, and personnel studies on the operations of the concern. They advise the managers, directors, and owners of enterprises on new policies and techniques to bring about greater over-all production at less cost per unit, with resulting higher profits. Management thus has become a specialized profession, separated from ownership in nearly all large-scale economic operations. The owners (stockholders) and creditors (bondholders) are scattered to the four corners of the world. They have no direct concern with the operating policies or productive process unless their profits (dividends) or interest payments (coupons) fail to be forthcoming.

Nearly all of the basic management problems of today were present in the operation of the plantation system of the Old South, although they were not handled by personnel operating as cogs in an elaborate functional and organizational chart. There were two outstanding differences, however, as compared with today: first, owners of plantations usually were managers also, and second, the members of their labor force were not guaranteed collective bargaining and were not free to pick up their worldly goods and move on to other employment. The tradition of the cultured old Southern gentleman sipping a mint julep, while sitting on the veranda of a magnificent plantation edifice, surrounded by magnolias, live oaks, and crape myrtle trees is largely incorrect. The limited number of plantation owners who could indulge in such living had previously put in long years in building up a competent organization of overseers, managers, and co-operating relatives, who profited from the older man's extensive experience and knowledge in the running of the plantations.

Even efficiently run plantations required a surprising amount of personal attention from the manager. Many basic decisions as to finance, supply, planting schedules, treatment of the growing crop, and marketing arrangements had to be made by the responsible manager. More often than not this manager was the owner, the planter himself. He had to ride the rounds of his fields, checking the progress of the crop. His practiced eye detected inefficiency in the labor force, poor cultivation techniques, lack of adequate water, etc. This was especially true on rice plantations where the growing of the crop was subject to multiple hazards not present in the production of clean culture crops.

Overseers generally functioned as executive officers for the owners, not as deputy managers. They saw to it that the owners' carefully prepared instructions were followed.[28] Those owners who gamboled off to Europe or some resort for a year or so, leaving the overseer in charge, often returned to face near disaster. Some owners attempted to solve this difficulty (especially when they possessed more than one plantation) by installing a son, son-in-law, or some very efficient younger member of the planter class as operator during their absence. Occasionally this technique was successful, as exemplified by the brilliant administration of James Hamilton Couper at Hopeton. But it may be concluded that successful planters generally found it necessary to be on the job, supervising the over-all life of the plantation at all times. After all, a capitalistic enterprise with $100,000 to $500,000 of invested capital and a labor force of 100 to 1,000 must be adequately directed or it will deteriorate rapidly. This was especially true in any such undertaking as rice culture where a recalcitrant labor force, a lazy or inefficient overseer, or an unkind nature could do such tremendous economic damage in the space of a few short days.

The basic management problems of preparation of the rice fields, planting and culture of the crop, finance, and supply have been discussed. Other outstanding problems on which decisions had to be made were, first, securing, training, and controlling the labor force, and second, supervision of winter activities on the plantation. Supervision of the preparation of the crop for market and the scheduling of shipments of the crop to the factors were also management problems of significance. They can best be discussed later in connection with the over-all problem of the marketing of rice.

The volume of printed words on American Negro slavery is so tremendous that it may seem futile to review its operation on Georgia rice plantations. Although some scholars insist that the definitive work on slavery in the Southern States has still to be written, the interested reader has his choice of a great variety of

[28] See Phillips, *Plantation and Frontier*, I, 109-30, for examples of instructions to overseers.

fine works on the subject which have appeared in the past half century. Of these the two volumes of documentary source material and two volumes of interpretative history on the subject from the pen of Professor Phillips would seem to be the best summaries.[29] There is little need here to quarrel with the conclusions of that great student of Southern life, even though variations in detail may be discernible to one who has conducted intensive research in the limited field of Georgia rice plantations.[30] He does, however, fail to point up the fact that the slave system in rice-growing areas differed in some important respects from other regions. These differences are hinted at in some recent works[31] and in the traditions which are still repeated along the Georgia coast. They can be reduced to the following concepts:

1. There was limited interchange of slaves between rice-growing areas and other types of plantations. Natural increase provided a rather adequate supply of hands, with little or no surplus to be sold off. Where more slaves were needed because of the opening up of new lands, the new hands were usually acquired from other rice plantations, especially estates in the process of being settled.

2. Rice plantation slaves were not content when transferred to plantations of other types and were of little use in the cotton fields, which usually operated under the gang system.

3. Discipline was more stringent on rice plantations than elsewhere. This was supposedly owing to the fact that the Negroes alone remained on the plantation at night during the growing season and thus any transgressions must be promptly and severely punished to prevent runaways, thievery and licentiousness.

A study of the records of numerous rice plantations in Georgia suggests that all of the above traditions are basically correct. The Elizafield Journal has very few entries of the purchase or sale of slaves during a period of twenty years. Other records support the concept that while rice slaves were sometimes sold from one rice plantation to another, especially when estates were settled, yet they seldom were fed into the general slave market and transported to labor on distant cotton, tobacco, or sugar fields.

[29] *Ibid.;* and his *American Negro Slavery* and *Life and Labor in the Old South.*

[30] The U. B. Phillips MSS at Yale University Library were consulted by the writer in September, 1941. The sparseness of notes and primary materials on rice culture in comparison with those on cotton and tobacco was very apparent.

[31] Simkins, *The South, Old and New,* p. 46.

Rice hands became accustomed to a diet which included considerable rice and seemed to languish when forced to go without their favorite food. They also usually operated on the task rather than the gang system. Under the supervision of reasonable overseers and drivers this could result in tolerable working conditions. The very isolation of rice plantations may have made possible more liberty within the plantation area. Finally the necessity for a species of group self-discipline at night may have produced a happier living environment, although proof on such matters is not readily available.

In the 1840's and 1850's prime field hands on Georgia rice lands cost between $300 and $500, with an average of close to $450. When sold in family lots any children or old folks were rated as one-half or one-quarter hands and priced accordingly. An efficiently run rice plantation required one field hand for every seven acres of rice swamp cultivated.[32] Because of sickness and the presence of many children and older slaves, an overseer could seldom muster more than 40 to 50 per cent of the total slave population for duty in the field.[33] It required between $20 and $30 a year to provide a slave with adequate food, shelter, and clothing, depending on whether he was fed good rice at $2.50 a bushel or corn at $1.00 a bushel.[34]

Customarily in the slave plantation system the house and yard slaves were somewhat privileged. They performed a variety of housekeeping duties as cooks, washwomen, seamstresses, nurses, coachmen, carpenters and yard watchmen. Field hands (both men and women) were rated as prime when they could perform the expected task in the usual working day of nine to ten hours. Boys aged ten to fourteen and women with little physical vigor were rated as one-quarter or one-half of a prime hand. Some women were rated as "hoes," meaning that they could wield a hoe for a full day but could not perform other and heavier duties. Each plantation had one or more drivers who sometimes added a fancy title such as Prince to their given name to indicate that they were a species of sub-foreman. They fulfilled functions some-

[32] MSS Diary, Memo by C. Manigault dated 1844, Louis Manigault MSS, Southern Historical Collection, University of North Carolina Library.

[33] *Ibid.*, Memo dated January 1, 1845; Sick List, 1860, Ossaban Island Plantation Book, George Kollock MSS, Southern Historical Collection, University of North Carolina Library. The Elizafield Journal also confirms this ratio.

[34] Phillips, ed., *Plantation and Frontier*, I, 135, quoting C. Manigault MSS.

what similar to those of a pusher in present-day construction work in that they personally assigned tasks to individual hands and inspected the finished work before the hand was allowed to "knock off" work for the day. In addition, certain responsible slaves, known as "trunk minders," undertook to care for all trunks, gates, sluices, and canals. They had the use of a personal flatboat to enable them to get about over the extensive water system with facility. Older slaves, no longer valuable in the field, were assigned as bird minders and rat men to drive off or kill these pests which devoured the crop.

Tasks expected to be completed by a slave in one day's labor were not oppressive. They were figured on the expected performance of the "meanest full hand in nine hours, working industriously."[35] The day's task was seldom increased and work in excess of the task was frowned upon, yet the task once assigned had to be completed. Sample tasks expected on rice plantations ran somewhat as follows:

1. The standard task was one-quarter of an acre, a square 105 feet on a side. This applied regardless of whether the operation was trenching, hoeing, cutting the rice crop, and tieing or carrying off the newly tied sheaves to the flats. This task might be increased under stress to meet a planting or harvesting schedule but not decreased. Likewise if the crop were largely free of grass as the result of covered planting, the hoeing task might be increased.

2. Excavation of ditches and canals—the task was 600 cubic feet. This might be decreased slightly if freshly cleared land were being worked on.

3. Threshing with flail stick—the task was 600 sheaves or twelve bushels of rice. When slaves got smart and tied very thin sheaves because they knew they would have to thresh 600 of them, the planters shifted their measuring unit and demanded twelve bushels of rough rice at the end of the day.[36]

The planter usually managed his planting schedule so that a portion of his labor force would be free to plant food crops on

[35] *Ibid.*, p. 117, quoting Rules on Rice Estate (1856) of P. C. Weston, South Carolina, as published in *DeBow's Review*, XXI (January, 1857), 38-44.

[36] Slave List and Plantation Notes, Mackey-Stiles MSS, and Slave Record Book, C. Manigault MSS, both in Southern Historical Collection, University of North Carolina Library; and Legare, "Synopsis of the Culture of Rice—on Black River," *Southern Agriculturist*, I (1841), 80-81.

the highlands and hammock lands in the intervals between plantings of rice. Corn was planted as the first food crop, followed by crops requiring a shorter growing season. Potato slips were not planted until after the rice plantings were completed in May. Generally, few if any of the food crops were harvested until after all of the rice was cut and stacked in the yard in late September. All food crops received whatever attention could be spared them during the growing season, but it was always understood that the good health of the rice crop was the primary consideration of the planter.

Since all harvesting was not completed until November, the four winter months were almost too short a period for the accomplishment of the variety of work which had to be finished before the first planting in March. In addition to threshing, pounding, and periodically shipping the rice to market, all the fields had to be worked over in preparation for the new year.

The first problem was that of volunteer rice. There was often danger that a spell of warm weather might cause the grains which fell during harvesting or from the stubble during the winter to sprout a winter crop of unwanted rice. The methods of control were several and, one might say, equally ineffective. Sometimes the fields were burned off. Other planters plowed deeply so as to bury the fallen rice where it would not be likely to germinate. Still others purposely flooded the field in November so as to force the volunteer rice to sprout. When it had been nourished to the proper height, they either plowed it under or cut it off and threw away the straw. This last technique was used more frequently in Georgia than in the Carolinas because the milder climate made it possible. Finally some planters, in desperation, kept their fields covered during most of the winter with a considerable depth of water to prevent any plant life from getting started.

Regardless of what technique was used to control volunteer rice, the fields had to be plowed (or turned) and harrowed during the winter. Trunks, canals, and ditches also had to be cleaned of all the refuse which had collected during the growing season. If the planter possessed uncleared lands he used his labor during the winter to construct new rice fields. Some planters found that work available on their own lands was not enough to keep all the slaves busy during the winter. If so they were willing to hire out some of their hands to private contractors building such projects as the Brunswick-Altamaha Canal or to neighbors who were building large new embankments or clearing unusually large stretches of new land.

At the end of the year when the planter was in a position to total his expenditures, gaze at his crops in storage, and attempt to measure the progress made in the preceding twelve months, he often had cause for satisfaction. A bountiful nature and good management may have produced fine results in both rice and food crops. Repairs to his buildings and the maintenance work on his fields and banks might have progressed rapidly, but he still was unable to estimate his financial position definitively. He still had the enormous task before him of preparing his crop for market. He remained at the mercy of brokers, agents, shippers, and factors, operating in near-by and distant markets. His final profit for the year depended on prices; prices charged for services and supplies, and the prices he received for his crop. He could only wait to see what his fate would be.

# Chapter Four

## THE MILLING AND MARKETING OF GEORGIA RICE, 1830-60

IN ANY CAPITALISTIC INDUSTRY the marketing of products manufactured is the final and in many ways the most important step in the entire process. Final net return is dependent upon the market price received, less production, transportation, and marketing costs. Prices are set largely by the relationship between supply and demand in the primary markets. However, marketing conditions in these near-by or first-instance commercial centers are themselves dependent upon the countless economic factors and forces which operate in distant trading areas. This was especially true of a commodity such as rice, whose price was set largely in the world market. The net return to the rice planter was also seriously affected by the nature, types, and extent of transportation facilities available to carry the crop to market safely, cheaply, and promptly during periods when demand established favorable prices in near-by markets. Finally, net income was continuously influenced by the extent and nature of the facilities provided as well as by the expenses, charges, and commission rates of the middlemen who handled the crop on its long journey from plantation to consumers.

While it is possible for planters operating in isolated areas to fare well by shipping to distant markets, the chances of increased net return are obviously enhanced if an adequate commercial center is available near-by. The proximity of such facilities makes possible more appropriate timing of shipments of crops to catch the peaks of market prices. It also encourages closer working relationships with factorage houses and other middlemen concerned. This was especially true of the transportation problems of the Georgia rice planters, since they were largely dependent on the dispatch, by their factors, of coastal sloops, or itinerant coastal tramp vessels of light draft which could pull up at plantation wharves to load and unload.

Until sometime in the decade of the 1830's, the rice planters of Georgia did not have adequate marketing arrangements available in their home state. Up to that time the facilities of Savannah were incapable of handling the large-scale marketing of plantation crops. A few of the sea-island planters still followed British colonial traditions and carried on all commercial transactions with agents in England. A few more shipped and bought from Savannah, but most planters reflected their early status as colonial adjuncts to the rice center of the United States by consigning their total production to factors in Charleston, South Carolina.

In the three decades before 1860, Savannah achieved adequate stature as a commercial, shipping, credit, and transportation center. As the number of docks and locally owned sloops, schooners, terns, and brigs increased, the number and resources of commission houses, merchants, agents, counting rooms, and warehouses operating along Bay Street expanded and provided sufficient services for the rice coast and the rapidly spreading inland and upcountry cotton region.[1] As the result of this development, the growing metropolis had, by 1860, achieved control of 60 per cent of the rice produced along the Savannah River (including the product of the Carolina banks of the river) and a near monopoly of all the crops of the rice plantations located on the banks of all the other large rivers which emptied into the Atlantic between South Carolina and Florida.[2]

Georgia planters shipped the great bulk of their crops to market during the winter months, in the weeks between the end of the harvest season and the first planting in the spring. In these months the labor force alternated between the tasks of preparing the crop for market and the routine plowing, cleaning of the fields, and destruction of volunteer rice previously described. As the bound sheaves were unloaded from the flats, they were sorted,

[1] See *Directory for the City of Savannah*, 1859, for an itemized listing of commercial establishments and other marketing agencies operating in that year. Consult also C. H. Olmstead, "Savannah in the '40's," *Georgia Historical Quarterly*, I (September, 1917), 243-52.

[2] MSS Diary, January, 1860, Louis Manigault MSS, Southern Historical Collection, University of North Carolina Library.

and those which were dry were stacked in the yard. All wet sheaves were carefully opened and dried before being added to the remainder of the crop. Experience and tradition determined the size and construction of the yard stacks of rice. Since the grain often remained in these stacks for many weeks, every precaution was taken to make them safe from the hazards of wind and weather. Usual outside measurements called for a stack 45 feet long, 12 feet wide, and 10 to 12 feet in height to the point where the top of the stack began to slope upwards. Such a stack would produce approximately 1,000 bushels of rough rice when threshed and shipped to market. Stacks were always built running north and south, so that each side would receive the benefit of the sun for half a day.[3]

After the yard stacking had been completed and some attention given to the harvesting of provision crops, the tedious and somewhat delicate tasks of threshing, cleaning, and pounding the rice grain were begun. As the marketable rice accumulated, it was often loaded directly on ships tied up to the plantation wharf. Otherwise, it was stored temporarily in the mill. Market shipments commenced in late October or early November, and the last ships were usually loaded by mid-March, although there are records of some sales as late as the last week of April.[4] The majority of Georgia planters made their shipments in the form of rough rice. This was loaded into sacks at the mill or storage barn and carried to the plantation dock by the Negroes. There they emptied the grain directly into the hold of waiting vessels, which carried it in bulk to market. Others who owned and operated their own rice mills shipped clean rice in barrels of about 600 pounds, which were usually referred to as tierces or casks.

The preparation of the rice crop for shipment to market was not a simple, single operation. Various steps were required for the processing of the grain, with considerable supervision, labor, and even machinery involved. Threshing, the first step, produced a mixture of chaff and the grain in its outer shell. Cleaning, the next process, produced rough rice, which was the clean grain with both its inner and outer shells intact. Pounding or grinding cracked the outer shell, blew it away as chaff, and left a residue

[3] Pocket Notebook, 1852, Louis Manigault MSS, Duke University Library.

[4] See Hugh Fraser Grant's accounts with his factors for confirmation and illustration of this scheduling of market shipments.

known as shelled rice. When this was beaten and polished by the completion of the milling process, the result was clean white rice of two sizes, large and small, plus the powdered fragments of white rice which were known as rice flour. Rough rice was figured by the bushel, averaging forty-five pounds each. Clean white rice (large) weighed about sixty-two pounds per bushel, and prices on it were quoted in units of 100 pounds each. Thus a price of 2½ meant $2.50 per hundredweight.

A few of the larger Georgia plantations were equipped with complete milling facilities, notably Hopeton on the Altamaha River and Gowrie on the Savannah River. This involved a capital investment of from $6,000 to $10,000 for buildings and machinery.[5] A few also possessed steam threshers which, operating from a fixed installation, performed the primary step of separating the grain from the stalks. These were crude forerunners of modern grain threshing machines and operated on the same principles of cutting and chewing up the stalks, while blowing or sucking off the chaff.

The bulk of Georgia rice was, however, threshed by slave labor wielding flail sticks on rice stalks spread out on especially constructed threshing floors. An efficient threshing floor was 110 feet long and 60 feet wide, composed of three ranges of boards which were constructed separately and could be moved about in sections. Extra boards were pegged along the outer edges of the combined floor, as well as at the two places where the three ranges touched. Such a floor provided working space for twenty-five hands simultaneously. The daily task for each hand was twelve bushels of uncleaned grain. Some planters set the daily task at 600 sheaves, which yielded twelve to fifteen bushels, depending on the size of the grain. However, since the Negroes were cunning enough to know that what they harvested in the field they would have to thresh, they sometimes tied small sheaves. Planters then attempted to remedy this situation by counting 110 sheaves as 100 in figuring the daily task. Most planters found it more satisfactory to go entirely by measure, by placing a large tub on the threshing floor which, when full of threshed rice, particles of straw, and tailings, would produce twelve bushels of winnowed rice. This did not stump the smarter Negroes,

[5] Memorandum by C. Manigault, 1845, in MSS Diary of Louis Manigault, Southern Historical Collection, University of North Carolina Library, estimates the value of his rice mill at Gowrie (Savannah River) at $7,500.

who circumvented this requirement by mixing the greatest possible amount of cut straw with the grain which was destined for the measuring tub.[6]

Seed rice, however, could not be threshed satisfactorily by either the steam thresher or the flail stick, since the blows inflicted from either method cracked the shells of the grain and ruined it for seed purposes. Cracked seed, when planted, allowed water to seep in and rot the grain before it could sprout. The only safe method called for a careful shaking and beating of individual sheaves on the edge of rice barrels until all the ripe grain fell into the barrel. With two hands working on each barrel and as many as six barrels being filled at a time, it was possible to thresh all the seed rice needed for the next season in a week or two.[7]

After the threshing of any portion of the crop was completed, each planter had to decide whether to ship his grain to market as rough rice or as pounded, clean rice. Comparative prices offered and the comparative costs of transportation and handling were significant. Yet the cost, nature, efficiency, and extent of the milling facilities available on the planter's own or a near-by plantation were primary elements in his decision. Rice mills represented a considerable investment in buildings and machinery. They were operated for limited periods only during five months of the year. The equipment though ingenious was primitive and somewhat fragile, judged by modern standards. Repairs were needed continuously, and extended interruptions of production could result in a degree of inconvenience which might approach the status of near economic disaster, if vital parts could not be replaced readily by near-by equipment dealers. The number of slaves who could be trained to operate the milling process was limited, and many foremen who were excellent growers of rice were not too adept, despite the Yankee ancestry of many of them, at operating machinery. This situation often meant that the planter himself had to serve as "plant superintendent and chief mechanic."

This recital of the risks, responsibilities, and requirements involved in the operation of an efficient rice mill helps to explain why all planters did not attempt to maintain complete milling equipment. In addition, past practice, dating from earlier periods when

[6] See 1844 in *ibid.* for a further description of threshing floor and tasks.

[7] C. Manigault to Louis Manigault, January 10, 1856, Louis Manigault MSS, Duke University Library.

centralized milling in marketing areas was general, served to discourage the rapid development of plantation milling facilities. All rice plantations worthy of the name, however, had at least one building devoted to the threshing, cleaning, and storage of rice. Rudimentary machinery, including screens and a wind fan to carry away the chaff, was installed. Power was supplied by the tides, a steam engine, animal power, or the wind. Regardless of the type of power employed, operations usually were conducted on windy days to enable nature's breezes to assist in the cleaning process.[8] Threshing and cleaning mills were sometimes incorporated into the building which housed the pounding and polishing machinery. If so, they occupied a room or section of the building which could be connected easily with the common source of power. They actually performed the preliminary processing in an assembly-line type of operation which was designed to produce clean rice ready for the market.

Rice mills usually were located near the banks of a river, branch, or creek. This was to facilitate the loading of the produce on board the light-draft coastal vessels which carried the crop to market. Location near a tidewater stream was also necessary, if the tides were to serve as the main source of power.

Brick was the favorite material used in the construction of rice mills. Substantial chimneys and sheds containing the steam engine and boiler were attached to the main structure. The milling process required a room some 60 feet in length and about 40 feet in width. Thus the over-all dimensions would often run as high as 100 feet in length and 50 feet in width.[9] The combination type of mill included rooms or sections devoted to threshing, to pounding, screening, and cleaning, and to barreling, loading, or storage.

The primary operation in the *milling process* was the cracking

[8] The Elizafield Journal of Hugh Fraser Grant shows that Elizafield was provided with such equipment but not with full milling machinery. James H. Couper makes continuous reference in his Agricultural Notes, Southern Historical Collection, University of North Carolina Library, to the velocity and direction of the wind on days when his mill was cleaning rough rice. See also R. F. W. Allston in *DeBow's Review*, I (April, 1846), 340, for a description of the adaptation by Calvin Emmons of New York of the threshing mill invented by Dr. Robert Nesbit.

[9] The Slave Record Book of Gowrie plantation gives the dimensions of the rice mill as 82½ feet by 40 feet with 13 pestles operating. See Manigault MSS, 1833, Southern Historical Collection, University of North Carolina Library.

of the outer shell of the rice without damaging the inner core of the grain. This was usually accomplished by machinery designed to raise a series of slotted timbers, called pestles, a short distance above a mortar filled with rough rice, which were allowed to drop on "the deep contents of the mortar."[10] Experience and observation of results indicated the necessary adjustment of the machinery so that the pestles would fall from the exact height required to produce the precise degree of pressure needed to break the outer shell but not harm the inner grain. These pestles were lifted by the spokes of wheels attached to an overhead shaft which rotated 6 to 8 feet above the mortars. Each revolution of the wheels lifted the pestles four times. The pounding pestles themselves varied in length from 4 to 5 feet and in diameter from 2 to 4 inches. James Hamilton Couper of Hopeton recorded in his "Agricultural Notes" that the main crank shaft of his steam engine made 32 revolutions per minute. This was connected in turn with the drive shaft running to the overhead shaft, so that the pestle wheel made approximately 12 revolutions per minute and produced 45 strokes by the pestles each minute. This hookup delivered from 10 to 12 horsepower at the pestle wheels.

Rough rice was fed into the mortars by hand, and the contents spilled over after each fall of the pestles. The mortars were 30 or more inches high and 18 to 24 inches in diameter. The pounding well within the mortars was hollowed out about 12 inches deep and slightly more at the mouth. The mixture of shelled rice and chaff was subsequently passed through a series of sifting, sanding, and brushing screens which deposited the grain at the further end of the building, where a wind fan, which turned at a rate of as high as 400 revolutions per minute, drew off the chaff and tailings. The screens separated the mill product into three categories of large rice, small rice, and rice flour.

The labor force requirements were small for the threshing. Two or three hands to feed and several more to supply the feeders, plus one hand to fire the boiler were sufficient. This was not true however of the larger pounding and cleaning mills, where

[10] The general description of the milling process is founded on the brief account contained in Phillips, *Life and Labor in the Old South*, p. 116. The details of measurements and arrangement of machinery were supplied by an interview with the late Marmaduke Floyd of Savannah and by the very extensive data set down by James H. Couper in his Agricultural Notes, pp. 54, 56-58, J. H. Couper MSS, Southern Historical Collection, University of North Carolina Library.

as many as seven prime hands and ten or more boys and girls could be kept busy.[11] While the process cannot be classified as entirely mechanical, yet the arrangements of all shafts, pestles, mortars, screens, and fans was such that a minimum of hand labor was required.

The output of these mills was considerable and surprising. James Hamilton Couper of Hopeton recorded the results of a time study of the operation of his threshing mill under ideal conditions in 1835. He estimated that, even when he was compelled to rethresh as much as one-third of his rice straw, the mill turned out 50 bushels of rough rice per hour or 500 per day. Another study in 1837 of operations under somewhat adverse circumstances showed an output of approximately one-half that of the 1835 study.[12] One commercial manufacturer of rice threshing machines estimated that any parcel of rice was worked through the entire process in about one minute.[13] Output, of course, varied with the type of power used. Wind power was variable, while animal power generally produced less than one-half that of steam.

Evidence as to the exact volume of the output of Georgia pounding mills is scarce. However, Governor R. F. W. Allston reported the output of a pounding mill in South Carolina which operated 20 pestles as 3,000 bushels of rough rice pounded in 60 hours. He also described a phenomenal 2,000 bushels pounded in "one day" by the famous Chisholm Mill.[14] The capacity of the plantation mills in Georgia probably did not approach that of the Carolina mills, with the possible exception of that operated by James Hamilton Couper at Hopeton on the Altamaha. Rather it was more common to find small mills in Georgia with fewer pestles working at slower speeds using tides or small steam engines for power. One of these at Gowrie in the Savannah River turned out "8 to 10 barrels with each tide," with a total of 460 barrels

[11] *Ibid.*, p. 54, and Slave Record Book (Gowrie), 1833, Manigault MSS, Southern Historical Collection, University of North Carolina Library. See also memorandum by C. Manigault in MSS diary of Louis Manigault, in the Southern Historical Collection.

[12] Agricultural Notes, pp. 54, 55, J. H. Couper MSS, Southern Historical Collection, University of North Carolina Library.

[13] Reference is to "directions supplied by one M. Honet for his rice machine," installed by James H. Couper at Hopeton and recorded in Agricultural Notes, p. 62.

[14] Letters of Benjamin King and A. W. Chisholm to R. F. W. Allston, November 16, 1843, and November 21, 1843, respectively, in R. F. W. Allston, *Memoir on the Introduction and Planting of Rice* (Charleston, 1843), p. 63.

pounded in three months in 1832-33.[15] This was possibly typical of the average production of Georgia mills using tide for power. Those employing steam would doubtless be able to double this daily production on a good day.

All mills in Georgia pounded their rice with pestles until the introduction of Deforest's mill machinery in the mid 1830's. This operated on the principle of crushing the rice shells between revolving and fixed stone cylinders. Each "machine" stood 5 feet high and was 3 feet square. Machines were placed in groups of four so that a single spin wheel could activate all four machines. One set of four machines milled about twenty-five bushels of rough rice per hour. This was superior to the pestle method in terms of speed but was inferior in that it produced a much higher percentage of small rice and rice flour than the usual pestle process. This, of course, reduced the net value of the yield.[16] Such criticism, however, could not be leveled at Honet's Clean Rice Mill which employed the stone roller principle and turned out a slightly greater percentage of prime clean rice than the older pestle operations. Some speed in production may have been sacrificed by the Honet system, and operating expenses may have been higher; yet James Hamilton Couper felt called upon to record its favorable characteristics.[17]

A balance sheet showing the *weight* of the output of typical threshing and milling operations might read as follows:

1. Rice sheaves when threshed yielded by weight about one-fourth straw and three-fourths rough rice mixed with small straw.
2. When cleaned a bushel of rough rice weighed approximately 45 pounds.
3. Twenty-one bushels of rough rice when pounded by pestles and cleaned and polished yielded:
   a. 600 pounds or one tierce of prime clean rice (59 per cent)
   b. 66 pounds of clean small rice ( 7 per cent)
   c. 75 pounds of rice flour ( 8 per cent)
   d. 245 pounds of chaff and tailings (26 per cent)

These figures and percentages would, of course, vary with the

[15] Slave Record Book (Gowrie), 1833, Manigault MSS, Southern Historical Collection, University of North Carolina Library.

[16] Agricultural Notes, p. 55, J. H. Couper MSS, Southern Historical Collection, University of North Carolina Library.

[17] *Ibid.*, p. 62.

quality of the rice grown and the type of milling machinery employed, but they served as the basis for the planter in making a rough estimate of the volume and value of his crop yield.[18]

Obviously a planter who did not possess complete milling facilities or have them available near-by could not ship clean rice directly to his factor in the marketing center. But even those who were so equipped occasionally sold a portion of their crop as rough rice. Many economic factors entered into the making of this decision. These included comparative gross prices for rough or clean rice and transportation costs, as well as the possibility of being relieved of the necessity of paying for the various charges and services involved. Net return was usually the deciding factor, but since the preparation of rough rice was an uncomplicated operation while the production of clean white rice was an extended and complex process, the varying temperaments of the planters concerned was often a significant element in the decision. It was a rather simple matter to ship rough rice to the factor and turn over to him all of the headaches of milling, cooperage, insurance, storage, weighing, drayage, loading, and unloading. Of course, the cost of all these services was charged back to the planter, but he need not concern himself with their accomplishment. On the other hand, planters who possessed complete milling facilities stood to receive a greater net return if they sold the finished product. But, they were also letting themselves in for a succession of milling, transportation, and marketing problems which required close supervision and considerable patience. [19]

Planters whose milling equipment was inadequate and who were considering the advantages of establishing an efficient plantation mill had to balance the pros and cons of the proposition with care. Such benefits as might result from milling clean rice

[18] *Ibid.*, p. 49. These figures are confirmed in part or in their entirety by all sources consulted during the course of this study which gave data on the problem.

[19] This general evaluation of the problem of rough rice vs. clean rice is founded on an analysis of the situation in South Carolina as set forth in a report to the Agricultural Society of South Carolina entitled "Expenses on Preparing Rice for Market," which was published in the *Southern Agriculturist*, 2d Series, III (December, 1843), 456-58. However, the basic pattern is confirmed by numerous items in Georgia sources such as the Elizafield Journal of Hugh Fraser Grant, and more especially in the detailed calculations and analysis of the alternatives recorded by James Hamilton Couper in his Agricultural Notes, pp. 50-53, covering the years 1834-37, J. H. Couper MSS, Southern Historical Collection, University of North Carolina Library.

on the plantation had to be balanced against the costs. The advantages were numerous and included the following:

1. Rice flour, which was worth around 15 cents a bushel and composed one-third of the mill product by measure and one-seventh by weight, could be consumed on the plantation by the labor force and the livestock. It was nearly worthless in the metropolitan market because of its bulk when transported any distance.

2. Planters could build their own tierces, casks, or barrels at a cost of about 50 cents each and not be forced to pay 87 cents for them at the rice toll mill.

3. Mill tolls varying from 7½ to 9 per cent of the market price of the clean rice produced by milling could be saved.

4. Finally, freight charges would be somewhat reduced, since neither the chaff produced by the milling process nor the rice flour would be subject to transportation. These items represented somewhat more than one-fourth of the weight of the original rough rice.[20]

In the face of such possibilities for increased net return, it may seem strange that all Georgia planters did not mill their own rice. But when the original cost of rice mill buildings and machinery is considered, it is obvious that the balance would be in favor of plantation milling only if a rather large crop were produced. Likewise, the traditions of factor-planter relationships were strong. Some planters may have been forced by circumstances to follow the advice of their factors who operated their own mills. Thus, it is possible that some who contemplated establishing complete milling facilities on their plantations were dissuaded.

Rice prices were quoted in Savannah and Charleston for both rough and clean rice.[21] Yet world prices for the grain were usually announced solely for clean rice, and by weight only. The price of rough rice, which was sold by the bushel, was figured by measure but was based on the average weight of the clean rice which probably would be produced from it when milled. The price relationship was generally "one to four"; that is, if *100*

[20] Couper, Agricultural Notes, pp. 50-53.

[21] For price quotations in Savannah, see the Savannah Shipping and Commercial List published in 1840's and 1850's by the *Daily Georgian*, and the Prices Current published by the Savannah *Weekly Republican* during much of the same period.

[22] This ratio was used by James H. Couper in his calculations mentioned in note 19 above.

*pounds* of clean rice were quoted at $4.00, the price of a *bushel* of rough rice was usually about $1.00.[22] Since a bushel of rough rice weighed approximately 45 pounds before milling, it might be more accurate to say that the price of rough rice was about half that of clean rice by weight. Yet the planters, millers, factors, and merchants all preferred to use the "one to four" quotation, even though this practice involved mixing prices based on measure with those figured by weight.

Merchants and agents of northern and European importers and exporters customarily purchased and shipped out of the ports of Savannah and Charleston clean rice only. Usually this was polished to a shiny whiteness, but some areas of the world which possessed their own milling facilities, notably Great Britain, preferred to purchase rough rice.[23] Since the market generally demanded clean white rice, it is apparent that, regardless of whether or not the planter shipped rough or clean rice to his factor, the normal ultimate goal was the production of clean rice which was appropriately polished and packaged in wooden casks, tierces, or barrels, usually weighing around 600 pounds each.

There were at least four different arrangements for producing this end result. The *first* method has been discussed somewhat, namely: complete milling on the plantation and shipment of clean rice to the factor, who handled all matters in the city marketing area, from the original dispatch of a "boat" to the plantation for the purpose of transporting the shipment to market until the final sale of the cargo to a merchant or agent. This program, it should be remembered, could be followed only by those larger plantations which were equipped with adequate milling facilities.

The *second* procedure was identical with the first, except that the last portion of the milling process—namely, pounding, cleaning, and polishing—was completed at the mill of a near-by plantation equipped for the task. The mill tolls and inter-plantation transportation arrangements and costs were taken care of by the planter who grew the rice.[24] All other steps in the process were quite like those described in the first method above.

[23] Savannah Shipping and Commercial List, September 1, 1842, estimated that Charleston had exported 300,000 bushels of rough rice in the previous year. This was unusual and considered noteworthy.

[24] Hugh Fraser Grant makes various references to tolls which he paid at Butler's Mill.

The *third* procedure was that followed by the majority of the smaller Georgia plantations. Under this arrangement the planter shipped rough rice to the factor, who handled all milling, freight, and marketing problems and charged their cost back to the planter when the rice was sold to a merchant. These combined costs, which included expenses, charges, and commissions, often totaled as much as 25 per cent of the gross price paid by the merchant to the factor for the shipment.[25]

The first step in the *fourth* method called for the planter shipping rough rice to a factor, mill, or commission house, where it was purchased outright at a price figured by the bushel. It might then be sold to a merchant or agent for eventual use by the rough rice areas of the world market. Under this plan the original rice grower had to bear the primary freight costs from plantation to market of 5 to 7 cents per bushel, depending on the distance involved. He also was charged the usual factor's commission of 2½ per cent of the gross price received. By employing this procedure the percentage of the gross return which was charged back to the planter was reduced to about 12 or 13 per cent. This figure was about one-half (in terms of percentage of gross return) of the charges levied against the planter by the third method described above. However, because of the lower prices quoted for rough rice, the planter received 5 per cent less net return than would have been his due if he had paid the seemingly endless marketing costs totaling 25 per cent which were exacted by the more usual marketing pattern. This adverse differential of 5 per cent on the net return grew to 14 per cent or one-seventh of the net return if planters sold rough rice in preference to complete milling on the plantation where possible.[26] Thus, it becomes apparent that as long as the prices of rough rice and clean rice retained their customary "one to four" relationship, most large planters would not find it advantageous to use this fourth alternative. This method would appeal largely only to those planters who did not want to be bothered with all the problems connected with the production of clean rice, to those whose relations with their current factors were not satis-

[25] This was described most thoroughly in "Expenses on Preparing Rice for Market" mentioned in note 19 above.

[26] Details of cost and percentages are set forth with great care by Couper in his Agricultural Notes, pp. 50-53, J. H. Couper MSS, Southern Historical Collection, University of North Carolina Library.

factory, and to the managers of plantations who were serving somewhat ignorant absentee owners living in the North or in the resort regions of Europe.

It has been noted that by the 1840's and 1850's the majority of Georgia rice planters sold their crops in Savannah. Many of them had sold previously in other markets, notably in Charleston. Their shift in primary markets reflects the growth of Savannah and raises the question of just what facilities had been developed in that city to induce and take care of the change. Or again, the question might read: What additions to the economic life of a prosperous small seaport were necessary to enable it to shift from a classification of *distribution center* to that of *commercial center?* Finally, considering the special nature of this study, the inquiry would be: What were the requirements for, and characteristics of, an adequate rice-marketing center? Continuous references have been made to factors, commission houses, merchants, agents, insurance agencies, warehouses, docks, and shipping facilities. What were the functions of each in the marketing process? How much time elapsed before rice which left the plantation in November was sold to eventual consumers? Most significant of all: Who received the lion's share of the net income from this extended, complex, and seemingly endless trading process?

In all literature devoted to a discussion of the credit, supply, and marketing practices of the coastal plantations, factors and factorage houses dominate the picture. Too few writers have attempted to learn or recount the sources of the factor's credit and supplies or the types of customers who bought the crops entrusted to him. The system has not been studied adequately beyond the urban-rural locale where the individual factor had his business establishment and planter clients. The term factor has usually been employed as a catch-all phrase to include all functions which should more accurately be associated with credit agencies, commission houses, merchants, or purchasing agents performing services for outside dealers. True, some factors performed most if not all of these functions in the eighteenth century, but the growth in the volume and value of various plantation staples in the first half of the nineteenth century, helped to produce a rather high degree of specialization among the middlemen who handled the credit, supply, and marketing services in such growing centers as Savannah.

Without doubt factors were the key figures in the marketing of Georgia rice. They had pre-emptive rights to the crops of the plantations of their planter customers. They made recommendations to particular planters as to the timing, volume, and types of grain to be shipped to the primary market. Their suggestions were usually followed up by the dispatch of coastal vessels to the plantations to pick up the cargo and bring it to Savannah.[27] In that city the factors took over control of the grain and followed it step by step through the trading process until it was either sold to a merchant or agent or loaded on an ocean-going vessel for dispatch to a purchaser in the West Indies or some northern or European port. The shepherding of the planter's property through the routine of milling, weighing, grading, coopering, storage, insurance, "starting,"[28] and loading was the responsibility of the factor and his clerical and countinghouse personnel. Each procedure had to be checked by careful supervision and an accurate account retained as the documentary basis for the itemized statement of charges, expenses, and commissions which would later be sent to the planter to justify the deductions from the gross price received for the planter's rice. In performing this function the factor served as the agent of the planter, theoretically subject to his instructions and desires. The factor paid such "expenses" as freight brokerage and insurance; such "charges" as drayage, cooperage, and weighing; then levied a 2 per cent "commission" for himself on the entire transaction. By 1859 Savannah, then a city of about 22,000 had eighty-two such establishments performing these services for planters, one of the largest and oldest of which was the firm of Robert Habersham & Son.

Factors' establishments were often listed as commission houses. The operations of a majority of them justified this nomenclature; that is, they fulfilled the various requests of their customers and charged 2 per cent of the total amount involved in the purchase or sale connected with the task for which they had been commissioned. However, the label "commission house" was most appropriately used when their service involved the securing of

[27] R. Habersham & Son to Louis Manigault, February 26 and 28, 1853, Louis Manigault MSS, Duke University Library, illustrates this practice.

[28] A term now somewhat archaic which refers to the "drawing of the contents from a containing cask." This often resulted from the necessity of transferring the grain from whole casks to half-casks or bags for seagoing shipment.

supplies of various types for customers, rather than the carrying out of a commission to market produce. Occasionally, factors served as part-time correspondents or agents for dealers in New York, Boston, or Liverpool, by purchasing specific amounts of rice of specified quality at stated prices on the order of these dealers. Under such circumstances they were "doing a commission business and acting as forwarding agents."[29]

Rice merchants usually purchased tierces of rice from the factors on the basis of prices quoted and bid on separate transactions. They sometimes bought with their own funds, which included credit supplied by local or northern banks, and held the produce for a time. This procedure makes it appropriate to call them speculators. However, they often had a prospective purchaser in mind when they bought from the factor. In fact, they frequently had standing orders to fill for northern or European dealers. If not, they could usually interpret the trend of the market so as to be able to sell in a few hours or days to the resident agent or correspondent of these outside dealers. If no such purchaser appeared within a reasonable period of time, they often consigned the rice to one of these outside dealers for a joint-account sale. This meant that they authorized their business contact in New York, Liverpool, or Boston to sell the produce for whatever it would bring when it arrived at the distant market.[30]

Merchants who bought "on order" for a northern or European dealer were actually fulfilling a commission which had been assigned to them. On such deals they could be listed as commission houses. If they executed a succession of orders from the same outside dealer and actually had a working agreement for the delivery of definite quantities of rice over a definite period, they took on the functions and characteristics of a resident agent or correspondent of the dealers to whom they shipped rice. But the more they entered into such arrangements the less they deserved to be referred to as merchants. While there were very few establishments which confined their business solely to acting as agents for one or two houses in the North and Europe, it is obvious that

[29] See circular of R. Hutchinson of Savannah announcing the opening of his new commission business establishment at Savannah in 1840, in Godfrey Barnesley MSS, Duke University Library.

[30] The Letter Books, Sales and Invoice Book, Invoice Books, and Cash Book of C. F. Mills of Savannah covering the years 1835-55 contain numerous items which illustrate this pattern, in C. F. Mills MSS, Southern Historical Collection, University of North Carolina Library.

most merchants were sometimes agents, sometimes commission houses, and maybe even factors if they developed a binding economic relationship with any planters. All these activities were in addition to their supposed primary business as buyers and sellers of rice, namely rice merchants. It is also apparent that in the nineteenth century few factors had the funds, facilities, or business connections to allow them to participate in the trading process all the way to New York, Boston, or Liverpool. They were too busy nursing along their many planters and attempting to meet their myriad demands to engage in such extensive enterprise. They could not stretch their limited financial resources to enable them to compete at both ends of the rice business. They were already heavily involved with credit and services to planters. Most of them were glad to devote themselves to their primary clients and allow other trading and shipping personnel to handle the grain after the original sale was completed.

This discussion of the trading process is partially confirmed by a memorandum in the Manigault papers from R. Habersham & Co. listing the merchants in Savannah who had purchased Gowrie plantation rice during the 1852-53 trading season. It mentions such prominent firms as Cohens and Hertz, S. H. Fiske, Brigham Kelley & Co., Cohen & Fosdick, and Scranton, Johnston & Co.[31] Another step in the marketing operation is substantiated by the fact that Cohens and Hertz appear in the records of a Boston rice dealer as the source of various shipments of Savannah rice in the same general period.[32]

Some merchants were involved in so many activities at the same time that they might be referred to more aptly as tycoons. C. F. Mills of Savannah kept rather extensive records which show his varied enterprises and activities.[33] In the 1850's he was a director and leading figure in the Marine Bank of Savannah. He discounted his own notes there and used the proceeds to buy and sell rice and cotton. He sometimes purchased these staples from factors on order of Boston and Liverpool dealers. He also sold rice to agents and other merchants in his home city. He owned one or more ocean-going vessels and established one of his relatives to serve as master of the ship and his agent in dealing with

[31] Louis Manigault MSS, Duke University Library.

[32] Larkin and Stackpole MSS, June 13, 1854, Harvard Business School Library.

[33] See note 30 above.

importers and exporters in foreign ports. This vessel often carried a cargo of these staples consigned to particular foreign dealers for joint-account sale. On the return trip from Liverpool his ship brought cargoes of salt, which he sold to numerous commission and supply houses for resale to Georgia residents or transshipment to the West Indies. He had no direct dealings with planters and does not seem to have operated his own insurance agency to cover his many dealings, but otherwise he was active at all points along the extensive and complex trading process.

In addition to considerable numbers of factors, commission houses, merchants, and resident agents, the marketing center for the second most productive rice-growing area in the United States in the mid-nineteenth century required considerable physical equipment such as docks and warehouses. Likewise, skilled labor for such operations as the coopering of rice barrels was needed, as was considerable floating common labor for longshoremen's tasks. Because fate and the forces of nature could damage rice rather easily, the crop was insured constantly during handling. This called for new insurance coverage every time any portion of rice changed hands, which meant that the insurance agents had a field day. The companies which they represented had their home offices in New York, New England, Liverpool, and London, but local agents usually placed the policies.[34]

As the volume and value of the rice produced increased, it became apparent that the consumer needs of Georgia's coastal population could no longer be satisfied by factors placing individual orders with supply houses in New York, Boston, or Europe, for tools, leather goods, fancy foods, and household needs. This, in turn, brought about a demand for the development of supply houses, clothing dealers ,and fancy goods shops stocked with inventories of some size.[35] Some plantation supplies could then be bought by shopping expeditions rather than by the

[34] The Savannah Directory, 1859, lists thirteen insurance agents operating in the city. C. F. Mills evidently placed the insurance on his ships with a Boston firm and requested N & B. Goddard, his cotton dealers in Boston, to pay the premiums for the same and deduct from his credit balance. C. F. Mills to N & B. Goddard, January 19, 1855, C. F. Mills MSS, Southern Historical Collection, University of North Carolina Library.

[35] The Savannah City Directory, 1859, lists 30 clothing establishments, 26 dry goods stores, 168 grocers, 12 jewelers, and numerous ship stores and ship chandlery shops.

combined shopping and express services previously operated by factors. A bustling though small metropolis no longer could afford to wait for goods to arrive on order from afar.

The appearance of numerous supply houses and dealers selling directly to consumers probably would not have been possible to any great extent without the development of local sources of commercial bank credit. It was feasible for the old-style factorage system to operate entirely through drawing accounts with outside suppliers, and by credit and exchange secured from northern and European banks. Factors were able to balance their accounts by offering drafts, sixty-day bills, and acceptances due them from the purchasers of the crops which they sold. But this was finance and commerce by remote control and left the operators at the perimeter of the trading region at the mercy of policies and developments at the heart of the activity. Professor Ulrich B. Phillips commented on this situation in the unpublished draft for an article as follows:

> Sparsely settled agricultural communities usually tend to be out of touch with money markets and undisturbed by crises because their industry is usually democratic and their employment of capital and credit slight. But in the ante-bellum South, or at least in the plantation districts which largely determined financial conditions for the whole South, the reverse was the case. Relatively little capital, it is true, was invested in buildings, drainage and machinery, but the investment in land was large and more notably, the ownership of labor itself in the slavery regime involved the use of great amounts of capital and very extensive dependence upon credit. When to these considerations it is added that that industry was devoted to the production of staples mainly cotton, in which the crops and prices were subject to wide and active fluctuations, the factors begin to appear which made the ante-bellum South one of the most sensitive of all modern communities to the movements of money and credit.[36]

Thus, it is not surprising to learn that by 1859, Savannah had the use of ten local banks, with branches and resources extending into the heart of the state. The combination of well-stocked local supply houses with numbers of local banks operating in the interior sounded the death knell for many old-style factors. The heart of their service functions to their clients—namely, credit

[36] Undated Manuscript draft, Ulrich B. Philipps MSS, Yale University Library.

and supplies—was largely cut out of their operations as a result.[37]

Extensive commercial, brokerage, and credit contacts in the world market were mandatory if a primary market center were to escape from the narrow confines of mercantilist colonialism. Of course, the freedom to buy and sell in any market and the supposed alternatives of action actually may not have been enhanced when their relationship with the centers of world trade was transformed to a species of free enterprise capitalism. However, the illusion of independence was there, and it was pleasant to contemplate the satisfaction of participation in the great movements of world trade. Real autonomy would depend on the success of any primary marketing center in building up competitive bidding for its products and competition among shipping lines and independent freight handlers for the right to transport these products to the various ports of the world. Single staple ports were at a disadvantage in this effort, except when there existed a world-wide shortage of their chief export item. Ports which could send several exports into the stream of world commerce in well-established combinations such as rice and sugar, rice and cotton, or rice and lumber were in a superior position. Their trading power was augmented still more if, as the result of their own imports and transshipments, they could export other basic combinations such as rice and salt, rice and ice, or rice and fish—all of which were in demand in the West Indies or along the Gulf Coast.

The weekly "Prices Current" list of the Savannah *Daily Georgian* and the "Shipping and Commercial List" of the Savannah *Republican* in the years 1840 to 1855, as well as the records of Savannah merchants, agents, and factors, show that city was quite fortunate in developing multiple trade relationships. In the early decades of the nineteenth century, rice and sugar was the favorite combination shipped to northern ports and Europe. Later, these same world markets received rice and cotton from the Georgia port. Meanwhile, a thriving trade with the West Indies was built around the rice and lumber combination. The

[37] The Savannah City Directory, 1859, lists those establishments dealing in consumer goods and also ten local banks. The general shift in the pattern of supply and credit is confirmed by a study of the C. F. Mills MSS and Elizafield Journal and Account Book, and by a perusal of the Savannah press, especially the Savannah *Daily Georgian* and the Savannah *Republican*. These papers carried considerable advertising which was addressed solely to plantation populations.

manifests of vessels plying between Savannah, Cardenas, Matanzas, Guadeloupe, the Barbados, and Nassau from 1830 to 1855 continually list cargoes of rice in combination with light lumber, shingles, scantling planks, and staves.[38] In earlier decades this lumber-rice combination was a basic item in the Charleston-West Indies trade. The exhaustion of river-bank timber in the Carolinas allowed Savannah and Georgia to take over this trade because of the quality, quantity, and availability of Georgia light lumber.

By 1859 ten steamboat lines made Savannah a regular port of call. Nearly all the vessels engaged in the Atlantic coastal trade put in at the port, and the colonial trade routes between Savannah and the West Indies were maintained with an expanding and thriving trade. Finally, Savannah developed considerable two-way trade with such Gulf ports as Mobile and New Orleans.[39]

This extended discussion of the economic institutions, specialized services and personnel, and capital equipment necessary for the functioning of an adequate rice-marketing center should make it apparent that after 1840 Savannah qualified as such, despite its limited size. In 1820 it was still little more than a fair-sized town of about 7,500 souls. Its population increased 25 per cent each decade to 1860, when 22,500 persons were listed as residents.[40] It had long been the cultural and distribution center of the Georgia coast, but the character of its leadership and function changed rapidly and radically after 1830. In addition to an expanding rice-merchandising business, the building of early railroads and the establishment of branch banks allowed it to share in the increased wealth and economic activity resulting from the expansion of the cotton-growing regions of interior Georgia. By 1850 the commission houses, merchants, factors, and agents were handling more cotton (in volume and value) than rice. Yet, the peak years of rice production were in that same decade.[41] The declining importance of rice in the Savannah mar-

[38] Port of Savannah Records, 1820-56, Duke University Library.

[39] *Ibid.* See also Godfrey Barnesley MSS, Duke University Library, for data on trade with the Gulf Coast ports, and also C. F. Mills MSS, Southern Historical Collection, University of North Carolina Library, for references to coastal and West Indies trade.

[40] U.S. Census Office, Fifteenth Census, 1930, *Bulletin on Georgia Population*, contains statistics showing the growth of Savannah.

[41] C. Mildred Thompson, *Reconstruction in Georgia, Economic, Social and Political, 1865-1872* (New York, 1915), p. 304.

ket resulted somewhat from the industry's own failings and vicissitudes as well as from the spectacular advance of cotton. Plantation plagues of measles and cholera crippled the rice-plantation labor supply. Even before 1860 competition from Louisiana and Texas was undermining the comparative stability of the price of Georgia and Carolina rice. An excessive number of freshets also interrupted production. This resulted at least partially from the exploitation and rapid depletion of the stands of timber along the banks of Georgia rivers. The lessening of the timber supply in turn affected purchases of rice by the West Indies, since the rice-timber combination was a stable trading pattern.

An analysis of the destination of Savannah rice exports, as shown by a sampling of the Prices Current and Shipping and Commercial lists published by the Savannah press for the years 1841, 1842, 1844, 1846, 1847, 1850, 1852, 1853, and 1855, provides some significant and somewhat surprising data.[42] The market year in rice began on September 1 and ran to August 31. Some rice was usually sold during each month, although totals were small in September and the summer months. The great bulk of the produce was exported from December to April. In those sample years total shipments, to coastal and foreign ports, varied annually between 20,000 and 43,000 tierces of 600 pounds each. Prices ranged from $2.00 to $4.75 per hundredweight, or from 2 to 4¾ cents per pound, with both seasonal and yearly fluctuations.

About 75 per cent of the total shipments of rice was consigned to domestic coastal ports. That fact did not necessarily imply that all of the grain received by these ports was consumed there. It is highly probable that much of the rice exported from Savannah to Charleston, New York, and Boston was later transshipped to Europe. New York was the heaviest importer of Savannah rice. It alone took from 20 to 25 per cent of the total export, which was equal in amount to all rice shipped directly to foreign dealers from the Georgia port. Boston and Charleston each received about 10 per cent of Savannah's rice. New Orleans accepted from 5 to 10 per cent and Baltimore and Philadelphia from 5 to

[42] Savannah Shipping and Commercial List (Savannah *Daily Georgian*), September 3, 1841, September 1, 1842, September 1, 1847, September 2, 1850, September 2, 1853, and June 26, 1855; Prices Current (Savannah *Republican*), September 13, 1844, June 5, 1846, and July 2, 1852.

8 per cent each, while small amounts were purchased by dealers in miscellaneous smaller trading ports such as Mobile and Providence.

The West Indies alone received four-fifths of the total exported to foreign ports. This was 20 per cent of all Georgia rice and nearly as much as was sold in New York each year. Cuba with its three ports of Havana, Cardenas, and Matanzas bought the most, while smaller amounts went to Guadeloupe, Nassau, and the Barbados. The remaining one-fifth of the direct foreign exports, which was a mere 5 per cent of the total grain exported from Savannah, went directly to a large number of European ports. Liverpool led the list in this category, but appreciable amounts were shipped each year to Cowes, Cork, Marseilles, Havre, Bordeaux, Hamburg, St. Petersburg, and Trieste. The high percentage of Savannah rice exports consigned to domestic ports, the considerable volume of the West Indies trade, and the rather small percentage of direct overseas commerce in rice reveal the limitations of the Savannah business establishment and its continued dependence on the older and larger commercial centers of the Atlantic coast for markets.

It is enlightening to follow a hypothetical shipment of rice from a Georgia river plantation through the entire sweep of the trading and marketing process to eventual consumers in the North, Europe, or the West Indies. The handling costs which accumulated as a burden on the rice as it flowed along the course of the trade then become obvious. Such a study also throws some light on the duration of the time span from plantation to consumer and gives a nineteenth-century version of Thomas Jefferson's charge in colonial days that "southern planters were merely a species of property annexed to certain mercantile houses in London."[43]

Let it be supposed that on December 1, 1850, Hugh F. Grant of Elizafield Plantation, Altamaha River, Georgia, shipped 2,100 bushels of rough rice to R. Habersham and Son.[44] This cargo

[43] Quoted in B. B. Kendrick "The Colonial Status of the South," *Journal of Southern History* VIII (1942), 5.

[44] This description of costs incurred in marketing rice is patterned after the report to the Agricultural Society of South Carolina previously mentioned in note 19. It is supplemented by numerous manuscript entries in the Elizafield Journal and Account Book; the J. H. Couper and C. F. Mills MSS, Southern Historical Collection, University of North Carolina Library;

arrived in Savannah the next day and was accepted by clerks employed by the factorage firm. Freight expenses from Elizafield to Savannah amounted to 5 cents per bushel or a total of $105. If, as rarely happened, the total shipment was sold promptly to a rice merchant as rough rice, it brought 75 cents per bushel or $1,575. Freight expenses, various minor handling charges at dockside, and the factor's 2 per cent commission ($39.37) were all deducted from the $1,575 to produce a net return of about $1,375. If title to the grain was retained by Mr. Grant until it was milled and sold to a merchant, the financial picture was different. At a price of $3.00 per hundredweight, the resulting 100 tierces of clean rice brought a gross return of $1,850, including 50 cents each for 100 barrels. In this process, additional costs accumulated on the rice, as follows:

| | |
|---|---|
| 1. Freight, mill to market | $ 25.00 |
| 2. 100 barrels at 87½ cents each | 87.50 |
| 3. Handling and weighing 100 barrels at 10 cents each | 10.00 |
| 4. Coopering 100 barrels at 11 cents each | 11.00 |
| 5. Insurance | 18.00 |
| 6. Factor's commission at 2 per cent of gross proceeds | 45.00 |
| 7. Mill toll—9 per cent of net proceeds ($1,548.50) | 139.36 |
| Total | $335.86 |
| Grand Total (including $105 for freight from plantation) | $440.86 |

By the time this process was completed and the rice became the property of a merchant such as Cohens and Hertz or C. F. Mills of Savannah, two to four months had elapsed, depending on the activity of the market and the availability of money. Thus, by February, 1851, the merchant was ready to export his rice, but a ship to transport the produce to the desired port might not be tied up to the wharf at the moment. If not, the merchant re-coopered the rice at 14 cents per barrel and placed it in temporary storage, where he paid warehouse charges of 5 cents to 8 cents per barrel per week, plus new insurance charges. Added to these costs were drayage charges of at least $20. When the opportunity to load the casks on board ship arrived, there was an-

the Larkin and Stackpole MSS, Harvard Business School Library; and the Godfrey Barnesley MSS, Duke University Library. The last item includes several copies of the Prices Current and Shipping and Commercial Lists published by the Savannah press in the 1840's and 1850's.

other round of minor charges for drayage, wharfage, as well as starting and more cooperage costs if the rice was shipped in half-casks. These new costs easily totaled another $50 to $75. Freight costs per cask for shipping to Philadelphia were 75 cents or more, to New York 87 cents to $1.25, and to Boston $1.25 to $1.75. These costs and the premiums of marine insurance on the cargo (another $18) were borne by the importer if the goods were exported on order.

After the Savannah merchant had exported the rice, he drew a bill on New York, Boston, Baltimore, or Philadelphia payable at sight, or thirty or sixty days, and then discounted this bill in the local money market. If he had shipped on order he possibly received payment through funds placed at his disposal in New York by his northern dealer. Otherwise he charged the cost of discounting the bill to the dealer whose order he had filled. Discounting charges varied with the type of financial instrument employed, from one-fourth of one per cent for sight bills to 2 per cent for checks or sixty-day bills. By this time it was March or April, 1851. Some five months had elapsed since the rice left the plantation, and it was still being handled from dealer to dealer, with charges mounting. Its value was well over 4 cents per pound upon arrival in Boston consigned to Larkin and Stackpole. These wholesale merchants proceeded to pay the cost of seaborne freight and insurance, then had the casks trucked to their warehouse (more cost for trucking). They disposed of the cargo to local dealers in small lots of five to twenty-five casks for prices ranging between 4¼ and 4¾ cents per pound. Any casks not sold to regular customers were put up for auction on specified days. By May, 1851, the produce had come into the possession of Boston grocers and food processors. By June or mid-summer it probably ended up in the mouths of consumers at prices ranging from 5 cents upwards. The six to eight months required for the rice to reach actual consumers was, of course, increased considerably if the produce was shipped to Europe.

This description and discussion of the milling and marketing practices of the Georgia rice trade provides some understanding of the milieu in which these operations were conducted. It throws some light on how and why certain things were done as they were. It points up the ingenuity and enterprise of the planters in developing milling facilities. It stresses the endless procession of middlemen who handled the produce and helps to answer the one big query which is still unresolved, namely: Who received the lion's share of income and net profit from the rice trade? The planters most decidedly did not. The local middlemen in Savannah received a good living but not riches. They handled large amounts of grain and funds but were merely temporary custodians of both. Outside economic interests controlled supplies, credit, and prices. These interests called the tune, and the Georgia rice trade had no *real* alternative but to continue in a species of economic servitude. This is the thesis presented separately by Professors Louis M. Hacker and B. B. Kendrick some ten years ago.[45]

These introductory chapters showing the history of Elizafield and the Grant family, the problems of rice culture, and the practices of the rice marketing areas supply the background needed for an intelligent study of the documentary section of this volume which follows, namely, "The Journal and Account Book, 1834-61, of Hugh Fraser Grant of Elizafield Plantation, Glynn County, Georgia." In the reproduction that follows, the spelling, punctuation, and capitalization of the original manuscript have been preserved. The page layouts of Grant's entries have been followed as much as possible; however, the topical arrangement of the entire document reproduced on the following pages is a collation of material dispersed through the owner's manuscript.

[45] Hacker, *The Triumph of American Capitalism*, pp. 280-321, and B. B. Kendrick, "The Colonial Status of the South," *Journal of Southern History*, VIII (1942), 280-321.

# PART II

## The Journal and Account Book, 1834-61, of Hugh Fraser Grant of Elizafield Plantation, Glynn County, Georgia

1839

| | |
|---|---|
| March 11th | Commenced planting the upper twenty on W. S. C First planting West of Creek. |
| | 20,22,27,16,17 & 5 = 105 Acres |
| 26 | White frost |
| 28 | Second planting East of Creek |
| | 20,22,23,18 = 83 Acres |
| | " " West of Creek |
| | 15 . . . . . . . = 15 = 98 Acres |
| April 10 | Third Planting West of Creek 21,19,10,6 56 |
| 13 | White frost |
| 11 | Finished Planting . . . . . . . . . . . [Total] 259 Acres |
| 12 | Commenced hoeing Corn. Excessively dry |
| 15 | Commenced hoeing Rice in upper 20 Acre field |
| 23 | Slight showers of Rain |
| " | Gave out Osnabergs to the People |
| 30 | Not ½ inch of Rain this month |
| May 8 | Hoed entirely throug[h] the Crop once, and 105 Acres twice |
| 9 | Fine Rain, every thing revived |
| 14 | Fine Shower of Rain |
| 18 | Moved to the Sand Hills with my family. Delightful Weather |
| June 25 | The Whole Crop under harvest flow. From the excessive drouth the water was too Salt for use at New Hope and Broadfield but perfectly fresh at this place |
| July 1 | Young Rice just forming |
| Augst 17 | Commenced Harvesting. |
| Sept 9 | Finished Cutting Rice and Twenty one Acres in the Yard. |
| 14 | Fifty one Acres in the yard |
| 17 | Eighty acres in the yard |
| 24 | 164 Acres in the yard |

[September 1839]

25 173 Acres in the yard

Oct 2 Finished bringing in Rice. Their [sic] never has been known so dry and delightful a Harvest Season, only one Slight Shower Since the 17 of August.

2 The whole Country Suffering for want of Rain & the Southern Rivers dryer than ever before known, and much Sickness in all the Southern Cities except Savannah and Darien.

29 No Rain, No Rain, Salt water nearly as high as Barrington ferry. Very warm Mr Shoutz at August planted turnips in the bed of the Savannah River

Nov 7 Moved down from the Sand Hills with my family all well.

" Frost the first this season

8 Frost and some Ice

10 Gave out Negroe Shoes 84 pr

11 Sent Rice to Butlers Mill

25 Commenced clearing Land on Champneys Island

28 & 29 Rainy and unpleasant weather.

30 Rainy all day & warm

Decr 3 Cool & pleasant

4 Freshet in the River, which has driven out all the Salt Water from the South branch.
still brackish at Darien

9 Mr Spicer commenced working on the Engine

11 " " Commenced Mason work

12 " " " " "

9 Burning off stubble on E S Creek

10 " off 17 Acre field

12 Cleaned out all the ¼ drains on the plantation & large ditches in most of the fields

14 Turning & Ploughing in 17 Acre

21 Heavy Rain all day

28 Started my Engine for Thrashing

1840

Feb 1 & 2 Rainy all of both days
" Started my Windfan

[February 1840]

8 My thrasher & windfan clean an avarage [sic] of 300 Bushels of Rice per day

March 3 Heavy Shower of Rain

4 Commenced planting Rice in the 27 Acre field

12 Planted Lower 20

13 " Upper 20 & part of 16

14 " part of 16 & all of 17

16 " 15 and 10

17 " 5 & 4 & 2 Acres

19 Rain nearly all day

20 Received from Charleston 500 Bushels of Corn & 6 Barrels of Pork

23 24, 25, Rainy, some very heavy Showers

26 Clear and cold, *white frost*

27 Frost no harm done

30 Rain.

April 2 Rain & fine freshet in the River

6 Heavy freshet, 27 Acre trunk blown up

7&8 NE Wind, and fine Rain putting down the 27 Trunk

9&10 Rain Wind N. E.

11 Finished planting. Rice & Corn this day

13 Commenced hoeing in upper 20 Acre. Finished a new Flat for Canal

14 Hoeing Lower 20 Acre

15 " 27 Acre

16 " 17 Acre

17 " 16 Acre

18 " 15 "

22 Finished Hoeing through the first & Second planting of Rice

23 Hoeing & thinning Corn

24 Hoeing Corn & potatoes

25 Finished hoeing Corn & stopping leaks

26 Hoeing Rice in 19

26 Gave out Osnabergs

May 5 Left Elizafield for the Summer by paying a visit to the Island for a few days & then to the Sand Hills

13 Flowed all my Young Rice for 9 days

21 Taking off the water, the Rice very beautiful & Clean
Hoeing through the old Rice the third time.
June 29 All the Rice under harvest flow
July 1 Planted 12 Acres Peas
" Got 10⅓ Acres Potatoes Slips planted
4 27 Acre shooting out
9 5 & 3 " " "
May 28 [1] My House at the Sand Hills burned to the Ground, saved very little of the furniture, my family returned to Cartwright Point, and took Mr. Bryans House, his family being in Virginia—
July 4 Cool enough for winter clothing
Augst 1 All the Rice well eard out
11 Commenced Cutting Rice in 27 Acre
13&14 Bringing in 27 Acre to Barn yard
19 35 Acres in the yard
26 102 Acres in the yard
26 103 Acres of Rice in the yard
" Rainy & very squally for several days the wind N. E. & every prospect of a Gale
Sept 5 160 Acres of Rice in the yard
11 Finished cutting Rice
12 " Tieing up
12 180 Acres in the Barn Yard
" Delightful Weather
15 Very high tides wind N E broke the bank in the three Acre on the Canal and wet the Rice in the 21 Acre—not much damage, except two days loss of all Hands in mending break and opening Rice in 21.
25 Finished bringing in Rice. a very fine Harvest Season not one day lost from the commencement. Thank God for the same, and the Negroes all very healthy *Behold*
26 Breaking in Corn —— ——
Oct 26 Digging Potatoes

[1] This entry was recorded six weeks after the event which occurred off the plantation.

[November 1840]

Nov 2 Moved my family down from the Sand Hills, all well
4 Started my Thrashing Machine this day—
4&5 Cutting Rice for Provisions from Upper & Lower 20 Acres
8&9 Tides *very very* High
10&11 Tides higher than ever, one break in the three acre, ran over the Banks on Evelyn from one end to the other

1841

" 20 Loading Vessel for Charleston 2730 Bushels
Feb 12 For the last Month the weather very warm, the Peach trees & Jassamines in Full bloom, the Multicallis full of fruit and leaves.
13,14,15&16 Freezing weather all day in the Shade

## FRESHETS *1841*

1841

March 15 Light Frost. Delightful weather
18 Frost
" Very Heavy freshet in the River
19 Freshet all over the Land not a bank to be seen, unless the top of the Six mile Bank Water nearly up to the Barn floor and rising
20 Risen about 3 in since yesterday
21 " " $2\frac{1}{2}$ in since yesterday
22 " " $2\frac{1}{2}$ in since yesterday not a bank on the Plantation above water
23 Water fallen about 4 inches
29 Water fallen below the surface on Evelyn Side of the Creek & the high spots on the west side showing out, the Banks not so badly washed as might have been supposed—Stopped three Large Breaks
31 Fields all day—the Rice planted on the first tides in March, which was supposed to have all rotted. looks very well & is about two inches high.
April 1 Finished mending all the Breaks
June 29 All the Rice on West of Creek under Harvest flow

Augst 14 Commenced Cutting Rice in the 10, 3 & 19 Acre Fields.
Rainy & very bad weather
15 Heavy Rains from 3 o clock until bed time.
16 Heavy Rain from 12 " " " "
17 Showers in the evening & during the night
18 No rain tides *very very* high a small break at the flood gate
19 Very heavy Rain, & high tide a break on Evelyn side
20, 21,22,23 Fine weather. 15 Acres in the yard
24 Very heavy Rain
24 Very heavy Rain all day
25 " " Rain from 12 O clock M.
26 " " Rain all night & part of the day
27 " " Rain nearly all day
" 33 Acres Rice in the yard 120 Cut down
28 Delightful morning. 40 Acres of Rice in the yard. Rain in the Evening
29 Delightful Day
30 Delightful Morning 42 Acres in the yard
31 Heaviest & sharpest Thunder, Lightning & Rain I ever witnessed

Sept 1 Wednesday Heavy Rain
2 Delightful Day
3 fine morning rain in the afternoon & night
4 Delightful Morning 175 Acres cut down
5 Sunday, *no Rice birds yet on the place*
5 Tremendous Rain
6 fine morning heavy Rain afternoon
7 fine morning heavy rain all the afternoon
8 Rice birds numerous Cloudy, Rain in the evening
9 Rain in morning. 210 Acres Cut
10 Rain, Rain, Rain
11 No Rain fine day
12 Sunday fine day
13 delightful weather 75 Acres in yard
14 Heavy wind from N. E very high tide & Rain
15 Blowing almost a gale from N. E. enormous tides three breaks one in 27,12, & 23, every thing wet

16 N. E. Gale tremendous rains & tide & freshet every field under water, *and do not* run dry at low water

17 Delightful weather stopping breaks in 27

18 Delightful day stopping break in lower 20 all the fields still under water & the tide higher than yesterday by 3 inches
90 Acres in the yard

18 Breaks by the Gale. tide & freshet in the 27, Lower 20, 22, 17, 18 & 3 Acres squares the rice in the above been in water (Stacked) since Wednesday the 15th

19 Sunday

20 Breaks mended in 27 & lower 20 the Rice in the Stacks all sprouted, carried in, all the top of the stacks in 27 & Lower 20, & all pulled down and scattered in the upper 20 tides very high Wind N. E.

21 Delightful weather, tides very high N. E.

22 Cloudy, slight Showers. tides high S. W & mending break in 22 & 18, E. S. Creek

23, 24, & 25 Delightful weather. Cutting Rice in the 22 & 18 and carrying in—& cutting 23

26 Sunday. *I had chill & pretty severe fever* for a few hours

27 Delightful day, feel much better no fever 140 Acres Rice in the yard

28 Delightful Day, *fever again*

29 & 30 Delightful weather

Oct 1 Very unpleasant N. E Wind cold & damp
Considerable freshet in the River. Heavy Rain all night

2 Rain in the Morning. Cloudy & Cool all day North

3 Sunday Thermometer 57° fine day, freshet all over the Land at Eliza-field—

4 Delightful weather *very cool*

5 DO Do Do Land all dry

6 Do Do Do 175 Acres *in yard*

7 Do Do Do

8 Do Do killed a fine buck this morning
weighed when cleaned 85 pounds

9 Cutting New Ground Rice. the last to Cut
9 Finished Cutting Rice this day, would have finished a month earlier if it had not been for the Gale. High tides, freshets and incessent [sic] Rains.
10 Sunday. Cloudy & warm
11 Delightful Day
12 Do Do very warm
13 Do Strong Rain in the afternoon
14 Cold & Cloudy N. E wind *very very very* high tide
Recd this day from Savannah 200 bu Corn 4000 Laths
15 Delightful day. tides a little lower
16 Cloudy
17 Sunday to Sunday 24 Delightful weather
23&24 Light frosts
23 Cutting after Rice
26 Heavy frost Vines all killed & the Rice singed
27 Delightful day
28 Cloudy & warm
Cut after Rice in 27, 15, 10, & part of 17, & 19 for myself
" " " " upper and Lower 20s for Charles [2]

Nov 2 " Digging Slips 160 Bushels Large & 80 Small
3 Moved my family from Carterets all well
4 Digging Slips 157 bu Large 74 Small
Started my Engine for Thrashing
5 Digging slips 150 bu Large 20 Small
7 Sunday
8 Moulding up new ground bank & digging mud for the west bank of lower 20 Acre
9 Do Do
10 Sent a Flat Load of Rice to Butlers Mill—

Decr 1 Gave out Shoes
5 Gave out Clothes to the people
10 Sent 2395 Bushels Rice to Savannah to R H [abersham] & Son

[2] Grant's younger brother.

[January 1842]

Jany 15 Strawberry plants in bloom
17 Planted out 35 Fruit trees at Carterets
all the Multicallis in foliage
23 Frost killed all vegetation
Feb 25 Up to this date Raised the entire new ground Bank, the west of lower 20 north & west of 27, west of 21, check banks between upper & lower 20, d[itt]o between 10 & 15 d[itt]o from barn yard to the 17 trunk & the Canal bank, raised the line bank between D Tunno and myself cleaned out all the Large ditches & drains on the plantation & cleaned up the new Ground in very good order for planting Ditched 25 tasks in length on the hill for outside fence & the fence in fine order
24 Planted 4 Acres without covering and put on water for days
March 2 Planted 10, 15 & 5 Acres squares
8 to 12 " 27, 21, 19, 16, 17 Acre squares 133 Acres first
planting 3 Bushels per Acre
27 Hoeing Rice in 19 Acre
Received from Charleston 600 Bu Corn 3 barrels Tar
April 6&8 Light showers the first since the 1 March
13 Commenced hoeing Rice in earnest The Crop Generally the poorest & thinest stand I have ever had, in consequence of the Seed being inferior & bad management of overseer
14 Moved to Carterets Point
15 fine Shower of Rain
22&21 Cut up and replanted the 27, 21, & 23
the Rice not thick enough to treat for a Crop
22 Dashed the 15 & 16 Acres. very dry——
June 23 Ears Shooting out in the 4 Acre Square about 10 days earlier than usual
Augst 2 Heavy wind & Rain from N. E. no damage done
3&4 Clear & Cool wind N. E. fine all day in the house on the 2d, 3d & 4th
6 Commenced cutting Rice in the 10 & 4 Acres
8 10 Acres in the Barn yard

[August 1842]

| | | |
|---|---|---|
| | 10 | Cutting the 15 Acre |
| | 11 | " " 5 Acre |
| | 12 | 25 Acres in the yard & Cutting the 16 Acre |
| | 15 | 30 Acres in the yard<br>Cutting the 17 Acre |
| | 16 | Cutting the 19 Acre 48 Acres in the yard |
| | 17 | Cutting Lower 20 Acre 52 Acres in the yard Cutting upper 20 |
| | 20 | 80 Acres in the yard. Splendid weather this week not a Shower of Rain & no Sickness |
| | 24 | 94 Acres in the yard 135 Acre cut down |
| | 25 | Cutting 22 Evelyn side of Creek Heavy Rain in the evening |
| | 26 | 106 Acres in the yard |
| | 27 | Cutting Kesia Field Evelyn |
| | " | Thrashed 50 sheaves of Lower 20 made 2.03 Bu |
| | 29 | Finished Kesia field — Discharged the Overseer |
| | " | Cutting 18 Acre Evelyn |
| | 30 | Bringing in Rice 117 Acres in the yard. |
| | 31 | 122 Acres in the yard |
| Sept | 1 | 131 Acres in the yard |
| | " | Cutting 21 Acre field |
| | 2 | 140 Acres in the yard |
| | 3 | Cutting the 23 Acre Evelyn |
| | " | Rice birds coming in small flocks |
| | " | Delightful weather for the whole of this week some heavy showers all around us but none here |
| | 4 | Sunday Very high tides |
| | 5 | 151 Acres in the yard |
| | 6 | 166 Acres in the yard |
| | 7 | 175 Acres in the yard |
| | 8 | 192 Acres in the yard |
| | 9 | 209 Acres in the yard |
| | 10 | Cutting Rice in the 27 Acre. Birds rather numerous |
| | 11 | Sunday |
| | 12 | Cutting new Ground & tieing 27 Acre |
| | 13 | 217 Acres in the yard |
| | 14 | 228 Acres in the yard |
| | 15 | 244 Acres in the yard |
| | 16 | 269 " " " " Heavy Rain |

(Sept 4–8: Tides very High N. E. Wind)

17 273 And that is all
26 Rain every day since the 16th Inst
Women gleaning Men getting wood out of the New Ground
30 Cleaning up new Ground & Restacking in the yard

Oct 5&6 Heavy N. E. Gale for 36 Hours, the tide entirely over the whole plantation about 5 inches higher than the great freshet of 1841, March.
7 Wind still fresh from N. E. and tides very high three breaks one in 27, 18 & u 20
12 Commenced thrashing My Brother Allen maried [sic]
13 Cutting after Rice in 10, 15, 17, 16, 5 & 4
15 Making a new wind fan
29,30,&31 Heavy wind from N. E & much rain tides very high one break on canal north bank

Nov 5 Moved my family over from Carterets Point Thank God all well & have all enjoyed uninterupted [sic] health the whole summer
" Digging Slips, turn out very badly, scarsely worth digging
11 Heavy White frost, first this Season
21 Shipped 1847 bushels of Rice to Mess Mitchell & Mure of Charleston

Decr 4 Cleaned the old line ditch from the 27 trunk to the Spring, & cleaned out anew all the quarter & half quarter drains three feet deep in the 27, 21, 19, 15, 17 & 10 up to this date
6 About ½ done thrashing
16 Shipped 2150 bushels Rice to Mitchell & Mure
29 " 2050 "

1843

Jany 1
6 Finished ploughing 27 Acre and put on water
11 " " upper 20 " " " "
20 " " 21 Acre field
25 " " 10 Acre field
23 to 29 Burning off all the fields

26 Ploughing the 15 Acre field Moulding up the old line bank

Feb 1, 2&3. Very, Very Cold raw & uncomfortable, freezing all day in the Shade——

4 Ploughing the 9 Acre finished the 17 yesterday.

6 119 Acres ploughed

27 Planting 10, 9 & 17 Acre field

March 1 " 36 Acres

first Planting 36 Acres

6 Planted ¾ Acre Sugar Cane

7 Heavy Rain all day strong wind from N. E. Birds very bad

8,9,10&11 Rain every day & very heavy all night

9 A bright luminous appearance in the West after dark resembling a Comet

13 Trenched the 16, 15, 19, 21 & 27 Acres

12&13 Heavy Rain

14 Considerable Ice

15 Heavy frost & ground frozen delightful weather planted the 15,19 & 21 Acre fields

16 Heavy Rain night & day ——

17 Beautiful day thermometer in the house at 8 O clock 33° very cold thick Ice & frost

18,19,20&21 Rainy cold & unpleasant weather

Comets tail to be seen in the west at dark about 40° long

20 Planted to this date 150 Acres

21 Planting potatoes,

24 The coldest night this Season the fields all frozen hard & the water in canal & edges of the field ½ in. thick H. F. Grant[3]

26&27 Incessent [sic] torrents of Rain with thunder & Lightning, fields all under water from the Rain & over kitchen floor.

28 Delightful day rather windy from the West

29 " "

30 Cloudy & heavy Shower at mid day from S W.

[3] Mr. Grant evidently thought this entry was quite significant since he placed his signature after it for documentation.

| | | |
|---|---|---|
| | 29 | Planted Kesia field |
| | 30 | " Lower 20 Evelyn —— 43 Acres |
| April | 1 | Trenched 18 Acre Evelyn |
| | 2 | Cloudy from N. E |
| | 3 | Rain all day } no work done |
| | 4 | Rainy all day } |
| | 5 | Cloudy —— |
| | 6&7 | Delightful weather first planted rice just beginng to come up |
| | 7 | *Slight frost* |
| | 10 | Slight frost |
| | 13 | Dashed for one tide the following fields 27, 21, 19, 16 & upper 20. |
| | 14 | Finished planting |
| | 18 | Finished replanting —— |
| | 24 | Commenced hoeing in the 19 Acre |
| May | 15 | The following fields have been twice hoed Viz. 27, 21, 19, 10, 15, 16, 23, 18 & upper 20 and new Ground —— |
| June | 9 | All the Rice hoed four times |
| | 12 | Fine little Shower, planting a few Slips |
| | 15 | Catterpillars very thick in 19, & 27, a few in 21 |
| | 16 | Catterpillars covered the Rice in 19 perfectly black getting on Water. |
| | 18 | The 27 terribly eaten by the Catterpillar a few in upper 20, 15, 10 & 23. |
| | | Wind N. E. opened every door on the plantation |
| | 24 | " Took water off the 17, 9, 22, 23, 18 & Kesia field & lower 20. |
| | 26 | Took water of 16 & changed the water on 10, 15, 19, 21, 27 |
| July | 7 | Catterpillar did not spread much from the fields first attacked viz 19, 21, 27 from present appearance they have not done much harm |
| | 7 | Rice looks well |
| | " | Listing high Ground for Pease |
| | 12 | Planted 21 Acres Red Pease |
| | 17 | Heads shooting out in 21, 19, 15, 10, & 16 |
| Augst | 23 | Cut about 5 Acres in the 10 Acre |

26 Brought 5 Acres in the yard & finished cutting the 10
28 10 Acres in the yard
" Cut the 21 Acre 2d Square Cut
29 Cut the 15 Acre 3 Do Do
30 Cut the 19 Acre 4 Square Cut

Sept 1 20 Acres in the yard
2 Cut the 27 Acre 5 Square Cut
" 30 Acres in the yard
3 Sunday
4 Cutting Kesia field 6 Square Cut
5 " 22 Acre Evelyn 7 " "
6 Bringing in 15 Acre
6 45 Acres in the yard
7 Cutting 16 Acre 8 Square cut
" " A few large flocks of birds the first this season
8 Bringing in 19 Acre Square
" 65 Acres in the yard
9 Cutting Upper 20, 9th Square cut
" " 9 Acre 10th Do
10 Sunday Birds all gone
11 Cut 17 Acre 11 Square cut
12 " Lower 20 Acre 12 " "
13 " New Ground 13 " "
14 " Rainy Picking Pease
15 " Brought in 9 Acre Square
" 75 Acres in the yard
16 Cut part of 23 Acre Square 14 Square cut
17 Sunday
18 Cut 18 Acre 15th & last Cut

17 Sunday. My Dear and ever kind Father (Dr. Robert Grant) died this day at 8 O clock in the evening at St Simons Island in the 81st year of his age.

19 Brought 20 Acres in from the 27 Acre Square
" 95 Acres in the yard ——
22 124 Acres in the yard
23 138 Acres in the yard. Rain from 11 O clock until evening ——

26 165 Acres in the yard } Tides very high but no
27 185 Acres in the yard } damage done
30 230 Acres in the yard
Oct 5 Finished Harvesting this day 287 Acres in the Barn yard, only three days of interuption by Bad weather
6 Picking Pease
7 Holliday for the Negroes.
7 Killed a fine Buck at Carterets Point
9&10&11 Gleaning upper 20 & New Ground 6 Men getting Mud for break in New Ground & 6 cutting wood for the House
18 White frost, potatoes killed in patches
Commenced thrashing Straw with the Women
21 Men working at the New Ground Women thrashing
25 Cutting After Rice about 20 Acres
26 Bringing in after Rice
27 Rain all day

1843
Nov 6 Moved over with my family from Carterets, thank God all well
27 Commenced ploughing in Kesia field
20 Gave out Blankets & Shoes
29 Sent a flat load of 358 Bushels of Rice to Mr Butlers Water Mill made 12 bbls whole & 1 small
Decr 13 " Sent second load of 316 Bushels Rice to Butlers Mill made 12 whole barrels & 1 of small Rice
13 First Ice this season
21 Cleaning out drains in 22 & 18 Evelyn & clearing of the Stubble
Ploughing high ground
29 Second Ice this morning High Land ploughed 30 Acres

1844
Janry 8 Rain all day
9 Rainy
11 Rain all day
12 Misty & very unpleasant
13 " " " "

[January 1844]

14 Sunday. Rainy
15 Rainy
16 Rainy
17 Rainy
18 Delightful weather Ice
23&24 Heavy Showers of Rain
24 Turning 15 Acres with the Hoes 32 Hands

March 11 Commenced Planting in 10 Acre square
" Planted 9. & 10 & 17 Acre
12 " 15 & 19
13 " 16 & 21
14&15 " part of 21 & 27 And all under water & 3 Bu per Acre
Making 134 Acres

19 Sold this day the following Negroes viz Mingo Sebrinna Ben Nan & Child, Alick Flora Child Phillis, Julatta Lear, Jim, Charlotte & five Children

18 in all @ $ 415. round
18
3320
415
$7,470

22 Severe White Frost

24 By the grace of God, I was Confirmed this day in St Andrews Church, Darien by the Rt Revd Bishop Elliott, Jr. And may the Almighty ruler of the Universe protect me & keep me in the path of duty until my lifes end

HUGH FRASER GRANT

April 1,2&3 Heavy Wind from N E & a freshet in the Rice making very high tides and everything under water until the 7th one break in 21 & one in 27 back bank the first planting Rice just coming up
16 Finished planting this day
17 Commenced Hoeing

June 13 Planted 9 tasks Slips
15 Harvest flow on 27, 21, 19, 15, 10 & 9 Acres 101
The Crop as fine as can be ——

July 5 Ears Shooting out in 19 Acres ——

8 Ears Shooting out in 27, 21, 10, 15, 11, 9 & 17
June 15 8 Acres of Slips planted
July 18 3 " more of Slips planted
12 Acres of Pease The whole planting including everything is 323 Acres & at Carterets 61 *384* Acres
Augst 10 Cut 5 Acres in 10 & 5 in 9 Acres Square & breaking in Corn
12 Cutting 19 Acre Shower of Rain prevented tieing up
13 Cutting 15 Acre Rain every day
" 10 Acres in the Barn yard
16 20 Acres in the " yard
17 Cutting 17 Acre Square
" 25 Acres in the yard
18 Sunday Heavy Rain
19 Cutting 21 & tieing 17
" 35 Acres in the yard hired 17 hands from Dr. Tunno to bring in @ $1.50 per Acre
24 76 Acres in the yard heavy Rain yesterday
31 118 Acres in the yard —— Weather very cool fine morning & evening
Sept 5 162 Acres in the yard
4 to 8 Wind fresh from N.E. with occasional showers of Rain. Very Heavy Rain.
7 200 Acres in the yard
10th Wind fresh from S. W. Heavy Rain in the Morning
11 Wind N. W. Very delightful day
" 240 Acres in the yard
" Cutting New Ground John Square
14 Restacking in the yard & turning up New Ground
15 Sunday
16 Bringing in balance of 27, & Lower 20
16 253 Acres in the yard
17 Bringing in balance of 23 & part of New Ground
17 265 Acres in the yard
18 Bringing in New Ground
18 273 Acres in the yard
19 280 Acres in the yard & that is all The season has been very fine with the exception of about a week of NE Wind & Rain ——

[September 1844]

20 to 28 Rain every day

29&30 Very cold & *Slight frost in the Buffalo*[4]

Oct 1 to 9 Delightful weather. fine mor[nin]g & Ev[enin]g

8 Started the Engine runs very well

7 Commenced ditching in upper & Low 20 ——

25 Cut after rice in 27, 16 & part of 9 Acre 44 Acres

13 Dug half allowance Roots 1 task 40 Bushels

18 " whole allowance Roots 2 tasks 80 "

26 " ½ " " 1 task 40 "

The last week the weather has been cool, damp & hazy wind N W

24 Commenced Jinning Cotton at Carterets Pt

27 Sunday

30&31 Heavy frost and Ice

31 Digging Slips ——

Shipped this day 900 Bushels of Rice to Habersham & Son

Nov 2d Moved my family from Carterets this day. Thank God all well.

9th Purchased from A H Meriam Esqr Agent of the Brunswick Co a 15 Horse Power Piston Engine for $350.

Commenced putting it up the 9th of Decr

Decr 31 Burned off the 21 upper 20 & part of Lower 20

1845

Jany 30 Started the Engine everything worked well

Feb 5 Cold rain cleared off wind west very Cold

6 Very Cold wind W. N W

| | | | | | | |
|---|---|---|---|---|---|---|
| March | 6 | Commenced planting in | | | 27 Acre | |
| | 7 | Planted Lower 20 | | | 22 | |
| | 8 | " upper 20 | | | 17 | [Total] 66 Ac's |
| | 12 | Rainy all day | | | | |
| | 13 | Do Do | | | | |
| | 18 | Planted | 15½ | Acres in 21 | 15½ | |
| | " | " | 15 | " Square | 16¼ | |
| | 19 | " | 19 | " " | 19 | |
| | " | " | 10 | " " | 8¾ | |

[4] The Buffalo was a swamp area about five miles inland from Elizafield.

| | | | | |
|---|---|---|---|---|
| | 21 | " Kesia field | 21 | |
| | 22 | Planted 17 & 9 Acres | 26 | [Total] 106 ½ |
| April | 2 | Planted 18 Evelyn | 18¼ | |
| | 3 | " 22 " | 23 | |
| | 4 | New Ground point field | 12 | |
| | 5 | " " Johns field.... | 23½ | |
| | 17 | Planted 23 Evelyn | 23 | |
| | 18 | " 24 Evelyn | 24¼ | |

March 1 Whooping Cough on the place

15 Lost 2 Negroe Children from Cough

20,21,22 Frost each morning killed the Wampee [?] & Grass

24 Rainy all day

" Planted 2 Acres of Potatoes } 9¾ Acre Roots

April 10 " 7¾ " Potatoes }

19 Commenced Hoeing in 19, & 21

21 Hoeing 19 & 22¾

22 " upper 20, 22¾

{June 14th 7½ Acres Potatoes rotted in the ground from the Drought

23 Very High tide & excessively dry

May 1 No rain since 24th of March. the dryest spring I ever remembered

1 Put Long flow on the 27, upper & Lower 20s & 9 Acres

To this date hoed the following fields Viz 27, 21, 19, 8¾, 15, 17, 22, 17, 9, 21, Evelyn & 18 acr & the Potatoes

7 Shower of Rain first since 24th March

Moved to Carterets this day with my family

11&12 Fine Showers

17 Putting long flow on 21, 19, 15, 17, 10, Kesia 18

June 13 *Very very* dry. not a drop of water in any of the Ponds, everything on high ground suffering the Orange trees all curled up

14 Left with my family for St Augustine on a/c of Mrs. Grant's health. God grant she may improve

" The Rice Crop as fine as could be desired

28 Returned from St Augustine

21,22&23 Slight Showers
Rice all late in consequence of the excessive drought.
Water sweet in the River

July 3 Freshet in the River. Changed all the water on all the Squares——
4th Several Ears out in the 10 Acre
11 Fine shower of Rain. Planted 3¾ Acres Slips in 16 Acre & 3¾ Acre Peas. White Crowder
12,13,&14 Do Do
31 Heaviest Rain for 12 Months

Augst 2&3 Planted 2 Acres Slips
6 " 7½ Acres Red Peas
7 Rice Ripening very fast nearly ready for the hook
14 Commenced cutting the 10 & 15 Splendid weather
15 Cutting in 21, 19 & 27 20 acres cut
17 Sunday
18 Very Heavy Shower in the afternoon with Lightning
19 Finished cutting 27
" 30 Acres in the yard
20 Cutting 9, & the patches that were left in 10, 15 & 19
21 41 Acres in the yard
" Cutting Lower 20
22 53 Acres in yard
23 65 " " " finished cutting Lower 20
24 Sunday
25 76 Acres in the yard
26 88 Acres in the yard, heavy rain all round but none here
27 105 " " " "
28 117 " " " " Commenced cutting on Evelyn Kesia
29 125 " " " " Shower of Rain about 20 minutes
30 135 " " " "
31 Sunday Showers in afternoon

Sept 1 147 Acres in yard
2 159 Do Shower at midday
3 175 "
4 190 Do in the yard

| | | | |
|---|---|---|---|
| 5 | 203 Do D | | |
| 6 | 215 Do D Heavy Shower at 2 O clock | | |
| 7 | Sunday | | |
| 8th | 227 Acres in the yard, bringing in 24 Acres of Evelyn this Rice ready to cut in 4 months & 5 days from day of Planting 127 days! Rain or Shower | | Wind S.W S.W S.W |
| 9 | 238 Acres in the yard | | S.W |
| 10 | 250 " " " " | Heavy Rain | S.W |
| 11 | 260 | Started the Engine & Thrasher | N.E |
| Sept 12 | 273 | Works well | N E |
| 13 | 283 | Thrashed the 23 as came from the fields | N E |
| 14 | Sunday | | N E |
| 15 | 296 And that is all. a beautiful harvest season and not any sickness on the place. *thanks to God for all his mercies.* | | N E S E N E |
| 16 | Commence work for another Crop by cleaning of 28 Acre for my brother Charles | Rainy | N E N E |
| 17,18&19 | Cleaning off my yard & Cutting Engine wood | Rainy | N E |

20 Holiday for the Negroes

21 Sunday

22 Clearing off 28 Acre for Charles

23 Do

24 Do

26 Shipped 1700 Bushels Rice to Savannah

27 Ditching for fence on Hill

Oct 7 Taken sick & fever for 10 days & 3 of my Children Sick at same time

9 Shipped 1700 bushels Rice to Savannah

27 to Nov 3 Cutting & bringing in After Rice

Nov 1 Moved my family from Carterets Thank God all alive although two of the Children still quite sick. hope the change will help them.

3 No frost yet although vegetation checked from Cool Weather.

[November 1845]

4 Slight frost
5 Heavy frost
9&10 Heavy white frost Vegetation entirely killed
13 " " frost
" Gave out Negroe Shoes

1846

Jany Subsoiled the 17, 15 & part of 22 Evelyn
All the other squares broken up with the hoe

March 2&3 Planted Corn & 4¾ Acre potatoes = 7½ Acres potatoes,
4 Commenced trenching in 22 Evelyn
5&6 Finished trenching for first planting
Viz 22 E. 21 E. 17, 9 & 16 85 Acres
7 Planted 7½ Acres of Potatoes
8 Sunday
9 Commenced planting Rice 2½ Bushels per Acre
23 Second planting, 21, 19, 10, 15, 27 & Upper 20 = 105 Acres

April 12 Third planting Point, Johns field & Lower 22 = 73 Ac

May 1 Moved my family to Carterets point
2 Finished first Hoeing of Rice

April 28 A tremendous Thunder Storm Rain & Tornado & Hail Lightning killed two of my Mules and what is very remarkable two of them were chained together, one killed the other not hurt & the single one standing near by was killed

May 3 Gave out Osnabergs 7 yds each . . . .
5 Commenced Hoeing Second time.
9 Put Stretch flow on 17, 16 & 9 for 15 days
10 " " 22, & 21 Evelyn for days
20 " " " on 27 & U 20 for days
21 Finished hoeing 2d time Rice looks very fine
21 Stretch flow on 21, 19, 15, 10 & 2 New Ground
28 Left with my family for the Mountains for the health of my wife & children

Nov 7 Returned this day from the up country having spent a delightful summer, and all returned in fine health, for which we are truly thankful to the Author of all good —— the only accident occurring was Louisa breaking her collar bone.

*Remarks*

From all accounts the past summer has been most unhealthy for very many years, lost no negroes although nearly all have been sick —— the harvest season one of the worst excessive rains every day, the Crop all safe in the yard on 29 September On the 12 & 13 of Oct a very severe gale no loss but the banks much washed & broken ——

My Overseer Mr Benjamin Talbot of Boston Massachusetts *died* on the 13$^{th}$ of October of absess [sic] of the Lungs, opened by D$^{r}$ Sullivan. Talbot had been in my employ about upwards of four years; a very efficient man and a great loss to me =

8 Hands collecting mud to replace canal trunk, washed out by the very high tides of Last week

16 Started the Engine every thing works well
Dug all the Potatoes about 1500 Bushels

21 First frost of any consequence vines killed.

22 Sunday, Taken sick this day with Billious fever and confined to my Room 14 days

Decr 10 Rode into the field this day first since my illness
" Gave out Clothes this day

1847

Jay 1 Gave out Blankets all round
" " Shoes . . . .

March 1 Planted 9 Acre Square
10 Planted 16 & 17 Acre Square
11 Planted 23 & part of Kesia
12 Finished Kesia & all of Upper 20
15 Planted 22 Evelyn 125 Acres
25 Planted 10 & 15 Acres
26 " 19 & 21 "
27 " 27 Acres
"
26 Rain & Fresh blow from W

27 Ice & Wind heavy from N W
29 Planted Lower 20 Acre
April 13 Planted Point field $26\frac{3}{4}$ Acres
14 " Johns Square $23\frac{3}{4}$
12 Very heavy Rain & some Hail, Received 200 bushels white flint Corn from Sav[anna]h.
May 26,27,28,&29 heavy showers of Rain Working mostly on the hill
June 20 Planted $5\frac{1}{2}$ Acres Slips
July 1,2&3 " 6 " "
Showers almost every day for the last month
8 Ears shooting in 9 Acre
10 Dried down the 9 for 48 hours. Changed the water on all the fields
15 Finished picking all the Crop this day
21 Heavy wind from N.E. and tide very high
22 Small break in point field. Every square shooting out
Augst 14 Commenced Cutting the 9 Acre Square
21 Commenced cutting in earnest. Cut the 16 & part of Kesia
22 Sunday
23 Cutting Kesia
24 Cutting 23 Acre Evelyn. 25 Acres in the yard
} Delightful Weather
25 Cutting 22 Evelyn
28 Cutting 17. 55 Acres in the yard. Tides very high for 3 Days
} Rain 25, 26 & 27 Very Heavily
29 Sunday
30,31 Sept 1,2,3,4&5 Rainy every day & night
Sept 6 Delightful day. 83 Acres in the yard, delightful weather
7 Delightful weather
8 Do Do . 100 Acres in the Yard
9 125 Acres in yard
11 140 " " "
12 Sunday
13 Delightful weather
14 Do Do Restacking. Cutting & tieing

15 Wind N E and every appearance of a Gale. 150 Acres in the yard.

Birds in Millions in Johns Square

16 162 Acres in the yard Wind N E with Showers. Looks very Squally ——

1½ O clock Very heavy Rain from N. E.

19 Sunday " 17 Dry. 18 Rainy

20 From the heavy rains one of the Large ricks so much heated. had to take it down, & 21 Fine weather

22 Finished Cutting this day. Showry & looks squally

23 175 Acres in the Yard

24,25 Delightful weather 195 Acres in Yard

26 Sunday Delightful Weather

27 207 Acres in yard delightful Weather

28 224 Acres in Delightful weather.

29 228 " " Delightful weather

Restacking with all hands

30 240 Acres in Delightful day —— } Delightful Weather

Oct 4 282 " " & that is all ——

6&7 Breaking in Corn

8 Commenced thrashing Straw with the flails

Started the Engine, worked beautifully

9 Gave the People this day & went to S Simons myself to negotiate with John Demere for his place for Estate of Cater

13 From the 24 Sept to this date we have had most delightful weather not a Cloud & the atmosphere cool & delightful

13 Cloudy & few drops of Rain

14,15&16 Delightful weather.

20 Shipped this day 968 bushels Rice to Messrs R. Habersham & Son

Nov 3 Shipped this day Bushels Rice to Messrs R. Habersham & Son, Savannah

9 Moved from Carterets Point all well — } No Frost but vegetation checked from Cold weather

10 Finished digging Potatoes

25 Cumsey & Catherine blankets for Children

25 First frost to kill Gourd & other vines Ice

[November 1847]

26&27 Very Cold  Ice both mornings
28 Gave out Clothes & Shoes.

1848

March 1 A very dry winter, not more than two days rain until the 25, 26 & 27 of Feb. then three days Rain from N East
1 Planted this day, 9, 17 & five acres in the 16.
2 Finished 16 & Upper 20 Acres
3 Planted Lower 20 Acre  2½ Bu
9 Planted Johns Square  2 Bu
11 " Point field  2 Bu
April 17 Heavy white frost
21 Point flow on Kesia 22 & 23 for three days
25 Commenced Second hoeing, very dry & grassy
28 Stretch flow on 9, 17, & 16
" Point flow on two New Grounds & 18 — 4 days
May 3 Stretch flow on 10, 15, 19, 21, upper 20 & lower 20 & 27.
Moved to Summer quarters this day
18 Stretch flow on 23, 22 & Kesiah  Hoeing old Rice third time ——
20 Fine Shower of Rain, very much wanted. every Pond *dry dry*
Planted 15 Acres of Corn
21 Shower of Rain in the evening ——
June 16 Harvest flow on 9, 17, 11, Upper & Lower 20. Taking 14 day stretch flow off 18 & 2 New Ground both look well. I never saw anything to equal the grass on Elizafield except new ground ——
17 Planted 2 Acres Slips
20 Planted 3¾ Acres Slips
July 6 Ears out in 9 & 16 Acre  Catterpillars in nearly all the fields but very bad in 10 & some in 15 ——
15 All the Rice under Harvest flow
Augst 19 Commenced cutting in 9 & 16 acre squares. Splendid day ——
20 Sunday
21 Cut Lower 20

22 " upper 20 brought in 16 & 9 25 Acres
23 " 17 15 "
24 Brought in from Lower 20 15 "
25 " " " upper & Lower 20 12
26 80 Acres in the yard 17
Splendid weather the whole week all well
27 Sunday Rainy
28 Cut 21 Acre Delightful weather
29 Ricking & Gleaning Lower 20, Rice not ripe enough to cut
31 Delightful Weather

Sept 1 Stop cutting for 4 days Rice not ripe enough
2 Cut 19
3 Sunday Fine Day
4 Cutting 27 & tieing 19 —— 104 Acres in the yard
5 118 Acres in the yard
6 137 Do Cutting Johns Square
7 150 Do Do Wind N E & looks very squally occasional Showers of Rain
8 Delightful day
9 Do
10 Sunday — Do
11&12 Delightful weather
13 200 Acres in the yard delightful day
14 216 " in Shower of Rain at 11 O clock
17 Sunday
18,19,20 Delightful Weather
21&22 " " 21 Rainy
22 300 Acres in the yard, & that is all It has been one of the finest harvest seasons ever known—— Digging ½ Allowance Roots
23 Gave the Negroes to Rest
24 Sunday Rainy Wind N E & looks Squally
26&27 Pleasant started the Engine

Oct 6 Wind N E & very fresh with Showers
7,8,9,10 Do Do
11 Do
12 Pretty severe Gale Water entirely over the Plantation

13 Tides over the Land at Low water

14 Delightful day 8 Breaks Sent all Hands to assist Mr Forman save his crop

25 Cutting after Rice. Ditching out ¼ drains with the Men in 15 Acre

Dec 14 Employed J. J Morgan as Overseer —

12 to 16 Rainy & unpleasant weather

12 to 19 Rainy. *Very very* warm Summer Clothes comfortable. Rattoon Rice about 4 to 5 inches high in many parts of the field and the ground green with Grass ——

1849

Feb 5 Blankets given out this day —— Matilla, Looky, Judy, Hannah, Sue, N Jeany, Amey, Delia, Cart Bella, Sary, Susy. Bess, Phoebe, Mira,F Hannah, Adell, Patty, Dido, H Jeany, Cumsey, L Dinah, Catharine, Nanny, Haigar, Pussy, Margaret, Kate, Rina, Frederick ——

16 The Ground covered two inches thick with Snow, & Snowed until middle day

17 The North sides of the House still white with snow

March 5 Planted 9 & 17

6 " 16 & Kesiah

7 " 22 & 18 Evelyn

12 9 & 17 Water off & Rice coming up in 9. Went to S Simons this day for a change for Mrs Grant

25 Sunday Rainy

April 15 Heavy — frost & Ice

May 25 Left for Clarks Ville with my family on a/c of Mrs G.[s] health

Nov 9 Returned this day from Clarksville thank God all well & Mrs G[s] health quite restored

10 Fine white frost first of the season

27&28 Heavy white frost

Decr 2 Blankets given to the Children of the following Women

Nannys, R Hannah, Amaretta, Looky, P Kate, Sue, Haigar, Mira, R Kate, Catharine, P Hannah, Mira, R Kate

[December 1849]

10 Shipped this day 3300 bushels of Rice to Messr R Habersham & Son

Blankets given out to the following M John, April, Jack, D Prince, Richard, O Caesar, March, Hardtimes, Abraham, Fortune, Harry, George, D Scipio, Robert, J Stake, O Harry, Mark, Brister, London, Duncan, Duncan, Betty, Amaretta, Mary, Bella, Venus, Nancy, Nelly, F. Kate, Clora, R Phoebe, Molly, Abbey, Bobbett, Sarah, Grace, Jackson, Chance, Cyrus, William, Hannibal, L Caesar, L John, R Prince, Natt, Andrew, Pown, Piney = 47

1850

Jany 30 Up to this date little or no frost the Stubble all sprouting & the fields green as Spring. Commenced to hoe off the Stubble the first time in my life but driven out of the field by a very high tide 2 breaks in new ground & the doors all open for the next tide, ran over the banks in many places. Wind very heavy from N. E

Feb 4 First Ice this winter very cold all day finished repairing banks from high tides

| | | |
|---|---|---|
| March 6 | Planted | $2\frac{1}{2}$ acres Roots |
| 8 | " | All the High Land Corn |
| 11 | " | 9 & 17 Acres $2\frac{1}{2}$ Bush per Acre |
| | " | Johns Square 3 " |
| 12 | " | Point field 3 " |

| | | | |
|---|---|---|---|
| Augst 24 | Cut the 9 Acre | | No. Acres in Yard |
| 25 | Sunday | | |
| 26 | Cut Johns Square | Mr Morgan very sick | |
| 27 | " Point field | | |
| " | Brought in 9 Acre | | 9 Acres |
| 28 | " " $6\frac{1}{2}$ | | $15\frac{1}{2}$ " |
| 29 | " $8\frac{1}{2}$ | Heavy Rain in the morning N.E | 24 |
| 30 | " 16 | | 40 |
| 31 | " 9 | | 49 |
| Sept 1 | Sunday | | |

[September 1850]

| | | | | | |
|---|---|---|---|---|---|
| | 2 | Brought in 10 Acres | Light Rain | 59 | 59 |
| | 3 | Cut 17 & Lower 20 | | | |
| | 4 | Cut 27 Acre field | | 4 | 63 |
| | 5 | Tieing 17 & Lower 20 | N E | | |
| | 6 | Brought in 17 tide very high | N E | 80 | 80 |
| | 7 | " " 22 " " " | | 22 | 102 |
| | 8 | Sunday | | | |
| | 9 | Cut balance of 27, 21 & part of 19 | Rain | | |
| | 10 | " 16, Lower 20 | | | |
| | 11 | Magnificent Weather | | | |
| | 12 | " | | | |
| | 15 | Sunday | | | |
| | 19 | Brought in to date | | 180 | 180 |
| | 21 | Rainy Cutting 22 & 18 Evelyn | | | |
| | 28 | Brought in to date | | 235 | 235 |
| | 30 | Sept Heavy Rain wind N E | | | |
| Oct | 1 | Do Do | | | |
| | 2 | Brought in to date | | 241 | 241 |
| | 3 | " " " " | | 263 | 263 |
| | 7 | Brought in to date | | 290 Acres | 290 |
| | 9 | Brought in to date | | 300 & all | |
| | 20,21 | Light frost | | | |
| | 31 | Moved this day from Carterets | | | |
| Nov | 7 | Gave out Shoes | | | |
| | 17 | Ice & very cold | | | |

1851

| | | | |
|---|---|---|---|
| Aug | 19 | Commenced harvesting in Johns Square 4 Acre | |
| | 20 | Found the Rice not ripe enough | |
| | 24 | The Point field about ⅔ blown flat with the Ground & about half of John Square | |
| Sept | 25 | Cut John Square | |
| | 26 | " Point field | |
| | 27 | Tied up John Square the Wind and Rain heavy from N. E until the 29. Tides very high but no breaks nothing done for three days but raise low places in the banks | Wind |
| | 30 | Splendid day Cutting Lower 20 | N E |
| | 31 | Sunday | N E |

[September 1851]

| | | | | |
|---|---|---|---|---|
| | 1 | Cutting 17 & 9 tieing Lower 20 | | N E |
| | 2 | " upper 20 & part of 27 | | N E |
| | 3 | " 27 & tieing 17 & 9 brought in 13 Acres from Johns Square | | N E & Strong |
| | | | In yard | |
| | 4 | Tieing 27 & Upper 20 | Acres 13 | |
| | 8 | Brought in 27 & Johns Square | 54 | S E |
| | 9 | Cut 15 & 10 | | E |
| | 10 | Cut 19 & 21 & tied 15 | | E E |
| | 11 | Tieing 10, 19 & 21 | | N E |
| | 12 | " 21 & 16 Showers | | " |
| | 13 | Brought in to date | 77 | " |
| | 14 | Sunday | | |
| | 15 | Brought in to date & Cut 10 Acres in Kesia | 86 | N E, Rainy |
| | 17 | Finished Kesia, 22 & 23 | | N E |
| | 21 | Sunday | | N E |
| | 22 | Brought in to date | 140 | N E |
| | 23 | " " " " | 155 | N E |
| | 24 | " " " " | 165 | S W |
| | 25 | " " " " | 180 | N E |
| | 26 | " " " " | 196 | N E |
| | 27 | " " " " | 208 | S W |
| | 28 | Sunday | | N W |
| | 29 | Brought in to date very light frost | 226 | N W |
| | 30 | " " " " | 240 | N W |
| Oct | 1 | " " " " | 250 | N W |
| | 2 | " " " " | 270 | E |
| | 3 | " " " " | 280 All | W |

the weather during the harvest until the last week was very threatening for a gale with heavy N E Winds. still it was very cool & upon the whole it could not have been better

| | | |
|---|---|---|
| 4 | Dug ½ allowance of Roots from 18 —— 6 Acres manured Corn made 120 Baskets | |
| 5 | Sunday | N E |
| 6 | Election gave the hands this day | N E |
| 7 | Cutting Crab grass for two days & breaking in Corn at Carterets point | N E |

[October 1851]

| | | |
|---|---|---|
| 8 | Breaking in Corn | N E |
| 9 | Do Do Made 500 Bushels | N E |

10 Went to Savannah with My Mother & Eugenia and saw them off in the Alabama for New York

14 Returned from Savannah

21 Started the thrashing Machine having put in myself a cast iron bed—runs elegantly. Men cutting Canal through Johns square to the River about 15 tasks long

27&28 Frost both Mornings

28 Moved from Carterets pt all well at this time Myself, Fraser, Luly & Rose each had an attack of fever

29 Digging potatoes on the hill —— 587 Bushels

30 " "

31 Loaded Capt Stevens 2253 Bushels [rice]
Gave out Shoes ——

Nov 1 Weather very warm, 1 hit digging Slips in the Swamp

2 Went to Savannah with my family to meet my two daughters on their return from the North and the eldest from a tour over Europe

8 Returned from Savannah

1852

May 1 Crop Beautiful

4&5 Heavy N E wind tides over the whole place
1 Break in 9 Acre
2 " in 17
1 " Flood gate
1 " John Square
1 " Point
3 " Scipios
1 " 23 Acre
3 " 18 "

5 Mending break in 9 & 17 Acre

Augst 19 Cutting Rice in 16 Acre

20 " " " 17 & 9

21 15 Acres in yard

22 Sunday Rainy & high winds

23 Cut down 10 & tied 17 & 9 Cloudy } Weather Looks
24 35 Acres in yard Cloudy } suspicious

[August 1852]

24 Went to Macon for my daughters returned on 29
30 55 Acres Rice in yard
31 75 " " " " Splendid day
Sept 1 96 " " " " "
2 116 " " " " "
3 133 " " " " Slight Shower
4 *Very* heavy Rain cut Kesia & Upper 20 N E
5 Sunday Rainy N E
6 Tieing Kesia & Upper 20 —— N E
7 147 acres in yard Rainy N E
8 155 " " " " N E
9 172 " " " " N E
10 190 " " " " N E
11 196 " " " " N E
12 Sunday " N E
13 fine day
14 208 acres in yard Tides very high N E
15 215 Acres in the yard, Dry. The tides *very* high from freshet Spring & heavy East wind fortunately no breaks, but not able to draw the water for fear of breaks. Rice birds in millions
16 225 Acres in the yard Dry, tide very high N E
Cutting point field
17 Tides *excessively high and* the Wind blowing a gale from N East small break in Hopeton field, occasional showers ——
18 Rain every day to 25 and Rainy still
25 235 Acres in the yard Rice all sprouting in tops of the Ricks —— Rain Rain Rain
30 270 Acres in the yard No Rain N E
Oct 1 288 " " " " No Rain N E
5 325 " and that is all " " S W
Nov 11 Moved from Carterets today all well Rainy
9&10 Slight frosts
11 Digging slips turn out well
24 Mr Lockwood & 2 hands commenced work at 1 O Clock this day ——

[November 1852]

| | | |
|---|---|---|
| 29 | Robert commenced at Mr Hugers Machine —— | |

1853

| | | |
|---|---|---|
| Augst 16 | Cutting in Point field 25 Hands | Rainy |
| 17 | Finished cutting point " | Do |
| 18 | Cutting John Square | Do |
| 19 | Tieing in Point field Men from Canal | Fair |
| | Mulatto John died last night Rain in the afternoon | |
| 20 | Cutting Kesia & tieing John Sqr | Fair |
| 21 | Sunday | Fair |
| 22 | 10 Acres in the yard | Rainy |
| 23 | 14 " " " " | Rainy |
| 24 | 31 " " All of Kesia in the yard | Rainy |
| 25 | 49 " " the yard all of Point | Fair |
| 26 | 70 " " " " all of John | Fair |
| 27 | Cutting Buck & Lower 20 | " |
| 28 | Sunday | N E |
| 29 | Tieing 18 & Buck, Showry & Squally —— | N E |
| 30 | 82 Acres in yard Do & Do | N E |
| 31 | 90 " " " Splendid day | S E |
| Sept 1 | Rain all day Nothing done | S E |
| | Blew a gale in the Night from S E & Rain in torrents | |
| 2 | Rainy in Mrng 12 O clock some appearance of clear[in]g off —— | S E |
| 3 | Cloudy & wet Gleaning Showry | S E |
| 4 | Sunday Tied U 20 —— Showry | S E |
| 5 | 100 Acres in yard & tieing 16 | S E |
| 6 | 120 " " " light Showry | N E |
| 7 | Cutting 15 & 17 Acre | W |
| 8 | 131 Acres in yard Splendid day | S W |
| 9 | Cut down 21 Rain Rain poured | U & Down |
| 10 | " " 19 & 9 tied 17 Acre Rainy | S W Cloudy |
| 11 | Sunday | |
| 12 | Cut 23 Rain Rain Rain | N E |
| 13 | Nothing doing Every appearance of a Gale. Tides V High | S W |
| 14 | 142 Acres in yard | |
| 15 | 150 Acres in the yard fine day | S W |

16 170 " " " Do Rainy S W

17 190 " " " Do Rainy S W

18 Sunday —

19 210 " " " heavy Showry S W

20 220 " " " S W

21 240 " " " Splendid day Cool N W

22 260 " " Do Cool N W

23 270 " and that is all ——

Oct 4 Delightful cool weather to date Thrashed
Wind fresh from N.E tides very high break in Bucks Square & 9 acre

5 Thrashing

6 Do

7 Do

8 Rain all day —— N E

9 Sunday ———

14 Rainy

15 Charming day Mrs. G., Eugenia, Rose, Fraser, & Miller went to Darien ——

16 Sunday

20&21 Severe Gale from N E tides over everything several breaks &c

25 White frost

Nov 8 Moved from Carterets all well the whole summer ——

1854

Augs 19 Cut Johns Square & part of Point field Rain Rainy

20 Sunday Do Rainy

21 Finish cutting Point field & tied John Square

22 Cutting Lower 20 & tied a little in point Rainy

23 6 Acres in yard, tied point Clear

24 11 " " " tied Lower 20 "

25 33 " " " " —— "

26 40 " " " " Cut U[pper] 20 & 9 "

27 Sunday ——— Intence heat "

28 45 Acres in yard tieing U 20 & 9 hot "

29 60 " " " " —— Cloudy no Rain N E

30 84 " " " " Do " N E
31 90 " " " Cut 16 & part 17 Rainy in the Night
Sept 1 99 " " " Cut Kesia Fine day
2 Cut part of 23 & tied 16 Heavy Showers
3 Sunday Splendid weather
4 Finish cutting 23 & part of 22 tied Splendid day Kesia & part of 27
5 Finished cutting 22 & 18 Acre Splendid day
6 Cut Scipios Square & tied 22 & 18 Wind fresh from N. E.
7 120 Acres in yard Blowing a gale from N. E. tides very high but no damage yet —— Look for trouble this night ——
8 Dreadful Gale. Everything under water break in 16, 22, 18 & Kesia Scipio Square Every stack in the field blown and washed away. Loss entire 110 Acres of Rice about 6,000 bushels
9 Heavy clouds & Rain Thunder & Lightning most uncommon after a gale
10 Sunday all hands at Work very hot with distant Thunder
11 All Men at 16 break Women tieing up Scipio Square & drying Rice on the Creek
Pleasant but Hot
12 Cut 15 Acre working at Break Pleasant but Hot
125 Acres in yard — Do "
13 136 " in Cut part of 19 Heavy Shower
14 141 " " " 21 " Clear
15 150 " " " Tied 19 & 21 "
16 Cut 27 Acre Slight Shower
17 Sunday —— Heavy N E Wind & Rain every appearance of Gale
18 170 Acres in yard Rainy & every appearance of Gale N E
19 Rain Rain Rain
20 180 Acres in yard Showry N E
21 Cut 10 Heavy Rain N E
22 Lifting 27 Cloudy & drisling tides very high N E

| | | | |
|---|---|---|---|
| 23 | Tied 10 & lifted 27 | Beautiful day | N E |
| 24 | Sunday Tied 27 | " Do | N E |
| 25 | 190 Acres in the yard | Do " | N E |
| 26 | Very heavy rain | | S E |
| 27 | " " | Showry | S E |
| 28 | 200 Acres Rice in yard all that is saved from the Gale, the last 100 Acres will not yield more than half a Crop | | S E blowy |
| 29 | All hands in the yard restacking | | S E |
| Oct 1 | Sunday —— | Splendid day | |
| 2 | Finished restacking | Do do | |
| 3 | Cutting Hay & mending breaks | | Rain |
| 4 | Breaking in Corn at the Point | | |
| 5&6 | " | " " | |
| 7 | Cutting hay | Delightful for 4 days | very Cool |
| 26 | Heavy N E wind. Cool & pleasant 16 break so bad cant mend it. | | tides very high. |
| Nov 9 | Moved from Carterets Pt | all well | |
| 14 | First frost with Ice | | |

| | | | | | |
|---|---|---|---|---|---|
| Decr 25 | Bought from Mark | 10,300 | Shingles | due | $5 |
| | " " Abram | 9,000 | " | due | $1 |
| | " " Hardtimes | 10,000 | " | " | $3 |
| | " " Harry Troup | 3,300 = | | 32,600 | |

1855

| | | |
|---|---|---|
| Augst 10 | Left with Sarah & Miss Virginia King for Marietta to visit Fraser & remove him from Pratts School to Mr Gouldings.[5] Returned on the 18th the weather in the up Country intencely hot, delightful at home | |
| Aug 23 | Commenced cutting Rice Cut John Square & Point field | 49 Acres |
| 25 | Tied up the above two sqrs | |
| 26 | Sunday | |
| 27 | Cut No 4 Grantly<br>5 Acres in the yard from John Sqr | 25 |

[5] Pastor of church in near-by Darien, who also operated some type of boys academy. See the "Directory."

28 Cut No 5 Grantly 25
29 " 9 Acre & tied No 4 G[rantly] 9
17 Acres in yard
30 Rainy in the Morning
24 Acres in yard Cut U 20 17
31 40 " " "

Sept 2 Sunday
3 49 Acres in Yard Cutting 17 17
4 Cutting Lower 20 22
5 Cutting 27, & 21 Rainy no tieing done
6 " 19 & 15
7 Raining heavy all day No work done
8 Showry, 50 Acres in the yard too wet to tie
9 Sunday—Tied Rice all day
10 72 Acres in yard & Tieing
11 78 " " " Tieing
12 93 " " " tied Scipios Sqr
13 Cutting 3 & 2 Grantly 50
14 " 1 at Grantly & 16 Elizafield Finished Cutt[in]g
15 103 Acres in yard
16 Sunday
17 108 Acres in yard Finished tieing at Grantly
18 123 " " " Splendid weather
19 144 " " " Do——
20 163 " " " " Dry N E Wind
21 200 " " " Dry Do "
22 210 " " " "
23 Sunday Heavy Shower & wind N E
24 Heavy Winds from N. E. Loading flats at Grantly
25 230 Acres in yard Very high tides & Showry N E
26 250 " " " " " "
27 275 " " " Very cloudy West
28 & 29 Rainy nothing done
30 Sunday——

Oct 1 290 Acres in yard Warm weather W
2 215 Acres in yard Delightfully Cool W
At the Election yesterday between T. T Long democrat & T. B King Knownothing for Senate

T. T Long elected by *40 Majority* — The greatest triumph ever known in Glynn County [6]

| | | | |
|---|---|---|---|
| | 3 | Harvesting | |
| | 4 | Bringing in Rice | |
| | 5 | 330 Acres in & that is all. Very fine harvest Season | |
| | 6 | Breaking in Corn Showry | |
| | 7 | Sunday —— Very clear & Cold | |
| | 8 | Frost breaking in Corn | 647 Baskets 300 bu. |
| | 9 | Cleaning up my yard | |
| | 10 | Women thrashing Straw Rice. Men cutting Wood | |
| Nov | 8 | Moved from Sedgemoor spent a very delightful & healthy summer —— | |

1856

| | | | |
|---|---|---|---|
| Augst | 19 | Harvesting Corn made 250 Bushels | |
| | 23 | Cut Scipios Square 18 Acres | |
| | | Cut in Point field 13½ " | |
| | 24 | Sunday —— | |
| | 25 | Finished Cutting point & tied up Scipio & part of Point Showr in the ev[enin]g | |
| | 26 | Cutting 4 & 5 Grantly | |
| | 27 | Heavy N E wind & Rain all day | |
| | 28 | Cut John Square & No 1 Grantly | |
| | 29 | Tieing John & Point & bringing in from Scipios 9 Acres in the yard —— | |
| | 30 | Tieing 4 & 5 Grantly —— | |
| | 31 | Sunday Dreadful blow from S & SW | |
| Sept | 1 | 23 Acres in yard delightful day —— | |
| | 2 | 33 Acres in yard Cutting Upper 20 | N E dry |
| | 3 | Cutting Lower 20 & tieing U 20 | N E dry |
| | 4 | Cutting 17 Acre | N E |
| | 5 | Cutting No 2 Grantly Tieing Lower 20 | N E |
| | 6 | " " 3 " tieing 17 & 19 Acre | N E |
| | 7 | Sunday —— | |
| | 8 | Tieing 3 & 2 Grantly —— | S E |

[6] This entry is interesting because of its ambiguity. It is not clear whether the numerical majority of 40 was unusual or whether Grant deemed the defeat of the Know Nothing candidate to be of earth-shaking significance. If the former be the case, the entry also provides evidence of the limited participation in elections by Southern whites.

| | | | |
|---|---|---|---|
| | 9 | Cutting 27 | S E |
| | 10 | Cutting 21 & 19 | N E |
| | 11 | Cutting 24 & 16 and that is all. birds very bad | N E |
| | 12 | 43 Acres in Yard Splendid weather | |
| | 13 | 60 " " " " " | |
| | 15 | 77 " " " " | |
| | 16 | 89 Acres in Splendid weather | |
| | 17 | 110 " " " " | Very high tides |
| | 18 | 130 " " | N E & Freshet |
| | 19 | 144 Acres in Yard | |
| | 20 | 160 " " | |
| | 21 | Sunday——— | |
| | 22 | 175 Acres in the yard | Slight Shower early in mor[nin]g |
| | 23 | 195 " " " " | Do Do |
| | 24 | 213 " " " " | |
| | 25 | 230 | |
| | 26 | 250 —— Frost at Bethel Glynn County | |
| | 27 | 265 ——— | |
| | 28 | Sunday | |
| | 29 | 281 " | |
| | 30 | 307 " | |
| Oct | 1 | 308 " Heavy white frost vines well killed the earliest frost by 5 days within my recollection (Frost on the 26 Sept at Bethel, Glyn County —— H F G) —— | |
| | 6 | 349 Acres in & finished their [sic] never was so fine a Harvest season within the memory of any Planter on the River Not Rain enough in all Sept to wet or lay the dust | |
| | 10 | Showry, very refreshing —— | |
| | 18 | Frost | |
| Nov | 1 | Frost Moved from Sedgemoor thank God all well | |
| | 2 | Sunday | |
| | 3 | Showry & very oppressively hot. | |
| | 4 | Election for President, Buchannon [sic], Filmore & Fremont 3 Candidates. Good Rain. | |

[November 1856]

20&21 Rain all day——

23 For the first time Lay service was read in St Davids Church by H. F. Grant. May God in Mercy dispose of all our hearts to keep & walk in his ordineces [sic]——

1857

| | | Wind & Weather | | |
|---|---|---|---|---|
| Sept 1,2,3,4,5 | Heavy wind from No East & looks very Squally | | | |
| 3 | Commenced cutting Scipio & John Square | H[eavy] | N E. | D[ry] |
| 4 | Heavy Rain all day | H | N.E | R[ain] |
| 5 | Cutting John Square | H | N E | D |
| 6 | Sunday tieing Scipio Squr | H | N E | D |
| 7 | Cutting No 5 Grantly & part of Point Field tieing John | H | N E | D |
| 8 | Cutting L. 20 & finish point field | H | N E | D |
| 9 | Cutting U 20 & finishd L 20 & tieing No 5 | H | N E | D |
| 10 | Cutting 17 tieing Point & U 20 | H | N E | D |
| 11 | Tieing U 20 & part L 20 & brought in $7\frac{1}{2}$ Acres in yard from Scipio | L[ight] | N W | D |
| 12 | Cutting No 4 Grantly &c | L | N W | D |
| 13 | Sunday | L | W | D |
| 14 | Cutting in No 3 & tieing No 4 | L | S W | D |
| 15 | Cutting No 3 & No 2 & part of No 1 | L | S W | D |
| 16 | Finished cutting Grantly | L | E | D |
| 17 | Cut 10 & tieing at Grantly | L | E | (Cloudy) |
| 18 | Cut 15 & tieing at Grantly | L | W | D |

| | Day | Entry | | Wind | |
|---|---|---|---|---|---|
| | 19 | Cutting 19 & 21 tieing 10 & 15 | L | W | D |
| | 20 | Sunday Light Shower | | | |
| | 21 | Cut 27 “ Shower | | | |
| | 22 | Cut 16 and that is all —— Heavy Rain | | | |
| | 23 | 15 Acres in yard I [was] sick with fever | | N E | D |
| | 24 | 39 Acres in yard Very cool | | N E | D |
| | 25 | 60 “ “ “ “ “ | | N | D |
| | 26 | 80 “ “ “ “ Very ill this day | | | |
| | 27 | Sunday | | Rainy | |
| | 28 | 100 Acres in yard | | | |
| | 29 | 120 “ “ “ Splendid day | | N W | |
| | 30 | 143 “ “ “ Splendid day | | N W | |
| | | very Cool —— | | N W | |
| Oct | 1 | 165 “ “ “ Shower | | N E | |
| | 2 | 180 “ “ “ | | N E | |
| | 3 | 205 “ “ “ Showry ——— | H | N E | R |
| | 4 | Sunday heavy Rain | H | N E | R |
| | 5 | 220 Acre in yard Cool tremendous | H | N E | D |
| | 6 | 240 Acre in yard Cool high tides | H | N E | D |
| | 7 | 256 Acre in yard Do | H | N E | D |
| | 8 | 264 —— | H | N E | R |
| | 9 to 15 | I [was] confined by Sickness and the weather has been so wet that nothing could be done with the Rice | H | N E | |
| | 15 | Beautiful day | | N W | Cool |
| | 22 | In consequence of Sickness & other causes no entrys have been made | | Very cool & some frost in parts of the county — N E | |
| | | 320 Acres in the yard | | | |
| | 23 | 330 “ “ “ Rain at night | | N E. | R |
| | 27 | Finished harvesting this day Good Frost | | | |
| | 29 | I have another attack of Chill | | | |

[November 1857]

Nov 2 Moved from Sedgemoor

7 Another attack of Chill & fever

9 Do Do Very severe

11 Fraser — Eugenia & Sarah returned from the North this day all well

Also Sarah Hogan & Mr Fox from Columbus, the former for some weeks the latter a few days

1858

Nov 13 Returned this day with all my family from the Up Country where we have been since the 11th of June, on a/c of the health of Mrs Grant She very much improved in health. all the rest quite well. I was desperately ill with congestion at Catoosa Springs on the 18th of August, but Blessed be God he spared me a little longer & Oh may I improve the time.

Found all the people well & the Crop appearantly [sic] good. Lost March a prime Man aged about 32 years and two children & My fine Buggy Horse Caesar during my absence——

24 Having put in New Line shaft & overhalled Theresh-ing [sic] Machine We commenced threshing to day, worked well

29 Mr Wm Aikin Walker of Charleston arrived this evening on a visit to the family

22 Fraser commenced School in Brunswick this day boards at the Oglethorp Hotel at $25 per Month Fuel & Lights extra——

30 Rain all day, hands in their Houses——

Decr 14 Shipped Rice to day to N A Harde & Co. Planted 2½ acres Oats——

25 All my Barns, Machinery, Saw Mill &c & 7000 Bushels Rice destroyed by fire occasioned by carelessness, My House also took fire from the half burned shingles, Commenced immediately to erect New Barns & contracted with Messr Lachlison for entire new Machinery at $4000.

28 One New Barn 36 x 22½ finished for a Carrier Barn

As the result of considerable study of the Elizafield Journal, the fields which were usually planted by Hugh Fraser Grant are identified tentatively by the code given below. It should be recalled that in some years he planted *all* of the fields shown in this map, since he served as caretaker for the Evelyn and Grantly plantations when his brother Charles was unable to operate them. The reader is also reminded that as the result of floods and the destruction of some banks and trunks as well as changing growing conditions, it was possible and often profitable to rearrange the banks and ditches (especially for the smaller fields) so that the acreage of some fields varied from year to year.

| | | |
|---|---|---|
| A | 23 Acre Field | East of Creek separating Elizafield and Evelyn |
| B | 18 Acre Field | East of Creek |
| C | 22 Acre Field | East of Creek |
| D | 20 Acre Field | East of Creek |
| E | 27 Acre Field | West of Creek |
| F | 21 Acre Field | West of Creek |
| G | 19 Acre Field | West of Creek |
| H | Lower 20 Field | West of Creek |
| I | Upper 20 Field | West of Creek |
| J | 16 Acre Field | West of Creek |
| K | 15 Acre Field | West of Creek |
| L | 17 Acre Field | West of Creek |
| M | 5 Acre Field | West of Creek |
| N | 10 Acre Field | West of Creek |
| O | Point Field | West of Creek |
| P | New Grounds (or Johns Field) | West of Creek |

Planimetric Air Map of Elizafield, Evelyn, and Grantly Plantations

A section of U.S. Coast and Geodetic Survey Air Photo Compilation No. T-5122 (1933).

# FIELD JOURNALS

## HIGH LAND CROP[1]

1839

Mar 18 Planted — Acres of Corn
22 " 3½ " " Potatoes
22 " ½ Acre Baden Corn
April 2,3&4 Clearing Land in rear of House 4¾ Acres
12&13 Hoeing Corn
May 8 Hoeing Corn
9 Fine Rain. thinning Corn

1840

March 5 Planted 15 Acres of Corn
26 Planted 4 Acres Potatoes.
April 9 Ploughing Corn
11 Finished planting 19 Acres of Corn
25&26 Hoed all the Corn & potatoes.
July 1 Planted to this date 10½ Acres Slips[2]
" 12 Acres Peas
Harvested 500 Bushels of large Potatoes
" 250 " " Corn
Peas about made the seeds
Nov 10&11 Listed[3] all the high ground

1841

March 8 Planted 5 Acres of Corn
22 Coming up. Planted 4 Acres of Potatoes
June 19 Planted 5 Acres Crouders in the Corn
Augst 1 " 10 Acres Cow Peas
Planted 11 Acres of Slips

1842

March 14 Planted 4 Acres Roots
20 " 13 Acres Corn.

[1] The entries on this page and the next page are concerned with the production of provisions crops. Although they do not appear in the Elizafield Journal before those pages concerned with fields devoted to rice culture, it seemed desirable to list them at the beginning of this section on field journals.

[2] Sweet potato seedlings. [3] Refers to plowing with a list plow.

## CARTERETS P^t FARM[4]

| | | |
|---|---|---|
| 1841 | | Purchased at *$6,000* Cash. |
| Feb | 28 | Planted 3½ & 2½ Acres of Corn |
| Mar | 12 | Planted 5 Acres of Cotton. |
| | 20 | " 13½ Acres Cotton |
| | 25 | " 12 " " |
| April | 1 | " 9 " " |
| June | 24 | Planted 6 Acres of Peas |
| July | 30 | " 5½ Acres of Peas & 3 Acres of Slips |
| Augst | 7 | " 13 " of Peas in Multicalis Patch |
| | 12 | Commenced picking Cotton about 30 lbs —— |
| | 6 | Cotton in; low places taken the Rust |
| | 26 | 1000 lbs Cotton in Barn. Cotton almost ruined by the Torrents of Rain |
| Sept | 18 | three bags Cotton in barn |
| Oct | 27 | Six bags Cotton " " |

| | | |
|---|---|---|
| 1842 | | |
| March | 10 | Planted 10 Acres Cuba Corn |
| | 14 | " one acre Root potatoes |
| | 17 | " 10 Acres white flint corn yield 86 Bushels |
| | 21 | Commenced planting Cotton 8 Acres |
| April | 9 | Planted 7 Acres Cotton . . . . 7 |
| | | *15 Acres* |
| June | | 10 Acres White Gomased |
| | | Yield —— |
| | | 3 Acres Slips |
| | | 37 Acres Pease |

[4] This combination provisions and sea-island cotton farm also served as the summer home for the Grant family in the 1840's. It was located some six miles down stream on the South Altamaha River.

## CULTURE OF 18 ACRE E.C[5]

| | | |
|---|---|---|
| 1838 | | |
| March 12 | Planted and watered | |
| 30 | Rice all coming up | |
| May 8 | " Long flow | |
| July 7 | Harvest flow | |
| Sept 1 | Cutting | |
| 1839 | | |
| March 10 | Turning Land | |
| 29 | Planted and watered | |
| April 24 | Hoeing Rice | |
| May 14 | Second Hoeing | |
| 1840 | | |
| | Ploughing & Harrowing | [Seed] |
| April 11th | Planted and watered | 2.1 [6] per acre |
| June 27 | Harvest Flow | |
| 1841 | | |
| April 7 | Planted and flowed | 2.1 per acre |
| July 3 | Harvest flow | |
| Sept 24 | Cutting Rice | |
| 1842 | | |
| March 26 | Planted and watered | 2½ " " |
| April 11 | Point flow for 4 days | |

[5] East of creek.

It should also be noted that the preceding MS p. 13 of the Elizafield Journal, which contained the record of 23 Acre Field for the years 1838-42, was torn out. This may be confirmed by consulting the MS Index prepared by Grant and printed on page 294, of this book.

[6] This figure should be read as 2 bushels and 1 peck per acre.

## CULTURE 22 ACRE

| | | | |
|---|---|---|---|
| 1838 | | | |
| March | 8 | Planted & watered | [Seed] |
| July | 7 | Harvest flow | |
| Sept | 3 | Cutting Rice | |
| 1839 | | | |
| Jany | 9 | Burning Stubble | |
| Feb | 20 | Turning land | |
| | 21 | Put in a new trunk | |
| March | 28 | Planted and watered | 2 Bu per acre |
| April | 26 | Hoeing Rice | |
| May | 15 | Second Hoeing | |
| 1840 | | | |
| | | Turning with the Hoe and flowed | |
| April | 4 | Planted and watered | 2.1.0 per acre |
| June | 27 | Harvest flow | |
| 1841 | | | |
| April | 6 | Planted & watered | 2.1.0 per acre |
| July | 2 | Harvest flow | |
| Sept | 9 | Cutting Rice | |
| | 24 | Finished cutting this square. prevented by Gales & breaks | |
| 1842 | | | |
| April | 9 | Planted & watered new ground seed | 2½ Bu per |
| 1843 [7] | | | |
| March | | Broken between the old Stubble | |
| | 31 | Planted New Ground seed | 2½ Bu per Acre |
| May | 13 | Watered 3 Days } Hoed 4 times | |
| June | 9 | Watered for 14 days } Hoed 4 times | |
| July | 1 | Harvest flow | |
| Sept | 5 | Cutting 7 Square cut | |

[7] This field is henceforth referred to by Grant as 22 Acre Evelyn.

1844

| | | |
|---|---|---|
| Jany 1 | Finished ploughing & drains all cleaned out | |
| April 10th | Planted & watered | 3 Bu per acre |
| 20 | Hoed | |
| May 15 | Watered 8 days | |
| May 30 | " 12 " | |
| June 15 | Watered for days kept on for Harvest | |

1845

| | | |
|---|---|---|
| April 3 | Planted | $2\frac{1}{2}$ per Acre |
| 26 | Dashed for two days | |
| May 17 | Flow for 23 days. Decidedly injured by the Dash | |
| Nov 17 | Sinking large ditch & $\frac{1}{4}$ drains | |

1847

| | | |
|---|---|---|
| | Broke up entirely | |
| March 15 | Planted & Watered | $2\frac{1}{2}$ Bu per Acre |
| 21 | Water off | |
| April 21 | First hoeing | |
| May 10 | 2d Do | |
| 13 | Stretch flow | |
| 22 | Water off | |
| June 10 | 3d hoeing | |
| 12 | Harvest flow | |
| Aug 25 | Cutting | |

1848

| | |
|---|---|
| April 21 | Point flow |
| May 11 | Second hoeing |
| 18 | Stretch flow |

## Culture of 20 Acre EC Kezia[8]

1838

March 13 Planted and watered
May 8 Long flow
July 7 Harvest flow
Sept 5 Cutting Rice

1839

Feb 28 Turning Land
March 18 Harrowing
27 Planted and Watered — 2 Bu per Acre
April 27 Hoeing Rice
May 15 Second Hoeing

1840

Land all turned
April 3 Planted & Watered — 2.1.4 per acre
June 27 Harvest flow

1841

April 5 Planted & watered, N Carolina seed — 2.1. per acre
25 Bank broke and flowed for 3 days
July 1 Harvest flow
Sept 7 Cutting Rice

1842

April 7 Planted & watered New Ground Seed — 2½ ——

1843

March 15 Broke up between the old row's
29 Planted & watered — 2½ bushels New Ground
May 12 Watered for 4 days
June 8 Watered for 14 days
July 1 Harvest flow
Sept 4 Cutting Rice 6 Square cut
Nov 27 Commenced Ploughing

[8] Grant spells this Kesia in other places.

[December 1843]

Decr 10 Finished ploughing

1844

| | | | |
|---|---|---|---|
| April | 2 | Planted & Watered 8 days | 3 Bu pr Acre |
| | 20 | Hoed | |
| May | 15 | Watered 14 days | |
| June | 15 | Dashed for days Kept on for Harvest flow | |

1845

| | | | |
|---|---|---|---|
| | | Turned between the Stubble | |
| March | 21 | Planted & Watered | 2½ Bu per Acre |
| May | 17 | Long water for 23 days | |
| June | 22 | Harvest flow | |

1846

| | | | |
|---|---|---|---|
| Decr | | Ditched around the entire square. turned between the stubble | |

1847

| | | | |
|---|---|---|---|
| March | 12 | Planted & Watered | 2½ [bu per acre] |
| | 18 | Water off | |
| April | 19 | First hoeing | |
| May | 7 | 2d Do | |
| | 12 | Stretch flow | |
| | 22 | Water off | |
| June | 9 | 3 hoeing | |
| | 12 | Harvest flow | |
| Aug | 23 | Cutting | |

1848

| | | | |
|---|---|---|---|
| April | 21 | Point flow | |
| May | 15 | Second Hoeing | |

## Culture 27 Acre W.C[9]

1838

| | | | |
|---|---|---|---|
| April | 16 | Planted & watered | |
| July | 18 | Harvest flow | |
| Sept | 20 | Cutting Rice | |

1839

| | | | |
|---|---|---|---|
| Feb | 14 | Put down a new trunk | |
| March | 13 | Planted & watered | 2 Bu per Acre |
| April | 17 | Hoeing Rice | |
| May | 3 | Second Hoeing | |
| | 4 | Put on water for two days | |
| | 11 | Put on Water for 8 days | |
| June | 10 | Harvest Flow | |
| July | 12 | Ears Shooting out. | |
| Augst | 17 | Commenced Harvesting | |
| Nov | 27 | Cleaning ditches & drains | |

1840

| | | | |
|---|---|---|---|
| March | 4 | Planting & watered | Bu 2.1.0 per Acre |
| April | 5 | Trunk washed out the tide flowing in & out to the 9th Inst. has not been entirely dry since the Break owing to a heavy freshet | |
| May | 5 | Watered for 20 days | |
| June | 2 | Put on Harvest flow | |
| July | 4 | Rice shooting out | |
| Augst | 11 | Commence Cutting Rice | |

1841

| | | | |
|---|---|---|---|
| March | 15 | Planted | 2¼ per Acre |
| | 18 | Watered | |
| June | 2 | Harvest flow | |
| | 10 | Dry for 5 days & hoed | |
| Augst | 23 | Cuttin [sic] Rice | |
| Nov | 10 | Cleaning out north ditch & raising the Bank | |

9 West of creek

1842

| | | |
|---|---|---|
| March 8 | Planted & watered | 3 Bu |
| April 20 | Cut the Rice all up & replanting | 4 Bu |
| Nov | Cut ½ & ¼ drains & cleaned out all the old ¼s and cleaned out Large ditches | |

1843

| | | |
|---|---|---|
| Jany | Ploughed thoroughly & put on water | |
| March 18 | Planted Tunnos seed | 2½ per Acre |
| April 12 | Dashed one tide | |
| 26 | First hoeing | |
| May 12 | Watered for 20 days | |
| June 10 | Watered " 2 days | |
| 18 | Harvest flow. put on to kill the caterpillar | |
| Sept 2 | Cutting 5th Square Cut, this field as well as the others that were appearantly [sic] injured by caterpillar, have not sustained the least injury —— H. F. Grant | |

1844

| | |
|---|---|
| Feb 10 | Finished thrashing & find every square dreadfully injured from the effect of the Caterpillar, by keeping the water on too deep, those that were not eaten were more injured by the water than those that were eaten H. F. Grant |

1844

| | | |
|---|---|---|
| | Turned between the old stubble | |
| March 15 | Planted & Watered 8 days | 3 Bu per Acre |
| April 22 | First Hoeing | |
| May 3 | Watered for 9 days | |
| 28 | Watered 7 days | |
| June 14 | Put on Harvest flow | |

1845

|  |  |  |  |
|---|---|---|---|
|  |  | Land turned between old Stubble |  |
| March | 6 | Planted $2\frac{1}{2}$ Bushels per Acre |  |
| April | 6 | Dashed |  |
| May | 1 | Watered for 21 Days |  |
| June | 19 | Harvest flow |  |

1847

|  |  |  |  |
|---|---|---|---|
| Mar | 27 | Planted | $2\frac{1}{2}$ [bu per acre] |
| April | 26 | First hoeing |  |
| May | 15 | Stretch flow |  |
|  | 23 | Water off |  |
| June | 1 | 2[d] Hoeing |  |
|  | 3 | Hoeing |  |
|  | 26 | Harvest flow |  |

## CULTURE 21 ACRE W.C

1838

| | | | |
|---|---|---|---|
| April | 17 | Planted & watered | |
| July | 17 | Harvest flow | |
| Sept | 21 | Cutting Suffered from Birds | |

1839

| | | | |
|---|---|---|---|
| April | 9 | Planted & Watered | 2 Bushels |
| | 23 | Put in a new trunk on the Canal | |
| May | 2 | Hoeing Rice | |
| | 18 | Second Hoeing | |
| Sept | 7 | Cutting Rice | |
| Nov | 26 | Cleaning out ditches & drains | |

1840

| | | | |
|---|---|---|---|
| March | 31 | Planted & Watered | 2 Bushels per Acre |
| June | 27 | Harvest flow | |
| Sept | 29 | Ploughing in the green stubble | |

1841

| | | | |
|---|---|---|---|
| | | Partly Ploughed & turned | |
| March | 18 | Planted & Watered | 2¼ Bu per |
| April | 28 | Watered for 8 days | |
| June | 2 | Harvest flow | |
| | 10 | Dry for 5 days & hoed | |
| Augst | 21 | Cutting Rice | |

1842

| | | | |
|---|---|---|---|
| March | 7 | Turning & ditching in quarter drains | |
| | 9 | Planted & watered for 6 days | 3 Bu per A |
| April | 9 | Rice very thin | |
| | 22 | Cutting the Rice all up & re-planting | 4 Bu |
| Nov | | Cleaning out large ditches & ¼ drains & cutting half quarters | |

[1843]

| | | | |
|---|---|---|---|
| Jany | 20 | Finished ploughing | |
| March | 15 | Planted Tunnos seed | 3 Bushels per Acre |

[April 1843]

| | | |
|---|---|---|
| April 12 | dashed one tide | |
| 25 | First Hoeing | |
| May 12 | Watered for 20 days | |
| June 10 | Watered for 2 days | |
| 18 | Watered to kill Caterpillars & kept on for the harvest flow | |
| Augst 28 | Cutting Rice | |
| Sept 2 | All the Rice in the yard | |

1844

| | | |
|---|---|---|
| Feb 1 | Turned very deep with the hoe | |
| March 14 | Planted & Watered for 8 days | 3 Bu per Acre |
| April 22 | First Hoeing | |
| May 3 | Second Hoeing | |
| 4 | Watered 7 days | |
| 28 | Watered 7 days | |
| June 15 | Put on Harvest flow | |
| Augst 19 | Cutting | |
| Dec 31 | Burnt off cleaning out ¼ drains & the large ditches on the East and South well deepened | |

1845

| | | |
|---|---|---|
| March 18 | Planted 15½ Acres in this square | 2½ [bu per acre] |
| May 17 | Long flow for 23 days | |
| June 22 | Harvest flow | |

1847

| | | |
|---|---|---|
| Mar 26 | Planted | 2½ [bu per acre] |
| April 26 | First hoeing | |
| May 13 | Stretch flow | |
| 22 | Water off | |
| 30 | Second hoeing | |
| | 3d Do | |
| June 26 | Harvest flow | |

## Culture 19 Acre W.C

1838

| | | |
|---|---|---|
| April 18 | Planted & watered | |
| July 18 | Harvest flow | |
| Sept 18 | Cutting | |
| | Suffered from Birds | |

1839

| | | |
|---|---|---|
| April 10 | Planted and Watered | 2 Bushels. |
| May 4 | Hoeing Rice | |
| Sept 5 | Cutting Rice | Yield 67 Bu per Acre |
| Nov 25 | Cleaning out ditches & drains | |

1840

| | | |
|---|---|---|
| March 30 | Planted & Watered | 2 Bu per Acre |

1841

| | | |
|---|---|---|
| March 5 | Planted & Watered | 2½ Bushels pr Acre |
| 18 | Freshet over the land 11 days | |
| April 28 | Watered for 6 days | |
| June 2 | Harvest flow | |
| 12 | Dry partially & hoed in water | |
| 19 | Harvest flow | |
| August 14 | Cutting Rice | |

1842

| | | |
|---|---|---|
| March 10 | Planted & watered 7 days | 3 Bu per Acre |
| April 9 | Watered for 5 days. to throw it down the Rice very thin. | |

1843

| | | |
|---|---|---|
| | Cleaned out all the drains & large ditches | |
| Feb 20 | Broke up between the stubble | |
| March 14 | Planted New Ground seed | 3 Bushels per Acre |
| April 12 | Dashed one tide | |
| 24 | Commenced hoeing | |
| May 12 | Watered for 20 days | |

[June 1843]

| | | |
|---|---|---|
| June 1 | Picking out the Grass | |
| 10 | Watered for 3 days | |
| 18 | Watered to kill Catterpillar & kept on for Harvest flow | |
| Augst 20 | Cutting 4 Square down | |

1844

| | | |
|---|---|---|
| Feb 8th | Turned deep with the Hoe | |
| March 13 | Planted & Watered for 8 days | 3 Bu per Acre |
| April 19 | First Hoeing | |
| May 3 | Second Hoeing | |
| 4 | Watered 7 days | |
| 28 | " 7 " | |
| June 15 | Harvest flow | |
| Augst 12 | Cutting Rice | |

1845

| | | |
|---|---|---|
| | Turned between the stubble | |
| March 19 | Planted, Wards Seed —— | 2½ Bu per Acre |
| May 17 | Long flow for 23 days | |
| June 22 | Harvest flow | |

1847

| | | |
|---|---|---|
| Mar 26 | Planted | 2½ [bu per acre] |
| April 24 | First hoeing | |
| May 13 | Stretch flow | |
| 22 | Water off | |
| 29 | Second hoeing | |
| | 3d Hoeing | |
| June 26 | Harvest flow | |

## Culture Lower 20 W.C

1838

| | | |
|---|---|---|
| Jany 16 | Put down a new trunk | |
| Mar 20 | Planted | |
| June 21 | Harvest flow | |
| Augst 25 | Cutting Rice | |

1839

| | | |
|---|---|---|
| Jan 22 | Turning Land | |
| March 12 | Planted | 2 Bu per Acre |
| April 16 | Hoeing | |
| 22 | Second Hoeing | |
| May 4 | Put on water for two days | |
| 11 | Third Hoeing | |
| 13 | Put on flow for 5 days | |
| June 10 | Ears Shooting Out | |
| Augst 21 | Cutting Rice | |

1840

| | | |
|---|---|---|
| | Land all turned with the Hoe | |
| March 12 | Planted | 2 B. 1 pk per Acre |
| April 28 | Watered for 5 days | |
| June 2 | dashed with water | |
| Aug 19 | Cutting Rice | |

1841

| | | |
|---|---|---|
| March 13 | Planted | Bu 2½ per Acre |
| 18 | Watered 7 days | |
| May 30 | dashed for 4 days | |
| June 19 | Harvest flow | |
| Augst 25 | Cutting Rice | |

1842

| | | |
|---|---|---|
| March 24 | Planted New Ground seed | 2½ Bu pr Acre |
| April 7 | Point flow for 5 days. then kept the water on the low places to give it strength for days and then a full flow for days | |

1843

| | | |
|---|---|---|
| | Cleaned out all the drains 3 ft deep & parts of the old ditch | |
| Feb 10 | Breaking up between the old Stubble | |
| 20 | Put on water for a few days | |
| April 12 | Planted & Watered | $2\frac{1}{2}$ Bu per acre |
| June 1 | Watered for 9 days | |
| July 1 | Same as upper 20 Acre | |
| | Cutting 11th Square | |

1844

| | | |
|---|---|---|
| Jany 20 | Burning off the Stubble | |
| 22 | Ploughing.—— | |
| April 10 | Planted & Watered | 3 Bu per acre |
| 30 | Hoed | |
| May 30 | Watered 13 days | |
| June 27 | Harvest flow | |
| Oct — | Centerditched the whole bank & raised it two feet | |

1845

| | |
|---|---|
| Jany 2d | Burned off & clearing out $\frac{1}{4}$ drains the large ditch sunk very deep & the banks raised 3 feet all the Sword grass on the edge of the Creek dug up by the roots |
| | Broke between the Stubble |
| March 7 | Planted $2\frac{1}{2}$ Bu per acre—— |
| April 6 | Dashed two days. Hoed once before long water |
| May 1 | Watered for 23 days— |
| June 19 | Harvest flow |

1847

| | | |
|---|---|---|
| Mar 29 | Planted | $2\frac{1}{2}$ [bu per acre] |
| April 5 | Water off | |
| 11 | first hoeing | |
| May 29 | 2d Do Stretch flow | |

[June 1847]

| | | | |
|---|---|---|---|
| June | 5 | Water off | |
| | | 3 Hoeing | |
| | 26 | Harvest flow | |

1848

| | | | |
|---|---|---|---|
| Mar | 3 | Planted | 2½ [bu per acre] |
| | 13 | Water off | |

## Culture Upper 20 Acre

1838

March 22 Planted
May 21 Long flow
June 21 Harvest flow
Augst 27 Cutting

1839

Jany 20 Turning Land
March 1 Harrowing Land
11 Planted — 2 Bu per Acre
April 15 Commence Hoeing
20 Second Hoeing
May 4 Put on Water for 2 days
10 Third Hoeing
13 Put on flow for 5 days
June 10 Put on Harvest flow
July 10 Ears shooting out
Augst 19 Cutting Rice
Nov 28 Cleaning out ditches and drains

1840

Land all turned with the Hoe
March 13 Planted — 2.1. Bu per Acre
April 28 Watered for 5 days
June 2 Dashed with water
Augst 10 Cutting Rice

1841

March 12 Planted — 2½ Bu per Acre
18 Watered
April 28 Watered for 6 days
May 31 Dashed " 4 days
June 19 Harvest flow
Augst 27 Cutting Rice

1842

March 25 Planted — 2½ "
April 7 Point flow for days

1843

| | | |
|---|---|---|
| Jany | Ploughed | |
| March 20 | Planted Tunnos seed | $2\frac{1}{2}$ bu per Acre |
| April 11 | Dashed one tide | |
| May 12 | Watered for 10 days | |
| June 9 | Watered for 3 days | |
| 18 | Watered to kill Caterpillar for 8 days | |
| July 1 | Harvest flow | |
| Sept 9 | Cutting Rice 9th Square Cut | |

1844

| | | |
|---|---|---|
| Feb 16 | Breaking up with the hoe | |
| April 13 | Planted, Wards Seed | 2 Bu 3 pecks per acre |
| 30 | Hoed | |
| May 30 | Watered 12 days | |
| June 27 | Harvest flow | |
| Oct | Centerditched the whole bank & raised it 2 feet | |

1845

| | | |
|---|---|---|
| Jany 1 | Burned off & clearing ¼ drains the large ditches sunk very deep & raised the banks 3 feet broke up between Stubble | |
| March 8 | Planted | $2\frac{1}{2}$ Bu per Acre |
| April 6 | Dashed for two days | |
| | Hoed once | |
| May 1 | Watered for 23 Days | |
| June 19 | Harvest flow | |

1847

| | | |
|---|---|---|
| Feb 22 | Sunk the old trunk 2 feet deeper Broke between the Rows | |
| March 12 | Planted & Watered | $2\frac{1}{2}$ Bu |
| 20 | Water off | |
| April 15 | Cut up and replanted | |
| 18 | Water off | |
| 27 | Point flow | |

[April 1847]

|  |  |  |
|---|---|---|
| 30 | Water off | |
| May 20 | First hoeing | |
| 28 | Stretch flow | |
| June 5 | Water off | |
| July 9 | Harvest flow | |

1848

|  |  |  |
|---|---|---|
| March 2 | Planted | $2\frac{1}{2}$ [bu per acre] |
| 12 | Water off | |

## Culture 16 Acre

1838

| | | | |
|---|---|---|---|
| March | 22 | Planted | |
| June | 21 | Harvest flow | |
| Augst | 28 | Cutting Rice | |

1839

| | | | |
|---|---|---|---|
| Jany | 10 | Ploughing | |
| March | 14 | Planted | |
| April | 18 | Hoeing | |
| May | 1 | Second Hoeing | |
| | 4 | Put on water for 2 days | |
| June | 10 | Put on Harvest flow | |
| Augst | 27 | Cutting Rice | |

1840

| | | | |
|---|---|---|---|
| | | Land all turned with the Hoe | |
| March | 13 | Planted | Bu 2.1 per Acre |
| April | 30 | Watered for 5 days | |
| Oct | | Ploughing the green stubble in | |

1841

| | | | |
|---|---|---|---|
| March | 16 | Planting | $2\frac{1}{4}$ per Acre |
| | 18 | Watered | |
| April | 28 | Flowed for 7 days | |
| May | 30 | Dashed for 4 days | |
| June | 19 | Harvest flow | |
| Sept | 2 | Cutting Rice | |

1842

| | | | |
|---|---|---|---|
| March | 11 | Planted & Watered 6 days | 3 Bu per Acre |
| | 22 | Point flow 4 days | |
| April | 13 | Hoeing | |

1843

| | | | |
|---|---|---|---|
| Feb | | Broke up between the stubble | |
| March | 18 | Planted New Ground seed | |
| April | 12 | Dashed one tide | |
| | 27 | Hoeing | |

[May 1843]

| | | | |
|---|---|---|---|
| May | 12 | Watered for 10 days | |
| June | 10 | Watered " 3 days | |
| | 18 | Same as 15 Acre | |
| Sept | 7 | Cutting 8 Square cut | |

1844

| | | | |
|---|---|---|---|
| Jany | 23 & 24 | Sinking the ditch next the 17 Acre | |
| | 18 | Ploughed very deep | |
| March | 13 | Planted & Watered | 3 Bu per Acre |
| May | 3 | Watered 8 days | |
| | 28 | Water 12 " | |
| June | 15 | Harvest flow | |

1847

| | | | |
|---|---|---|---|
| Feb | | Put down a new trunk. Broke up between the rows | |
| March | 10 | Planted & Watered | 2½ Bu |
| | 17 | Water off | |
| April | 18 | First hoeing | |
| May | 7 | 2d hoeing | |
| | 11 | Stretch flow | |
| | 21 | Water off | |
| June | 8 | 3d hoeing | |
| | 10 | Harvest flow | |
| Augst | 21 | Cutting | |

1848

| | | | |
|---|---|---|---|
| Mar | 2 | Planted | 2½ [bu per acre] |
| | 12 | Water off | |
| April | 28 | Hoed twice & Stretch flow | |
| May | 16 | Third Hoeing | |

1843

Jany 26 Ploughing
28 Finished ploughing & beautifully done
March 14 Planted. Tunnos seed 3 Bushels
April 12 Put on point flow for 4 days
16 Rice beautifully up
28 Hoeing
May 12 Watered for 20 days
June 2 Hoeing & picking
9 Watered for 3 days
18 Same as the 10 Acre
Augst 29 Cutting Rice the 3d Square cut

1844

Jany 23 Burning off the stubble
24 Breaking up with the hoes. (thoroughly)
March 12 Planted & Watered for 8 days
April 18 First Hoeing
May 4 Watered 9 days
29 " 7 "
June 15 Harvest flow
Augst 13 Cutting Rice——

1845

Land turned between the stubble
March 18 Planted 2½ per Acre
May 17 Long flow for 23 days
June 22 Harvest flow. Changed the water on all the Rice
Augst 14 Cut 10 acres of this square

[10] MS pages 32-33, describing the culture of 15 Acre Field at Elizafield from 1838 to 1842, were torn out of the Journal, with small portions only of the left-hand margin remaining. The identification of this field as the 15 Acre section is confirmed by consulting the MS Index prepared by Grant and printed on page 294 of this book.

## Culture 17 Acre

1838

April 5 Planted
July 18 Harvest flow
Sept 14 Cutting

1839

Jany 10 Turning Land
Mar 15 Planted
April 19 Hoeing
30 Second Hoeing
May 4 Put on Water for two days
June 10 Harvest flow
Augst 22 Cutting Rice

1840

Burning off Stubble  Turning and Ploughing
March 14 Put on Water
Planted & Watered — Bu. 2.1. per acre
April 31 Watered for 5 days
May 15 Watered for 9 days
June 5 Harvest flow
July 9 Rice Shooting
Augst 18 Cutting Rice

1841

March 5 Turned between the Rows, planted — $2\frac{1}{2}$ bu per Acre
19 Freshet over the Land 8 days
May 30 Dashed for 4 days
June 19 Harvest flow
Sept 4 Harvesting or Cutting Rice

1842

March 12 Planted & Watered 9 days — 3 Bu per Acre

[1843]

Cleaned out all the drains and levelling the high places into the creeks

[January 1843]

Jany 30 Commenced Ploughing
Feb 5 Finish the field
27 Planting Tunnos seed — 3 Bushels
April 10 Point flow for 3 days
18 Cut up & replanted New Ground Seed — 2 bu per acre
April 28 Put on the point flow for days
June 8 Watered for 14 days
July 1 Harvest flow
Nov 15 Cut the after Rice for fodder
18 & put the water on to rot the stubble for 15 days
Decr 2 The weather continued so very warm that the stubble commenced growing instead of dieing

1844

Jany 18 Hoeing off & Burning the stubble —— Turned deep with the hoe
March 11 Planted & Watered 8 days — 3 Bu per acre
April 29 Commenced hoeing
May 3 Watered 9 days
30 " 14 "
June 15 Harvest Flow
Augst 17 Cutting Rice

1845

Turned between the stubble
March 20 Planted & Watered — 2½ Bu
May 17 Long water for 23 days
June 22 Harvest flow

1847

Turned between the Rows
March 10 Planted & Watered — 2½ Bu
20 Water off
April 18 First hoeing
28 2d Do
30 Stretch flow

[May 1847]

| | | |
|---|---|---|
| May 12 Water off | | |
| 22 Third hoeing | | |
| June 12 4$^{th}$ hoeing | Harvest flow | |
| Augst 28 Cutting | | |

1848

| | | |
|---|---|---|
| Mar 1 Planted | | 2½ Bushels |
| 11 Water off | | |
| April 28 Hoed twice | Stretch flow | |
| May 17 Third hoeing | | |

## Culture 10 Acre 8¾ Acres

1838

| | | |
|---|---|---|
| April 7 | Planted | |
| Sept 15 | Cutting | |

1839

| | | |
|---|---|---|
| Jany 25 | Turning Land | |
| April 11 | Planted & Watered | |
| May 6 | Hoeing Rice | |

1840

| | | |
|---|---|---|
| March 16 | Planted without turning | 2.1.0 per Acre |
| April 30 | Watered for 5 days | |
| Augst 17 | Cutting Rice | |

1841

| | | |
|---|---|---|
| | Turned up between the Rows | |
| March 4 | Planted | 2.2.0 per Acre |
| 19 | Freshet over the land 10 days | |
| June 2 | Harvest flow | |
| 19 | Hoed in water good flow | |
| Augst 14 | Commenced Harvesting | |

1842

| | | |
|---|---|---|
| Jany 26 | Ploughing & turning with the Hoe | |
| March 2 | Planted & watered for 6 days | 3 Bu per Acre |
| 16 | Point flow for 6 days. Rice up all over the field | |
| 27 | Hoeing —— | |
| April 23 | Water up to date 16 days | |
| 24 | Dry | |
| Augst 6 | commenced cutting Rice | |

1843

| | | |
|---|---|---|
| Jany 23 | Ploughing | |
| Feb 27 | Planting Tunnos seed | 3 Bushels |
| April 15 | Cut up & replanted New Ground seed | 2 Bushels |
| 28 | Hoeing | |
| May 12 | Watered for 20 days | |

[June 1843]

| | | | |
|---|---|---|---|
| June | 1 | Picking out Grass | |
| | 10 | Watered for 3 days | |
| | 18 | Same as 19 Acre | |
| Augst | 24 | Cutting Rice the first cut | |
| Nov | 10 | Put the cattle in to eat down the after Rice | |

1844

| | | | |
|---|---|---|---|
| Jany | 10 | Cleaning out Large spring ditch & ¼ drains | |
| Feb | 17 | Ploughed deep & thoroughly | |
| March | 11 | Planted & Watered for 9 days | 3 Bu per Acre |
| April | 17 | Commenced hoeing | |
| May | 1 | Second Hoeing | |
| | 4 | Watered 8 days | |
| | 28 | " 7 " | |
| June | 15 | Harvest flow | |
| Augst | 10 | 1st Cutting 5 Acres cut | |
| | 12 | Finished cutting the square | |

1845

| | | | |
|---|---|---|---|
| | | Turned between the stubble | |
| March | 19 | Planted | 2½ [bu per acre] |
| May | 17 | Long flow for 23 days | |
| June | 22 | Harvest flow | |
| Augst | 14 | Cut about 6 Acres | |

## Culture 6 Acre

| | | | |
|---|---|---|---|
| 1838 | | Planted in Potatoes | |
| 1839 | | | |
| April | 9 | Planted & watered | 2 Bu per Acre |
| May | 7 | Hoeing Rice | |
| Sept | 9 | Finished Harvesting this day | |
| 1840 | | | |
| March | 17 | Planted & Watered<br>one Acre has 3 bu seed the rest<br>2 bu. 1 pk per Acre | |
| April | 27 | Watered for 5 days | |
| 1841 | | | |
| March | 8 | Planted & Watered | $2\frac{1}{2}$ Bushels per Acre |
| | 19 | Freshet over the land 10 days | |
| April | 28 | Watered for 17 days | |
| June | 2 | Harvest flow | |
| August | 14 | Commenced cutting | |
| 1842 | | | |
| Feb | 24 | Planted without covering<br>Put the water on for 15 days | $2\frac{3}{4}$ Bushels per Acre |
| Augst | 6 | Commenced cutting | |

1840

Commenced Clearing

July 16 Men at work clearing for bank

Nov 16 Nearly all cut Down

| | | | | | | |
|---|---|---|---|---|---|---|
| | 13 | Men | Ditching | 18 | Women | chopping |
| 17 | 15 | " | Do | 18 | " | Do |
| 18 | 15 | Do | " | 17 | Do | " |
| 19 | 15 | " | " | 17 | " | " |
| 20 | 11 | " | " | 17 | " | " |
| 21 | 10 | Do | | 17 | " | |
| 23 | 10 | " | | 17 | " | |
| 24 | 10 | " | | | | |

26 13 Do 17 Women Large Ditch

27 15 Men, 13 Men

30 17½ Men

1841

April 17 Planted 15 Acres Savannah seed 3 per Acre

Oct 9 Cutting Rice. very much injured from standing so long

23 Ditching around the out side bank

1842

Jany 24 Burned the 27, 21, 19, 15, 16, 10, 17, ($2.20^{s}$) and put the water on the 19, 21, 15, 10.[11]

1843 [12]

Nov 20 Fine bank entirely around it & about ⅔ cut down

26 to 30 Loging & burning off

1844

Feb 12 Put down a splendid trunk

Not Planted

[11] This entry which obviously belongs in the Plantation Journal was incorrectly recorded here by Grant.

[12] This field is referred to by Grant as New Point Fields in 1843-46.

1845

| | | | |
|---|---|---|---|
| March | 25 | Cleaned & broke up 12 Acres | |
| April | 4 | Planted Carolina Seed | 2½ per Acre |
| May | 25 | Watered for days | |

1847[13]

| | | | |
|---|---|---|---|
| April | 13 | Planted | 2½ [bu per acre] |
| | 18 | Water off | |
| May | 14 | Very high tides came over the field for three successive tides | |
| M | 21 | First hoeing | |
| | | 2 do | |
| June | 26 | Harvest flow | |

1848

April 28 Point flow

[13] Henceforth referred to as Point Field and the acreage listed as 26¾ acres.

## 9 Acre Field

1843

| | | | |
|---|---|---|---|
| Feb | 4 | Ploughing | |
| | 22 | Harrowing | |
| | 27 | Planting. New ground seed | 3 Bushels |
| April | 11 | Put on point flow for 3 days | |
| | 18 | Cut up & replanted New Ground Seed | 2 Bu |
| June | 8 | Flowed for 16 days | |
| July | 1 | Harvest flow | |
| Sept | 9 | Cutting 10th Square cut | |

1844

| | | | |
|---|---|---|---|
| Jany | 6 | Cleaning out 6 mile large ditch & ¼ drains | |
| Feb | 16 | Turning deep with the hoes | |
| March | 11—19 | Planted & Watered 8 days | 3 Bushels |
| April | 1 | Point flow for 7 days | |
| | 17 | Commenced Hoeing | |
| | 30 | Hoed 2d time | |
| May | 3 | Watered for 5 days | |
| | 30 | " " 7 " | |
| June | 15 | Harvest flow | |
| Augst | 10 | 1st Cutting Rice 5 Acres cut | |
| | 12 | Finished cutting the square | |

1845

| | | | |
|---|---|---|---|
| | | Turned between the stubble | |
| March | 22 | Planted & Watered | 2½ Bu |
| April | 15 | Dashed two days. Hoed over before long water | |
| May | 1 | Watered for 23 days | |
| June | 19 | Harvest flow | |

1847 [14]

| | | | |
|---|---|---|---|
| March | 1 | Planted & Watered | 2½ Bu per acre |
| | 16 | Point flow | |
| | 20 | Water off | |

[14] This field is henceforth referred to by Grant as 9 Acre Square.

[April 1847]

| | | |
|---|---|---|
| April | 6 | First Hoeing |
| | 28 | 2d Do |
| | 30 | Stretch flow |
| May | 21 | Water off |
| | 27 | Third hoeing |
| June | 10 | Harvest flow |
| July | 8 | Ears shooting out |
| Augst | 14 | Cutting |

1848

| | | | |
|---|---|---|---|
| March | 1 | Planted | 2½ Bu |
| | 11 | Water off | |
| April | 28 | Hoed twice & Stretch flow this day | |
| May | 17 | 3d Hoeing | |
| June | 1 | Picking out grass — no hoeing except the hills | |
| | 16 | Harvest flow | |

## New Grounds 23½ Acres
### or
## Johns Field

1843

| | | |
|---|---|---|
| Feb 1 to 5 | Burning off Logs & trash | |
| April 11 | Planting Tunnos seed | 3 Bu per acre |
| July 3[d] | Under water for the first time since planted, suffered very much from high land Crab grass. | |

1844

| | | |
|---|---|---|
| Jany | Cut Six ¼ drains through | |
| Feb | Upsetting stumps & roots | |
| April 16 | Planted | 3 Bu per acre |
| May 30 | Watered 7 days | |
| June 27 | Harvest flow | |

1845

| | | |
|---|---|---|
| April 5 | Planted | 2½ Bu per acre |

1847

| | | |
|---|---|---|
| April 14 | Planted | 2½ [bu per acre] |
| 18 | Water off | |
| May 13 | First hoeing | |
| 21 | 2[d] Do | |
| 28 | Stretch flow | |
| June 5 | Water off | |
| | 3[d] hoeing | |
| 26 | Harvest flow | |

1848

| | | |
|---|---|---|
| April 28 | Point flow | |

## 18 Acre Evelyn

1843

| | | | |
|---|---|---|---|
| Jany | 20 | Cleand & sunk the large ditch entirely around the field | |
| Feb | 22 | Put down a new trunk. Turned between the rows | |
| April | 1 | Trenching | |
| | 3 | Planting New Ground seed | $2\frac{1}{2}$ Bushels per Acre |
| May | 31 | Watered for 6 days | |
| June | 18 | Watered for Caterpillar 14 days | |
| July | 1 | Harvest flow | |

1844

| | | | |
|---|---|---|---|
| Jany | 5 | Finished ploughing & ¼ drains all sunk 3 ft | |
| April | 1 | Planted & Watered for 8 days | 3 Bu per acre |
| | 25 | Hoed | |
| May | 15 | Watered 14 days | |
| June | 15 | " for days kept on for Harvest | |

1845

| | | | |
|---|---|---|---|
| April | 2 | Planted | $2\frac{1}{2}$ Bu per acre |
| May | 17 | Long water for 23 days | |
| July | 2 | Harvest flow | |

1846 & 1847

Loaned this [field] to my Brother Charles — for two years

## 23 Acre Evelyn

1843

| | | | |
|---|---|---|---|
| March | | Turned between the stubble & the drains all cleaned out | |
| April | 13 | Trenching | |
| | 14 | Planting New Ground seed | 2½ [bu per acre] |
| May | 1 | Watered for 6 days | |
| June | 18 | Watered to kill Caterpillar 9 days | |
| July | 1 | Harvest flow | |

1844

| | | | |
|---|---|---|---|
| March | | Turned with the Hoes | |
| April | 3 | Planted 13 Acres & driven out by the water until the 8th | |
| | 9 | Finished planting | B 3.1 0 per Acre |
| | 27 | Hoed | |
| May | 15 | Watered 14 days | |
| June | 1 | Watered until Harvest | |

1845

| | | | |
|---|---|---|---|
| April | 14 | Broke up between the stubble | |
| | 17 | Planted | 2½ Bu Wards seed |
| May | 29 | Long water for 16 days | |
| July | 3 | Harvest flow | |

1846

| | | | |
|---|---|---|---|
| Decr | | Cleaned & sunk all the quarters & the Large ditch entirely around the field & put in a new trunk | |
| | 11 | Breaking up the Surface | |

1847

| | | | |
|---|---|---|---|
| March | 11 | Planted & Watered | 2½ [Bu per acre] |
| | 18 | Water off | |
| April | 23 | First hoeing | |
| May | 9 | 2d Do | |
| | 12 | Stretch flow | |
| | 22 | Water off | |
| June | 10 | 3 Hoeing | |
| | 12 | Harvest flow | |

[August 1847]

Augst 24 Cutting

1848

Thoroughly ploughed early in the winter

April 3 Planted

21 Point flow  Second hoeing

# ACCOUNTS WITH FACTORS

THIS SECTION presents the record of the financial transactions of Hugh Fraser Grant with the various factors and commercial houses with whom he dealt over the years. On these pages appear the names of upwards of 350 agents, professional practitioners, neighbors, firms, and supply houses who provided services and goods for Elizafield Plantation. Most of these individuals and business establishments have been identified and described in the "Directory," which appears later in the volume. The interested student will usually be able to satisfy his curiosity as to the probable reason for Grant's payments to this or that creditor by continually referring to the "Directory." Individual entries will become more meaningful when this practice is followed and the seasonal scope of the expenditures for Elizafield will be apparent when the entries for an entire "crop year" are identified by this procedure.

It will be noted that yearly accounts with individual factors usually were recorded in a *two-page spread*, with the debtor account on the left-hand page and the contra or credit account on the right-hand page. In a few instances, the debtor or credit pages were torn out of the original document (as, for example, the debtor page in the first entry). Usually, each *two-page spread* contained the record of financial operations for an entire "crop year." Credit entries, consisting largely of returns from shipments of rice to the factor, usually were not very frequent or numerous. Thus a major portion of each right-hand page remained blank. The debtor entries for the same period often ran to such length that *all available space on* the left-hand page was exhausted. On such occasions the recorder found it desirable to continue the account on the lower portion of the right-hand or contra page, which otherwise would have remained blank. He seems to have desired to keep all transactions for the year within the visual limits of a *two-page spread*, so as to be able to evaluate his situation at a glance.

These accounts have been reproduced exactly as they appeared in the original accounts, except for a very few, rare items, where publication problems made necessary slight variations in the location of individual entries on some pages.

## ROBERTSON & THURSTON Cr

| | | | |
|---|---|---|---|
| 1838 | | | |
| Decr 15 | By | 1630 Bushels of Rice | 1914 26 |
| 1839 | | | |
| Feb 4 | " | my note @ 6 months for | 2771 81[1] |
| Mar 19 | " | 3447 Bushels of Rice @ | 3085 57 |
| June | " | My Note at four Months for | 4063 54 |

[1] This item was entered and then scratched out.

## D^r Hugh Fraser Grant in a/c with

|  | | |  |  | |
|---|---|---|---|---|---|
| 1839 | | | | | |
| April | 29 | To | Amount brought over | $ 7757.17 | $ 7757 17 |
| May | 14 | " | Order in favor of H. Harding | 50 00 | |
| | 16 | " | " " " " C. Grant | 80 00 | |
| | 26 | " | " " Poerier & Matthiesen | 160 00 | |
| Feb | 13 | " | " " P Wiltbergher | 177 09 | |
| " | " | " | " " J H Alston | 70 00 | |
| May | 30 | " | Saddle & Bridle | 26 75 | |
| June | 22 | " | Order in favor of J. F Meeker of N Jersy | 500 00 | |
| Decr | 3 | " | Order in fav of I. C. Plant | 450 00 | |
| | 24 | " | " " " R Habersham | 64 09 | |
| | | " | Elam Lynds & Son | 1275 00 | |
| 1840 | | | | | |
| Jan | 7 | " | B F Perham | 115 00 | |
| | " | " | R Walsh & Co | 16 00 | |
| | 8 | " | S Spicer Engineer | 322 75 | |
| | " | " | 300 Bushels of Corn 68¾ cents | | |
| | " | " | Drayage | 1 87 | |
| | | " | 4 bbls. Pork $ 13 | 52 00 | |
| | | " | 2 " Mackerel $ 9 | 18 00 | |
| | | " | ½ " " $ 9 | 9 00 | |
| | | " | 6 Sacks Salt $ 2 | 12 00 | (11,156 63) |
| | 29 | " | Order in fav J. B Gaudry | 60 48 | |
| Feb | 1 | " | " " " M W Moshier | 61 97 | |
| | 8 | " | " " " Jacob Mac Pike | 196 69 | |
| | 10 | " | " Claghorn & Wood @ 30 day | 216 00 | |
| | 15 | " | " J Anderson & Co @ 15 day | 66 47 | |
| | 6 | | Mumford & Tison | 143 90 | |
| | 6 | | S. A Hooker | 41 62½ | |
| | 11 | " | 103 lbs Hams @ 13½ cents | 13 80 | |
| | | | 107 " Sugar @ 17 Package 25 | 18 44 | |
| | | | 44 lbs 1 Box Soap 10½ cents | 4 62 | |
| | | | 10 Gals Oil $1,37½ Cans $1.50 | 15 25 | |

## MESSRS ROBERTSON & THURSTON CONTRA Cr/

| | | | | |
|---|---|---|---|---|
| 1839 | | | | |
| April 29 | By | Amount Brought forward | 4999 83 | |
| | " | My Note for | 4063 54[2] | |
| Decr 19 | " | 2903 Bushels Rice | 1985 47 | |
| 1840 | | | | |
| Jan 29 | " | 3200 Bushels Rice | 1663 36 | |
| Feb 20 | " | 3700 Bushels " | 1866 06 | |
| 26 | " | By Cash | 450 00 | |
| March 16 | " | By draft from John Ashe Alston | 250 00 | |
| | | | | $11,214 72 |

[2] This item was entered and then scratched out.

[ Dr *cont.*, February 1840 ]

| | | | | |
|---|---|---|---|---|
| 26 | " | Order in Fav J F Meeker for Mrs Wilson | 376 00 | |
| " | " | " " " R Grant at 30 days | 260 00 | |
| | " | 500 Bu Corn @ 65 | 325 | |
| | | 6 Bls Pork @ $14 | | |
| | | Paid Self | 200 00 | |
| | | | | 13,239 03 |

## Dr H. F Grant in a/c with

|  | |  |  | |
|---|---|---|---|---|
| 1840 | | | | 13,239 03 |
| March | 2 | Order in fav I. C. Plant | $ 177.00 | |
| | 18 | " for C. E Putnam @ 90 days | 300 00 | |
| April | 8 | " " Hayden & Gregg | 95 00 | |
| | 3 | " " Fisher Day | 98 12 | |
| Decr | 1 | Robertson & Smith | 225 95 | |
| | " | H B Gleason | 250 00 | |
| | | Bill on New York in Favor J F Meeker | 677 81 | |
| | | " " Nu Yrk Hogan & Miln | 188 13 | |
| | | Order in fav of R Habersham | 4000 00 | |
| 1841 | | | | |
| Mar | 23 | " " " | 2500 00 | |
| | | Wm Matthiessen | 84 50 | |
| | | By Balance to my Credit | 7865 94 | |
| | | Ingraham & Webb | 250 00 | |
| | | | $8115 94 | |

## Dr Hugh Fraser Grant in a/c with

|  | |  |  | |
|---|---|---|---|---|
| 1841 | | | | |
| Decr | 19 | To 300 Bushels of Corn 75¢ | $ 225.00 | |
| " | " | 10 do Salt 45¢ | 4.50 | |
| | " | 52½ lbs Hams 11¢ | 5.75 | |
| " | " | 7 Door Locks 3 at $2¾ 4 at $2 | 15.25 | |
| " | " | 8 pr Sashes 10 by 12 — 18 lights 17¢ | 12.24 | |
| | " | 1 pr Mill Stones | 14.00 | |
| | " | Repairing Lamps | 10.00 | |
| 1842 | " | 6 Bbls Lime $1½ | 7.50 | 293.74 |
| Jany | 10 " | John L Jones | 190.00 | |
| | " | Lamp Shades | 4.50 | |
| | " | Lamp wicks | .62½ | |
| | " | Tomb Stone | 39.00 | |
| March | 26 " | Ingraham & Webb | 40.00 | |
| April | 6 " | H. W Hudnall | 50.00 | |

## Messrs Robertson & Thurston contra Cr/

| | | |
|---|---|---|
| | By Amount bro't forward | 11214 72 |
| | " draft in fav of C. Putnam not presented | 300 00 |
| 1840 | | |
| Nov 24 | By 2730 Bushels Rough Rice | 1719 70 |
| " | " Woman Tina | 500 |
| " | " Order on Ingraham & Webb | 250 00 |
| 24 | " By Bond of T P. & C Alston | 7453 71 |
| Decr 24 | " " " " " | 7777 78 |
| 1841 | | |
| Feb 21 | Interest on the same 1 year | |
| | Balance due me 1 May 1841 | 544 |
| | Order in fav Dr Bond | 44 |
| | At my Credit | 500 |
| | | 420 |
| May 3 | Hogan & Miln Exchange $4.20 | 80 Cr |
| | Sam'l Palmer | 75 80 |
| | | 4 20 |
| | | 80 00 |

## Messrs Robertson & Thurston[3] Blacklock contra Cr/

1841

Jany 18 By 2000 Bushels Rice . . . . $

$ 171.67

[3] The name Thurston was entered by Grant and then scratched out.

## Dr Hugh Fraser Grant in a/c with

| Date | Item | Amount | Total |
|---|---|---|---|
| 1842 | | | |
| March 21 | To 600 Bu Corn 69¢ | $ 414 00 | |
| | " 3 Barrels tar $3 drayage | 9 08 | |
| | Commissions | 1 05 | 424.23 |
| April 21 | " Order in fav of Capt Luce | 38 25 | |
| Nov 21 | " 200 Bu Corn $130 & Sacks Salt 7.50 | 137 50 | |
| | 1 Bushel Measure | 3 | |
| | " Order in fav of J & S H Rokenbaugh | 50 | 228.75 |
| Decr 6 | 200 Bu Rice flour | 33 | |
| | 1 bbl Loaf Sugar 111 lb @ 13¢ | 14 68 | |
| | " " Brown Sugar 8½¢ | 22 34 | |
| | 9 Hams 10½¢ | 11 27 | |
| | Commissions & Charges | 6 19 | |
| 27 | " Order in fav of Wm Matthiesson | 90 00 | |
| | " " G N Reynolds & Son | 97 33 | 324.81 |
| 1843 | | | |
| Jany 2 | " " J & S H Rokenbaugh | 50 00 | |
| 3 | " C H Bradley | 150 00 | |
| 30 | " J. Lawton & Co | 300 00 | |
| | " R Habersham & Son | 700 " | 1200.00 |
| Feb 1 | " 500 Bushels Rice flour 16¢ | 80 " | |
| | 8 Sacks of Salt $1.25 | 10 | |
| | 400 Bu Corn @ 53 | 212 | |
| | Charges | 8 05 | |
| | Capt Hammond | 50 19 | |
| 10 | N B & H Weed | 41 62 | |
| 13 | Walter Button | 77 50 | 479.36 |
| March 10 | S Palmer | 228 67 | |
| May 5 | " C. Grant | 300 00 | 2885.82 |
| | " Geo Oates Agent Courier & Audabon | 41 50 | |
| 9 | " R Hogan | 300 " | 870.37 |
| | | | 3527.32 |

## MESSRS MITCHELL & MURE CONTRA $C^r$/

| | | | | |
|---|---|---|---|---|
| 1842 | | | | |
| Nov 21 | By | 1847 Bushels Rough Rice | $ 896 18 | @ $2.18¾ |
| Decr 16 | " | 2155 " " " | 777 47 | @ $1.81¼ |
| 29 | " | 2050 | 855 05 | $2.25 |
| 1843 | | | | |
| Feb 1 | | 1650 | 690 83 | @ $1.87½ |
| | | 7½ Bags Sea Island Cotton @ 15¼¢ | 355 13 | |
| April 19 | " | Cash from Est. of Cater | 342 82 | |
| | | | 3917 41 | |

## Dr Hugh F Grant in A/C with

| 1843 | | | | 3527.32 |
|---|---|---|---|---|
| May | 5 | By draft in favor C Grant | 300 00 | |
| | | " " Geo Oates for Audebons Birds & Charleston Courier | 41 50 | |
| | 9 | " Draft in fav of R Hogan | 300 " | 641.50 |
| June | 1 | " A Blue | 16 77 | |
| | 5 | " R Hogan ( S. Palmer 30 | 330 " | 330 |
| | 23 | " A Delaroche | 50 " | |
| | 26 | " W B Thomas | 43 68 | 410.45 |
| July | 23 | " R Hogan | 250 00 | |
| | 24 | " B Talbott for Corn | 45 00 | 295 |
| Nov | 11 | " J & S H Rokenbaugh | 50 " | |
| | 27 | " B. Talbott | 100 00 | |
| | 29 | " 150 lbs Hams @ — | | |
| | | " 300 Corn @ 55¢ | 165 00 | |
| | | 6 Sacks Salt @ $1.35 | 8 10 | |
| | | Drayage & Commission | 5 57 | |
| | | " Mrs Mac Masters bill | 33 06 | |
| Decr | 16 | " Capt Hammond | 41 " | |
| | 7 | To selling 36 Casks Rice | 22 69 | |
| 1844 | | | | |
| Jany | 1 | James Gould Esqr | 64 00 | |
| | 9 | Col Williams | 38 00 | |
| | 9 | G. R Hendrickson | 17 00 | |
| | 10 | Mumford & Tison | 51 | |
| | 14 | Locke & Davis | 19 50 | |
| | 19 | Mrs Mc Master | 7 64 | |
| Feb | 21 | R Habersham & Son | 200 00 | |
| | 27 | Joseph Lawton & Co | 200 00 | |
| Nov | " | " Fav of Rokenbaugh | 100 | |
| | | Self to Cash | 250 | |
| Decr | | John Lawrence | 325 | |
| | | Potatoes & Lime | 11 85 | |

## MITCHELL & MURE $C^r$/

| 1843 | | | | |
|---|---|---|---|---|
| May 1 | By | Cash in hand | $ 1012 95 | |
| June 9 | " | draft on Ingraham & Webb | 398 00 | |
| Nov 22 | " | 1 Negroe Man — Ned | Dead | |
| Decr 16 | " | 2466 Bushels Rice . . . | 1287 06 | .52 cents per bu |
| 1844 | | | | |
| Jany 23 | " | 2669 Bushels Rice | | |
| Decr 5 | By | 2290 Bushels Rough Rice making 105 tierces whole & 5 small at 2¾ & 1.93¾ | $ 1432 99 | |
| 14 | | 3 Bags S. I. Cotton 760 lbs @ 14¢ | 100 46 | |

Cr B[alance] $600

| | |
|---|---|
| S Palmer | $100 |
| W Mathieson | 117.25 |
| J B Gaudry | 84 |
| B F Smith | 30.84 |
| J D Piles- Reynolds | 69.72 |
| Reynolds | 73 |
| J C Tunno | 30 |

598.11 – 504.81 = $93.30 at my end 10 May 1845

S Palmer 50

$43.30

$13.89 due me 16 April 45

16 April 1845

SETTLED IN FULL

## Dr HUGH FRASER GRANT IN a/c WITH

| 1840 | | | | | |
|---|---|---|---|---|---|
| Feb | 26 | To | Cash advanced[4] | 4290.67 | |
| March | 6 | " | Order in favor of E. Titcum | 20.12½ | |
| | 11 | " | " " " C. E. Putnam | 300 00 | |
| | 18 | " | " " " S. Palmer | 121 75 | |
| | 21 | " | " " " Joseph Reith | 42 00 | |
| | 22 | " | " " G Harrington | 30 00 | |
| | " | " | " " Ruth Berton | 40 00 | |
| | | | | | 554.54 |
| | | " | 6 Barrels of Lime @ $2½ dray[age] | 14 11 | |
| | | " | Woodford Mabry on a/c Dr Troup | 255 75 | |
| | | | | | 269.86 |
| April | 12 | " | J. Snow P M | 23 00 | |
| | 24 | " | J. M Hall of Brunswick | 120 — | |
| | 28 | " | Dr R Grant | 237 87 | |
| | | | | | 357.87 |
| May | 1 | " | S D & J P Woodbury | 16 75 | |
| | 15 | " | Thos Oden | 34 00 | |
| | | " | 150 Bushels Oats @ | 75 | |
| | | | | | 125.75 |
| July | | " | Window Sashes | 41 04 | |
| | | " | 1 Keg Nails | 7 00 | |
| | | | | | 48.04 |
| Augst | 24 | " | Bill Articles ordered for Mrs Grant. | | |
| Nov | 1 | " | Order in fav J E Johnston. 30 days | 48 00 | |
| | 3 | " | 3 Kegs Nails @ 6½ | 19 50 | |
| | " | " | 1 Bag Duck Shot | 2 — | |
| | 14 | " | Order in favr of C Webb | 8 25 | |

[4] This illustrates one of the major preliminary steps in the financial relations between factor and planter. See pages 42-44.

## Robert Habersham & Son contra $C^r$/

1840

| | | | Nett Amt |
|---|---|---|---|
| March 24 | By | 2200 Bushels Rough Rice | $1418 42 |
| Decr 9 | " | 2878 " " " | 1548 10 |
| 26 | By | Cash | 1066 67 |
| | " | Cash | 3000 00 |

[ Dr *cont.*, November 1840 ]

| | | | | |
|---|---|---|---|---|
| 28 | " | 225 yds Grey Cloth @ 55 | 123 75 | |
| | " | 359 " Kerseys " 40 | 143 60 | |
| | | 2 pieces Blankets @ 29 | 58 00 | |
| | | 1 " " | 24 00 | |
| | | 1 Keg Nails | 6 50 | |
| | | 6 lbs Thread $5.40 100 Needles | 5 90 | |
| | | | | 437.50 |
| Dec 20 | " | Otis Johnston | 11 00 | |
| | " | Paid Self | 103 00 | |
| | | R Habersham & Son | 1066 67 | |
| 26 | " | 200 Bushels of Corn | 112 | |
| 1841 | " | 2 bbls Pork | 29 | |
| | | | | 1321.67 |
| Jany 5 | " | Rice Parker & Co | 98 04 | |
| | " | Est of B. F. Cater | 777 19 | 875.23 |

## D[r] HUGH F. GRANT IN A/C WITH

| | | | | | |
|---|---|---|---|---|---|
| 1841 | | | | | |
| Jany | 8 | To | Amount br[ot] forward | | |
| | | " | Order in favr S. L Collins & Co | $ 83 49 | |
| | | " | " " " D[r] Holmes | 54 25 | |
| | | " | " " " J S Atwell | 38 00 | |
| | | " | " " " S Palmer | 250 00 | |
| | | " | 5 Gals Lamp Oil $1.37½ | 6 87 | |
| | | " | 6 Barrels of Lime $1.50 | 9 00 | |
| | 11 | " | J Bancroft | 35 00 | |
| | 22 | " | C. Grant | 500 00 | |
| | 27 | " | W. T. Williams | 20 00 | |
| | | " | Calvin Emmons | 233 00 | |
| | 28 | " | T. C. Chick | 224 25 | |
| | 29 | " | D[r] Follen | 22 00 | |
| | | | | | 1469.99 |
| | 30 | " | 1000 Bushels Corn @ 52 cents | 520 00 | |
| | | " | 100 Bu Seed Rice | 96 00 | |
| | | " | 12 Bbls Pork @ $11 . . . . . | 132 00 | |
| | | " | 25 Bushels Salt | 10 00 | |
| | | " | 10 bbls Lime @ $1.50 | 15 00 | |
| | | " | 20 gals Oil @ $1.31¼ | 26 25 | 799.25 |
| Feb | 5 | " | Calvin Emmons | 10 00 | |
| | | " | R Burton | 20 " | |
| | | " | Mumford & Tison | 243 64 | |
| | 9 | " | J B. Gaudry & Sons | 141 13 | |
| | | " | 4 Kegs White Lead @ $3 | 12 00 | |
| | | " | 2 gals Paint Oil $1.25 | 2.50 | |
| | | | Mrs E Johnston | 40 00 | |
| | 10 | " | C Grant for S L Collins | 170 00 | |
| | | | M H MacAllister | 50 00 | |
| | 17 | " | C. E Putnam | 350 00 | 979.27 |
| March | 5 | " | John Mallery | 72 00 | |
| | | " | A Clark | 45 40 | |
| | 8 | " | C. E Putnam | 1930 17 | 2047.57 |

## R Habersham & Son contra Cr/

| 1841 | | | | |
|---|---|---|---|---|
| Jany | 8 | By | Amount Bro[t] forward | 7033 19 |
| | 9 | " | 27 Barrels Clean Rice | 465 49 |
| | | " | 1626 Bushels Rough Rice | 1164 70 |
| | | " | Premium on $2000 @ 3 percent | 60 00 |
| | | " | " " $1066.67 @ $2\frac{3}{4}$ percent | 29 33 |
| | | " | " " $1000 @ 2 | 20 |
| Feb | 15 | " | Dr Tunno's draft for $7500 & int [5] | 8175 62 |
| | 26 | " | 4000 Bushels of Rice | 2526 62 |
| March | 13 | " | Draft on Robertson & Thurston [6] | 2000 00 |
| | | " | Do Do | 2000 00 |
| | | | Premium on 4000 @ ¼ | 10 00 |

[5] This entry was recorded and then scratched out.

[6] These entries for March 13, 1841, indicate that Grant was in the process of transferring his assets from his Charleston factor to his Savannah factor. See pages 45, 58, and 70-75.

## D$^{r}$ HUGH F. GRANT IN A/C WITH

| 1841 | | | | | |
|---|---|---|---|---|---|
| March 11 | To | 1 Gal Sp[iri]ts Turpentine | $ | 00 75 | |
| | " | 2 Sides Calf Skins @ 2.50 | | 5 00 | |
| | | Repairing Harness | | 30 25 | |
| 19 | " | Walter Button | | 400 " | |
| " | " | Lewis Demere | | 1000 " | |
| 22 | " | T. F. Bryan for a Boat | | 60 " | |
| 23 | " | Robt Grant | | 2589 " | |
| " | " | R Habersham & Son | | 2000 | |
| 27 | " | J & S H Rokenbaugh | | 500 00 | |
| " | " | Pease & Tarbell | | 118 00 | |
| | | | | | 6703.00 |
| April 7 | " | H. W Hudnall . . . . . . . | | 66 70 | |
| 8 | " | S. B Jewett | | 52 20 | |
| 17 | " | James Anderson & Co | | 75 00 | |
| 23 | " | R Grant | | 426 40 | |
| 25 | " | 500 yds Osnabergs @ 12 | | 60 00 | |
| May 7 | " | Saml Palmer | | 200 00 | |
| 17 | " | 150 yds Osnabergs @ 12 | | 18 00 | |
| " | " | Repairing watches | | 7 00 | |
| " | " | Mrs Grants Clothes Bill | | | |
| 20 | " | J Snow | | 20 00 | |
| 25 | " | Turner & Johnston | | 100 00 | |
| | | Tax Collector | | 48 67 | |
| June 1 | " | D$^{r}$. A Delaroche | | 168 00 | |

MESSRS R HABERSHAM & SON CONTRA $C^r$/

| | | | |
|---|---|---|---|
| | By | Amount Brought for[d] | $ |
| March 23 | " | Order of Robertson & Thurston | $ 2500.00 |
| | " | Premium on 2500 @ ½ | 12 50 |
| | | | |
| 1841 | | Balance due H. F. Grant | |
| June 9 | | this date | $ 263 58 |

## Dr/ H. F. Grant in a/c with

| Date | | Item | Amount | Total |
|---|---|---|---|---|
| 1841 | | | | |
| June | 9 | To order in favor Alex Blue on a/c of J. & P Butler | $ 28 00 | |
| | 29 | " O. J. H. Dibble | 200 00 | 228.00 |
| Augst | 22 | " 5 lbs turnip seed | 7 00 | |
| | | 1 piece x bard Muslin 62½ | 7 50 | |
| | | 1 " Long Cloth 31 cent | 13 33 | |
| | | 2 yds Linen Cambrick $2.12½ | 4 25 | 32.08 |
| Oct | 6 | 200 Bushels Corn 75 | 150 00 | |
| | | 4000 Laths @ $4 | 16 00 | |
| | | Freight, &c . . . . . | 22 50 | 188.50 |
| Nov | 23 | By Cash | 200 00 | |
| | | " 500 yds all wool Kerseys 55 | 275 00 | |
| | | 6 lbs thread 100 needles | 5 90 | |
| | | " Order at 60 days in fav O. Johnston | 103 50 | |
| | 24 | " 6 Barrels Lime | 12 00 | |
| Decr | 1 | " order at 60 days S M Burnett | 50 00 | |
| | 11 | " " T. M & J M Turner, fruit trees | 18 06 | |
| | 22 | " 6 Casks Lime | 12 | |
| 1842 | | | | |
| Jany | 1 | " Order in fav J Snow | 20 00 | |
| | 11 | D. S. Waters | 42 00 | |
| | 21 | " W. T. Williams | 66 65 | |
| May | | " 8 Barrels of Pork | 61 | |
| Aug | 26 | T. G. Skinner | 37 76 | |
| [1843] | | | | |
| April | 4 | To Cash in a/c of Mortgage | 1034 97 | |
| | | " " paid self | 300 00 | |
| | 8 | " N B & H Weed | 62 50 | |
| | | " J Anderson & Co | 12 60 | |
| | 10 | " J & S H Rokenbaugh | 1782 95 | |
| | 15 | " James Gould Esq | 825 95 | |
| | 16 | Mess Houstons | 40 00 | |
| | | " J B Gaudry & Sons | 391 82 | |

## R Habersham & Son Cr/

1841

| | | | |
|---|---|---|---|
| June 9 | By Cash balance of a/c | | $ 263 58 |
| Nov 23 | " 18 Casks Rice | | 214 28 |
| Decr 11 | " 2395 Bushels Rough Rice 39½ Casks @ $2, 1 do $2⅜ 4½ do small @ $1⅝ ½ do light $1⅞ 74 Bushels Rice flour @ 12½ c 1 cask @ $14.04 | | 346 65 |
| | 45 Casks sent to New York | | 650 00 |

[1842]

| | | |
|---|---|---|
| Feb 1 | " By Cash | 700 00 |

Feb 2d 1843 Amount due by me to R Habersham & Son $1145.84

April 4th By Cash in R Habersham & Sons hands $4

[ Dr *cont.*, April 1843 ]

| | | |
|---|---|---|
| 25 | " S Palmer | 256 59 |
| May 13 | " Ditto | 200 |
| 15 | " Rokenbaugh | 100 |
| June 4 | " Hogan | 1000 |
| 26 | Padelford & Co | 157 10 |
| | | 6798 95 |

## Dr/ H. F. Grant in a/c with

| 1844 | | | |
|---|---|---|---|
| Decr | 1 | To a Windfan | 90 00 |
| | | " Cash paid for Engine | 350 00 |
| | | " 10 bbls Lime. . . . . . . . . | |
| | | " Cash paid Self | 50 00 |
| | | " 3 Sheets paper for Packing . . . | |
| | | " 2 Barrels Coal @ . . . . . . . | |
| | | 150 Bushels Corn @ 56¢ | 84 00 |
| | | " Draft in fav of Capt Stevens | |
| | | 600 Bushels Corn @ 50 | 300 00 |
| | | Mr Lacklisons bill | 118 71 |
| Feb | 28 | Cash self | 200 00 |
| March | 1 | " " | 25 00 |
| | | 3000 Segars @ $6. | 18 00 |
| | 7 | Draft in fav of Hogan & Finlay | 1500 00 |
| | | 40 Bushels seed Rice, bags &c | |
| | 25 | " Draft in fav of Locke and Davis | 25 00 |
| | | " " " " " Wm H Bullock | 25 00 |
| | | " " " " " Col Williams | 24 87 |
| April | 7 | " Luther Cudwith | 20 12 |
| | 16 | Prentice & Way | 273 25 |
| | " | V. L & Butler | 74 66 |
| | 21 | " J. D Piles Sheriff | 26 75 |
| | | " 100 Bu Corn | 56 25 |
| | | " Capt Stevens. . . . . . . . . | 20 00 |
| May | 13 | " Draft in fav Hogan & Finlay | 2500 00 |
| | 20 | " " " " B Talbott | 155 69 |
| | 24 | " " " " Mrs Beals | 50 00 |
| June | 11 | J & S H Rokenbaugh | 250 62½ |
| July | | " John F Green | 31 50 |
| Augst | 23 | " Alex Blue in a/c Est Butler | 25 75 |
| | 30 | " H Feris | 8 00 |

R Habersham & Son contra Cr/

| | | | |
|---|---|---|---|
| | | By balance old a/c | |
| | " | Sales of 899 Bu Rice $2 11/16 | $ 500 86 |
| 1845 | " | 4 Bags Sea Island Cotton @ 15 | 143 80 |
| | " | T. F Bryans draft for | 135 00 |
| Feb 12 | " | 3750 Bushels Rough Rice | |
| March 1 | " | 3400 " " " | 5568 17 |
| May 1 | " | 1047 " " " | 777 79 |
| June 8 | " | 1½ Bags S. I. Cotton @ 20¢ | 76 80 |

## Dr/ H. F. Grant in a/c with

|  | | | | | |
|---|---|---|---|---|---|
| 1845 | | | | | |
| Sept | 11 | Draft | in fav A K Moore | 70 00 | |
| | 20 | " | " E. J Harden T. G. H. S. | 30 00 | |
| | | " | " J. Dubignon Taxes | 90 71 | 190.71 |
| Oct | 6 | " | " S. Palmer | 50 | |
| | 24 | " | " Dr Roberts | 10 00 | 60.00 |
| Nov | 5 | " | " J Lawton & Co | 500 00 | |
| | 15 | " | Dr James Holmes professionally | 150 00 | |
| | 25 | " | 300 Bushels Corn @ 68½ | 205 50 | |
| | | " | 300 Bushels Rice flour @ | 15 00 | |
| | 27 | " | Paid myself | 300 00 | |
| | | " | Draft in favr of W. Warner | 80 00 | |
| | | | " " " N B & H Weed | 122 | 1372.50 |
| Decr | 1 | " | W. W Hazzard | 15 00 | |
| | 9 | " | Capt Stevens | 73 82 | |
| | 16 | " | S. Palmer a/c Blue | 203 65 | 292.47 |
| 1846 | | | | | |
| Jany | 1 | " | Self | 150 00 | |
| | | " | Audabon | 33 50 | |
| | | " | Messr Habersham & Son | 4000 00 | |
| | | " | Pincheon Stotesbury & Co | 31 63 | |
| | 12 | " | C E Putnam | 86 85 | |
| | 17 | " | S Palmer | 211 90 | |
| | 28 | " | B Talbot | 175 00 | 4682.88 |
| Feb | 16 | " | A K Moore | 303 40 | |
| | | " | Prentice & Way | 43 87 | |
| | | | N B & H Weed | 123 65 | |
| | | | A Minis | 19 46 | |
| | | | Col Williams | 15 75 | |
| | 23 | | S. Grant | 454 00 | |
| | | | Hogan & Finlay | 890 " | |
| | | | C M Bell | 1196 00 | 3046.13 |
| April | 8 | | Wood & Claghorn | 312 | |
| | | | A K Moore | 63 | |
| | | | 400 bu Corn 75¢ | 300 00 | |
| | 17 | " | A S Hillard | 120 | 795 |

## R HABERSHAM & SON CONTRA Cr/

| | | | | |
|---|---|---|---|---|
| 1845 | | | | |
| Sept 10 | By Balance of a/c | | $ 600 99 | |
| 26 | " 1700 Bushels Rough Rice @ $4\frac{5}{8}$ | | 1757 42 | |
| Oct 10 | " 1586 " " " | | 1788 00 | |
| | " Balance of Note of $10,000 | | 1618 23 | |
| Nov 28 | " 3000 Bushels Rough Rice | $4 | 2799 94 | |
| Decr 9 | " 1500 " " " | $4.12½ | 1296 00 | |
| [1846] | | | | |
| Feb 13 | " 2568 " " " | @.87½¢ | 2165 23 | 12,024.82 |
| | | | $12024 82 | |

## Dr/ Hugh Fraser Grant in a/c with

| | | | | |
|---|---|---|---|---|
| 1846 | | | | |
| April 21 | Order in favr of J & S H Rokenbaugh | $ 137 10 | | |
| | " " " Mitchell & Collins | 183 09 | | |
| | " " T P Pease | 79 82 | | |
| May 16 | " Dr Troup | 42 56 | | |
| 26 | " S Palmer | 59 47 | | |
| June 2 | " Paid myself | 1500 00 | | |
| | " V. L & Butler | 58 79 | | |
| | " W. Warner | 365 00 | | |
| Oct 15 | " J. J. Giers $74.20 & B Cleveland $90 | 164 20 | | |
| | " J A Hibler | 160 00 | | |
| | " Tax Collector | 82 33 | | |
| | Paid Myself | 150 00 | | |
| | " T Allen | 214 37 | | |
| | | $ 3196 73 | | |

| | | | | |
|---|---|---|---|---|
| 1846 | | | | |
| | To Balance of a/c | $878.04 | 878 04 | |
| Nov | J. R Johnston | | 50 00 | |
| Decr 16 | 100 bushels Rice flour | | 75 | |
| | 5 pr Sashes | | 11 88 | |
| 1847 | Geo Schley, 1 Jany/47 | 217.35 | 217.35 | |
| Jany 4 | Paid Bishop Elliott | | 200 | |
| 8 | Paid myself | | 50 | |
| 23 | " Check in favr R Hogan | | 125 | |
| | " 100 bu Corn | | 75 | |
| Feb 1 | " Denslow & Webster | | 16 75 | |
| | G R Hendrickson | | 48 82 | |
| 2 | W T Williams | | 6 " | |
| | Miss Kendrick | | 54 70 | |
| 8 | " A K Moore | | 100 00 | 1940.82 |
| 27 | " C. M Bell | | 626 | |
| | S. Palmer | | 100 | |
| March | A T Bowne Druggist | | 5 00 | |
| | J. F Meeker | | 250 | |
| | Mitchell & Collins | | 144 76 | |
| April | 200 Bushels Corn | | 200 | |

| | | | |
|---|---|---|---|
| 1846 | | | |
| April 8 | Amount brought over | $ 12024 82 | |
| " | 1500 Bushels Rice by Georgia = | 1187 20 | |
| | 214 Bushels Rice flour | 20 86 | |
| | | 13232 88 | |
| 1846 | | | |
| | | | Freight off |
| Decr 16 | By 4075 Bushels Rough Rice | 2704 08 | 2506.18 Nett |
| 1847 | | | |
| Jany 14 | By 3034 Bushels Rough Rice | 3170 34 = | 3022.14 |

## D$^r$/ H. F. Grant in a/c with

| 1847 | | | | | |
|---|---|---|---|---|---|
| April 23 | Cash | Self | $ 150 | | |
| | " | J S Rogers | 94 96 | | |
| | " | Wood & Claghorn | 226 75 | | |
| | " | V. L & Butler | 125 66 | | |
| | " | J Anderson & Co | 156 76 | | |
| May 6 | " | R Hogan | 637 50 | 1051.20 | |
| | " | My Self | 50 | | |
| | " | N B & H Weed | 68 76 | | |
| | 300 Bu | Corn @ 87¢ | 261 00 | | |
| | 100 " | " 87 | 87 00 | | |
| | " | L M Smith | 44 28 | 511.04 | |
| | " | E W Sylvester | 25 50 | | |
| | | S Palmer | 25 | | |
| July 12 | " | Interest on my note to date | 241 92 | | |
| | " | Paid on note of $6480 | 2192 76 | | |

BALANCED

## R Habersham & Son Cr/

| | | Nett |
|---|---|---|
| April | By Balance brought over | $ 5528 52 |
| May 7 | " 1456 Bu Rough Rice | |
| 15 | " 826 " " " | 2382 07 |
| | BALANCED | $ 7910 77 |

1847

| | | |
|---|---|---|
| July 12 | By balance at my Credit | $ 100 00 |

## D^r/ H. F. Grant in a/c with

| | | | | | |
|---|---|---|---|---|---|
| 1847 | | | | | |
| Augst | 7 | To | Order in favr James Holmes | $ 50 00 | |
| | 17 | " | " " J W Moore Tax Col-lectr | 87 | |
| | | " | Iron Shafts &c | 96 65 | 233.65 |
| Oct | | " | 1 Five bushel tub | 5 | |
| | | " | 2 Tons Coal | 19 63 | |
| Nov | 17 | " | Cash My Self | 200 | |
| | | " | Bull & Andrews | 66 44 | 266.44 |
| Decr | 13 | " | M. A Price | 50 " | |
| | | " | T L Smith | 40 | |
| | 29 | " | P. R Yonge & Sons | 13 | 111.41 |
| | | " | G W. Johnston | 8 41 | |
| | | " | Farmers Library | 5 00 | |
| 1848 | | | | | |
| Jany | 3 | " | E W Sylvester | 13 97 | |
| | 6 | " | My Self Cash | 350 " | |
| | 8 | " | Dr H. A. Grant | 918 99 | |
| | | " | Hamilton & Symmons | 67 37 | |
| | | " | P Wiltberger | 110 00 | |
| | 14 | " | Wood. C[laghorn] & Co. | 340 64 | |
| | | " | G W Johnston | 80 " | |
| | 22 | " | J S Rogers | 200 57 | |
| | | " | N B & H Weed | 82 76 | |
| | | " | Miss Kendrick | 36 60 | |
| | | " | Mitchell & Collins | 67 34 | |
| | | " | A K Moore | 55 70 | |
| | | " | W. T. Williams | 23 38 | |
| | | " | Denslow & Webster | 41 31 | |
| | | " | J S Sullivan M D | 84 50 | 2405.71 |
| Feb | 1 | " | D B Nichols | 68 88 | |
| | | " | A A Solomons | 16 24 | |
| | 23 | " | Miss Bell | 900 | |
| | | | S Palmer | 210 44 | |
| | | | T P Pease | 87 89 | |
| | | | Miller for Castings | 276 52 | |
| | | | J F Meeker | 225 | 1784.46 |

## Messr R Habersham & Son contra Cr/

| | | | |
|---|---|---|---|
| 1847 | | | |
| July 12 | By Balance at my Credit | $ 100 00 | |
| Oct 21 | " 968 Bushels Rice . . . | | |
| Nov 3 | " 2200 " " | | |
| 18 | " 1650 " " | 3157 39 | |
| Feb 1 | " 3361 " " @ 90¢ | 2761 23 | |
| | | $ 5918 62 | Nett |

## D[r] H. F. Grant in a/c with

| | | | |
|---|---|---|---|
| 1848 | | | $ 4831 67 |
| Feb 20 | To | 4 Sides Band leather | 32 70 |
| | " | 1 Calcutta hide | 2 " |
| March 9 | " | Mr Miller 1 Spur wheel | 20 00 |
| | " | 500 bushels Corn & 7 Bbls Pork | 300 90 |
| | " | S H Harris | 70 89 |
| 7 | " | P Wiltberger | 50 " |
| 14 | " | My Self | 100 " |
| | " | 6 Bbls Pork @ $9 | 54 |
| | " | Expences on Corn | 8 51 |
| | " | 1 Cask Small Rice | |
| 29 | " | Mrs Hogan | 105 |
| | " | Bacon for (Trezevant) | 11 31 |
| April 3 | " | T. L Smith | 40 00 |
| 5 | " | J M Sturtevant | 125 " |
| 26 | " | James Anderson & Co | 30 " |
| 27 | " | V. L. & Butler | 158 24 |
| 29 | " | S H Harris . . . . . . . . . . | 81 14 |
| May 10 | " | M A Price | 50 00 |
| | " | J M Sturtevant | 39 00 |
| 23 | " | 1 Qr. Cask Madeira | 70 00 |
| | " | J. W. Morrell . . . . . . . . . | 27 97 |
| 27 | " | A. N Miller | 109 00 |
| 30 | " | Miss Gardner . . . . . . . . . | 4 25 |
| June 20 | " | T S Bond for myself | 50 00 |
| 22 | " | H H Stotesbery | 173 77 |
| 27 | " | C. C Moore for Ponys [7] | 30 " |

[7] This entry was recorded and then scratched out.

R HABERSHAM & SON CONTRA Cr/

| 1848 | | | |
|---|---|---|---|
| Feb 23 | By | amount brought over | $ 5918 62½ |
| April 17 | " | 1965 Bushels Rough Rice | 1277 66 |
| 24 | " | T. P Huger draft on Ravinel Brother & Co of Charleston | 244 " |
| | | Balance to new a/c | $ 562 25 |

Dr/ H. F. GRANT IN A/C WITH

1848

| | | | | |
|---|---|---|---|---|
| June 27 | To | Draft in fav C. C Moore | $ | 30 |
| July 8 | " | J. A Beals | | 39 |
| | " | W Warner | | 7 |
| Augst 30 | " | J D Piles Tax Collector | | 116 65 |
| Sept 19 | " | Solomon Cohen | | 25 |
| Oct 2 | " | A Scranton | | 16 |
| 4 | " | Cash sent me | | 300 |
| 1 | " | Paid my note to R Habersham & Son | | 4373 10 |
| | " | Remitted H. A Grant | | 4090 45 |
| Nov 6 | " | M. A Price | | 125 |
| | " | My Self | | 250 |
| | " | J. W. Morrell. *Piano* | | 431 |
| | " | Freight of Sundry articles from New York | | 6 62 |
| | | &c &c | | 5 90 |
| Decr 4 | " | C Stevens | | 18 75 |
| | " | 150 Bushels of Corn | | 97 50 |
| 12 | " | Wm H Smith & Co | | 136 31 |
| | " | P Wiltberger | | 419 83 |
| 16 | " | Geo Schley | | 65 07 |
| 25 | " | S Palmer | | 225 |
| 26 | " | C B Andrews | | 6 30 |
| | " | 100 Bushel Oats . . . . . . . | | 51 20 |

1849

| | | | | |
|---|---|---|---|---|
| Jany 1 | " | Heald & Burt | | 50 63 |
| 6 | | H A Crane | | 107 25 |
| 1,, | " | A T Bowne | | 10 " |
| 16 | " | Dr Holmes | | 50 " |
| 18 | " | A A Solomons | | 15 " |
| | " | M Eastman | | 20 75 |
| | " | Robinson & Camp | | 101 75 |
| | " | A Ponce | | 64 02 |
| | " | Denslow & Webster | | 98 07 |
| | | P Wiltberger | | 143 21 |
| | | | | 11403 13 |

## R Habersham & Son contra $C^r$/

| 1848 | | | | |
|---|---|---|---|---|
| July | 1 | By | Balance to new a/c | 562 25 |
| Oct | 6 | " | J. Barretts draft for $10,000 int off | $9,970 94 |
| Decr | 4 | " | 2200 Bushels Rice @ | |
| | 22 | " | 1400 " " @ | 3894 40 |
| | | | 1890 | |

## D[r]/ H. F. Grant in a/c with

1849

| | | | |
|---|---|---|---|
| Jany 20 | | De Witt & Morgan | 12 56 |
| | | D B Nichols | 167 75 |
| | | Myself | 300 |
| | " | 200 Bushels of Corn | 114 50 |
| | " | 5 Sacks Salt | 8 75 |
| | " | 2 Hhds Bacon | 83 64 |
| | " | S. Palmer | 133 22 |
| | | H H Stotesbury | 143 50 |
| | " | N B & H Weed | 128 78 |
| | | 150 Bushels Rice flour | 18 75 |

[1848]

| | | |
|---|---|---|
| Dec 14 | Freight on 2165 bushels @ 5¢ | 108 25 |
| | " " 1402 | 70 10 |
| | " 1967 | 98 35 |

| | | | |
|---|---|---|---|
| Feb 16 | " | C. Trezevant | $ 154 88 |
| 22 | " | W[ood] Claghorn & Co | 465 49 |
| March 2 | " | Miss Kendrick | 84 93 |
| 9 | " | Capt Stevens | 15 25 |
| | " | 400 Bushels of Corn | |
| April 2 | " | P Wiltberger | 100 00 |
| 7 | " | J F Meeker | 220 " |
| 17 | " | J Barrett | 61 76 |
| May 8 | " | P Mc Kinlay for D[r] Troup | 15 |
| | " | Mess. Cohen | 20 |

R HABERSHAM & SON CONTRA $C^r$/

By Amt brt over $ 14427.49

---

1849

| | | |
|---|---|---|
| Feb 12 | Balance to my credit | $ 1665 40 |
| Aprl 7 | By 1668 Bushels Rice. . . . . . . . . . | |
| May 16 | Making Tierces @ $2\frac{7}{8}$ . . . . . . . . . | 1306.51 |

## Dr/ H. F. Grant in a/c with

| | | | | | |
|---|---|---|---|---|---|
| 1849 | | | | | |
| Decr | 8 | To | Balance of a/c to date | $ 3100 88 | |
| | 18 | " | Draft in favr C Grant for Parsonage | 205 " | |
| | 22 | " | Draft Dr Holmes | 151 " | |
| 1850 | | | | | |
| Jan | 8 | " | J S Hervey | 100 00 | |
| | 12 | " | 200 Bushels Corn 68¢ | 136 00 | |
| | | | Porterage | 2 00 | |
| | 25 | " | To Cash | 100 | |
| | | " | W. Warner | 26 | |
| | | " | M Eastman 33.80 | | |
| | | " | 8000 Laths $1.85 | 14 80 | |
| Feb | 8 | " | Heald & Burt | 15 " | |
| | 9 | " | James Morgan on a/c Barrett | 148 00 | |
| | 27 | " | J S Rogers | 400 " | |
| | | " | Myself Cash . . . . . . . . | 225 " | |
| March | 2 | " | Wood Claghorn & Co | 264 04 | |
| | | " | Denslow & Webster | 22 98 | |
| | 11 | " | J W Morrell | 59 37 | |
| | 14 | " | T P Pease | 32 86 | |
| | | " | Mitchell & Collins | 80 22 | |
| | 16 | " | E H Hogan | 105 00 | |
| | | " | J. F Meeker | 125 " | |
| | 18 | " | Wm T. Williams | 39 76 | |
| | | " | A. A Solomons Agt | 49 81 | |
| | | " | T. P. Pease . . . . . . . . . | 32 86 | |
| | | " | Robinson & Camp | 151 25 | |
| | | " | N B & H Weed | 48 07 | |
| | | " | F Kendrick | 114 72 | |
| | 22 | " | J Parmely | 58 00 | |
| | | " | J Champney | 34 | |
| | 25 | " | J A Alston | 100 | |
| | | " | W. Warner | 123 50 | 6064.58 |

R HABERSHAM & SON Cr/

| | | | |
|---|---|---|---|
| 1849 | | | |
| Decr | 8 | By 3300 bushels rough Rice | |
| | | | $3989 67 |
| 1850 | | | |
| Jany | 4 | 2500 " " | |

## Dr/ H. F. Grant in a/c with

| | | | | | |
|---|---|---|---|---|---|
| 1850 | | | | | |
| March | 27 | To amount brought forward | 6064 58 | | |
| | 28 | " 2 Orders in fav of J J Morgan | | | |
| | | $175 & 60 | $ 235 00 | | |
| April | 17 | " Jacob Barrett | 552 00 | | |
| | 23 | " Capt Stevens | 128 56 | 6980.14 | |
| | | " Sashes Blinds Brick & Laths | 125 | | |
| | | " 500 Bushels Corn | 325 | | |
| | | 100 " Rice flour | 20 | | |
| May | 1 | J S Heald P M | 12 50 | | |
| | 9 | V. L & Butler | 116 63 | | |
| | | " G S Nichols | 67 58 | | |
| | | " H A G for Mrs S Grant | 264 " | | |
| | | " MySelf | 130 " | 1135.71 | |
| July | 17 | " G C Dent | 50 " | | |
| | | Tax Collector J Piles | 92 58 | | |
| | | Post Master | 10 | | |
| | | 4000 Laths @ $2 | 8 00 | | |
| | | 2 Doors | | | |
| Nov | 5 | Cash Myself | 125 " | | |
| | 11 | 200 Bushels Corn @ 75¢ | 150 " | | |
| | | 150 Rice flour @ 20¢ | 30 | | |
| | | Drayage &c | 2 | | |
| Decr | | W. W. Hazzard | 35 | | |
| | 5 | James Sullivan | 13 81 | | |
| | | Mrs S Grant to R Hogan | 110 " | 658.81 | |
| | | James Dickson | | | |
| | 6 | " Freight per America for 2689 | | | |
| | | Bushels Rice | 134 45 | | |
| 1851 | | | | | |
| Jany | 9 | Miss F Kendrick | 64 94 | | |
| | | Wm T Williams | 29 75 | | |
| | 11 | Jacob Barrett | 700 00 | | |
| | 18 | James Sullivan | 7 13 | 935.47 | |
| | | | | 9710.13 | |

MESS R HABERSHAM & SON [Cr/]

| | | |
|---|---|---|
| | By amount brt forward | $3989 67 |
| 1850 | | |
| April 23 | By 2340 Bushels Rice | 1678 79 |
| Nov 18 | " 2689 " " | 1959 61 |
| | " Cash from C Grant | 500 " |
| | | $8128 07 |
| 1851 | | |
| Jany 4 | " 2800 | |

## Dr/ H. F. Grant in a/c with

| Date | | Item | Amount | Total |
|---|---|---|---|---|
| 1851 | | | | |
| Jany 23 | To | Amt brt over | 9710 | |
| | To | draft J. W. Morrell | 204 97 | |
| | " | " Wood Claghorn & Co | 723 10 | |
| | " | 200 Bushels of Corn @ 78¢ | 156 | |
| 28 | " | Wm Matthiessen | 28 50 | |
| Feb 6 | " | G H Griffin | 54 " | |
| 8 | " | J S Rogers | 757 28 | |
| | " | A A Solomons & Co | 66 65 | |
| | " | Robinson & Camp | 51 13 | |
| | " | Miss C M Bell | 1000 | |
| 10 | " | Dr Holmes | 150 " | |
| | " | Dr Kollock | 10 " | |
| 14 | " | De Witt & Morgan | 13 81 | |
| 15 | " | Mitchell & Collins | 187 39 | |
| | " | S Palmer | 55 40 | 13168.23 |
| 25 | " | E H Hogan | 105 " | |
| | " | T P Pease | 34 36 | |
| March 1 | " | J F Meeker | 140 " | |
| | " | Capt Stevens freight on 3125 | 156 25 | |
| 6 | " | J J Morgan | 157 " | |
| | " | Dr Troup —— | 42 70 | 635.26 |
| | | | | 13803.49 |
| 12 | " | Myself $1832 | 500 | |
| | " | Marshall & Aiken | 268 11 | |
| | " | A Ponce —— | 82 24 | |
| | " | Freight Cap Stevens 2625 @ 5¢ | 131 25 | |
| 23 | " | J Rokenbaugh & Son | 562 56 | |
| | " | G S Nichols | 20 " | |
| | " | 300 bu Corn 75¢ | 225 | |
| | | 6 cases Claret $ 3½ | 21 " | |
| | " | S M Stover | 60 | |
| April 20 | " | 400 Bushels Corn 75¢ | 300 | |
| | " | Bbls Lime | 6 25 | |
| | " | Dr Daniell for Horses | 300 00 | |
| | | | | 16179.91 |

## R Habersham & Son contra $C^r$/

| 1851 | | | | |
|---|---|---|---|---|
| Jany 23 | By Amt brt forward | | $ 8128 07 | $8128.07 |
| 4 | " 2900 Bushels Rice —— | | 2232 96 | |
| 30 | " 3140 " " | @ 78¢ | 2376 56 | |
| Feb 6 | " Cash deposited by me | | 3700 | |
| 26 | " 2625 Bushels Rice | 77¢ | 2021 22 | |
| | | | | 19427.81 |

## Dr/ H F Grant in a/c with

1851

| | | | | |
|---|---|---|---|---|
| April 20 | To | 1 Box Oranges | | |
| | " | 1 " Lemons | | |
| | " | 2 doz Pine apples | | |
| | " | 1 Bunch Bannanas | | |
| | " | Freight &c &c —— | | |
| 28 | " | Dr B H Troup | 500 | |
| May 7 | " | N B & H Weed | 79 62 | |
| | " | W. L & Butler | 197 | |
| | " | J Anderson & Co | 50 | |
| | " | Agt of Magnolia | 50 | |
| | " | P Wiltberger | | |
| | " | Mess Sturtevant | 31 69 | |
| | " | Hetty Garey | 41 | |
| | | Repair Carriage wheels | 5 13 | 17184 |
| June 17 | " | J Sullivan | 3 50 | |
| 28 | " | J S F Heald P M | 15 " | |
| | " | S M Stover | 60 " | |

R HABERSHAM & SON Cr/

1851

| | | |
|---|---|---|
| April 20 | By Amt brt forward | 19427 81 |
| | " 1325 Bushels Rice | |

## Dr/ H. F Grant in a/c with

| | | | | |
|---|---|---|---|---|
| 1851 | | | | |
| Augst 14 | To | Cash sent G H Clark | $ 65 — | |
| Sept 13 | " | John Lamb for taxes | 81 " | |
| 15 | " | T. Eden for Dr Stuntson | 5 " | |
| | " | P. O Stamps | 3 " | |
| Oct 11 | " | Cash. . . . . . . . . . . . . | 575 " | |
| Nov 6 | " | Cash | 100 " | |
| 12 | " | J J Morgan | 21 | |
| | " | Freight on 2219 bu @ 5¢ | 111 95 | |
| | " | Do Do 3380 " 5¢ | 169 " | |
| | | | | 1119.95 |
| 1852 | | | | |
| Jany 6 | " | draft E. Blount. Mongin Schooner | 75 00 | |
| 10 | " | H B Harris for J J Morgan | 37 33 | |
| 14 | " | N K Barnum & Co | 73 63 | |
| | " | W. T Williams | 41 06 | |
| | " | M J Solomons | 288 56 | |
| | " | W Claghorn & Co | 470 60 | |
| 10 | " | Myself Cash | 100 " | 1086.18 |
| 22 | " | De Witte & Morgan | 181 88 | |
| | " | J. W Morrell & Co | 206 15 | |
| | " | Robinson & Camp | 47 " | |
| | " | Aikin & Burns | 63 48 | |
| | " | Myself Cash | 450 " | |
| | " | D B Nichols | 198 13 | |
| | " | McClosky & Norton | 136 49 | |
| | " | Myself Cash | 100 " | |
| | " | Georgian Office | 25 " | 1708.13 |
| | " | M C B Wright | 30 77 | |
| 27 | " | Jacob Barrett | 700 " | |
| | " | J F S Heald | 10 59 | |
| | " | W. T Williams | 41 06 | |
| | " | Hilton S Jones | 8 88 | |
| | " | E B Baker | 11 19 | 802.49 |

## R Habersham & Son contra $C^r$/

| 1851 | | | | | |
|---|---|---|---|---|---|
| July | 1 | By balance of a/c | | $ 713 77 | $ 713.77 |
| Nov | 1 | By 2253 Bushels of Rice | $3 | 1669 59 | 1669.59 |
| Decr | 4 | " 3380 " | @ 77¢ | 2537 53 | $ 2537.53 |

## Dr/ H. F. Grant in a/c with

| Date | | Particulars | Amount | Total |
|---|---|---|---|---|
| 1852 | | Amt Brought over | | $ 4316.75 |
| Jany | 27 | To Miss F. Kendrick | $ 71 37 | |
| | 29 & 30 | " J J Morgan | 274 79 | 4662.91 |
| | " | " Freight on 3130 Bushels | 156 50 | |
| Feb | 3 | " Horton & Rikeman | 35 " | |
| | 16 | " Charles Stevens —— | 123 47 | |
| | 17 | " T P Pease | 214 46 | |
| | | " Mitchell & Collins | 292 51 | 1168.16 |
| | | " Repair Wheel | 2 62 | |
| | | " Freight &c on 2950 | 147 50 | |
| | 23 | " C. M Bell | 1010 67 | |
| March | 1 | " E H Hogan | 105 " | |
| | | " J F Meeker | 150 | |
| | | " Dr Holmes | 50 | 1465.79 |
| | | " 150 Oranges @ $2.50 | | |
| | 12 | " J Parmely Jr | 25 " | |
| | 16 | " Telegraph dispatch | | |
| | | " ¼ Cask wine 72.38 | | |
| April | 6 | " J S Rogers | 600 " | |
| | 9 | " A Ponce | 39 50 | |
| | | " Geo Parrott — | 50 | 714.50 |
| | | | | $ 7665.20 |
| | 24 | " A A Solomons & Co | 69 13 | |
| | | " W H May | 63 68 | |
| | | " Verstelle & Butler | 147 90 | |
| May | 8 | To Balance carried down | 1689 48 | |
| | | | $ 9192.30 | |

R Habersham & Son contra $C^r$/

| 1852 | | |
|---|---|---|
| | By Amount brought over | $ 4920 89 |
| Jany 8 | " 3250 Bushels Rice | 2432 54 |
| Feb 10 | " 2999 Bushels Rice | 1838 87 |
| | | $ 9192 30 |

| 1852 | | |
|---|---|---|
| 9 May | By Balance to my credit | $ 1689 48 |

## Dr/ H. F Grant in a/c with

| | | | | | |
|---|---|---|---|---|---|
| 1852 | | | | | |
| May | 8 | To | J Barrett omitted in a/c Current | $ 700 00 | |
| | 14 | " | T. M Forman | 26 " | |
| June | 21 | " | Cash Myself | 100 " | |
| July | | " | R Grant | 25 " | |
| | 26 | " | H D W Alexander for J C Thornton | 76 " | |
| | | " | 2 Barrels Pitch & freight | 5 50 | |
| Augst | 3 | " | James D Morgan | 20 99 | |
| | 14 | " | F Poncil | 39 " | |
| | 19 | " | R Grant | 16 63 | |
| | 25 | " | My Self Cash | 100 " | |
| | 28 | " | P Wiltberger & Son | 50 " | |
| Oct | 5 | " | A A De Lorme P M— | 10 " | 1019.12 |
| | 7 | " | Mess A. Brown | 100 " | |
| | 16 | " | Mrs S Grant | 90 " | |
| Nov | 2 | " | J Piles Jr. Tax Collector | 45 94 | |
| | 15 | " | Dr H B Troup | 150 | 1405.06 |
| Decr | 9 | " | Mrs S Grant | 100 | |
| 1853 | | | | | |
| Jany | 17 | " | Camfield | 126 " | |
| | | " | A Ponce | 71 47 | |
| | | " | G M Griffin | 46 " | |
| | | " | J B Hale | 22 64 | |
| | | " | James Sullivan | 28 44 | |
| | | " | Horton & Rikeman | 150 24 | |
| | | " | My Self | 100 | |
| | 21 | " | Jacob Barrett | 700 | |

R HABERSHAM & SON CONTRA Cr/

| | | | |
|---|---|---|---|
| 1852 | | | |
| May | 8 | By Balance to my credit as per a/c/ rendered this day | $ 1689 48 |
| 1853 | | | |
| Jany | 7 | By 3300 Bushels Rice making Barrels @ $4. cwt | 3109 09 |
| | | | $ 4798 57 |

## Dr/ H. F Grant in a/c with

| | | | | | |
|---|---|---|---|---|---|
| 1853 | | | Amt brt forward | 4746 | |
| Feb | 9 | To | draft in favr Mitchel & Pease | 246 07 | |
| | 15 | " | " McCleskey & Norton | 63 24 | |
| | 17 | " | " Mrs Sarah Grant | 100 " | |
| | | " | " Dr Holmes for Sarah Grant | 75 | |
| | 21 | " | Mess G Sturtevant | 41 57 | |
| | 28 | " | T P Pease . . . . . . . . . | 428 39 | |
| | | " | Paid freight on 3225 bushels | 161 25 | 5861.52 |
| March | 2 | " | J F. Meeker | 150 " | |
| | 8 | " | J J Morgan 2 dfts of $ 130 each | 260 " | |
| | | " | 5 Hhds Bacon | 354 54 | |
| | | " | Freight on 1323 bushels @ 5 | 66 15 | |
| | | " | " " 684 " " 5 | | |
| April | 2 | " | Robinson & Camp | 35 50 | |
| | | " | A A Solomons & Co | 49 53 | |
| | | " | Freight Rice per America | | |
| | | " | J Rokenbaugh & Sons . . . . | 137 26 | |
| | 26 | " | C H Camfield | 71 75 | |
| | 30 | " | Charles Stevens [8] | 263 15 | |
| | | | | $6620 90 | |

---

| | | | | | |
|---|---|---|---|---|---|
| May | 2 | " | To draft in favr Charles Stevens | $ 263 15 | |
| | 18 | To | dft for L T Bennett & Co @ 30 days | 275 50 | |
| | | " | " " Verstelle & Butler at 30 " | 92 14 | |
| June | 7 | " | Mrs Sarah Grant | 50 | |
| July | 13 | " | T. W Collins | 202 50 | 883.29 |
| Augst | 1 | " | 1 Hhd Bacon 878 9¼¢ | 81 37 | 965.16 |
| Sept | 24 | " | Road Commissions | 115 " | |
| | 26 | " | Tax Collector | 214 56 | 1294.22 |
| Oct | 13 | " | dft T M Forman for Horses | 400 " | 1694.22 |
| | 24 | " | 4 bundles Laths @ 40¢ | 1 60 | |
| | 28 | " | James Sullivan | 17 " | |
| Nov | 8 | " | Capt Wiggins | 12 | |
| | 10 | " | Myself | 400 " | |

## R Habersham & Son contra Cr/

1852

| | | | | |
|---|---|---|---|---|
| Feb | 4 | By | Amt brt forward | $ 4798 57 |
| | 7 | " | 1323 bushels Rice per America.. | 1301 85 |
| | | " | 684 " " " " | 616 16 |
| April | 4 | " | 640 " " " " | 638 16 |
| | | " | G. C. Dents draft for | 375 " |
| | | | | $ 7729 74 |

1853

| | | | | | |
|---|---|---|---|---|---|
| May | 1 | By | Balance to my credit | $ 1108 84 | |
| | 10 | " | draft on Wm M Tunno | 2029 76 | |
| | 18 | " | Cash deposited | 640 50 | |
| June | 6 | " | " Sent | 540 " | |
| July | 14 | " | " " | 800 " | |
| Aug | 11 | " | " " | 500 | 6619.10 |
| Sept | 16 | " | " " | 470 75 | 6089.85 |
| Oct | 21 | By | 3000 bushels Rough Rice | 2761 87 | |
| | | | | $ 8857 72 | |

[ Dr *cont.*, November 1853 ]

| | | | | | |
|---|---|---|---|---|---|
| | 30 | " | 100 Bushels Corn | 90 | |
| Decr | 7 | " | W H W[iltberger] & Co | 60 " | |
| | 15 | " | L W Wall | 90 | 2364.82 |

[8] This entry was recorded and scratched out.

## Dr/ H. F Grant in a/c with R Habersham & Son

| | | | | |
|---|---|---|---|---|
| 1853 | | To amount brought up. . . . . | 2364 82 | |
| Decr | 17 | To dft in favr J J Morgan | $ 50 " | |
| | | " 100 bushels Rice flour | | |
| | | " 8 bbls Lime | | |
| | | " M E Grant | 20 | |
| | 26 | " M Coburn | 25 50 | |
| | 30 | " A Galloway. . . . . . . . | 15 " | |
| 1854 | | | | |
| Jany | 5 | " E. P Brown | 25 " | |
| | | " Jacob Barrett | 5700 " | |
| | 16 | " W. H Wiltberger & Co | 75 | 8274.32 |
| Feb | 3 | " Myself | 100 " | |
| | | " W H May & Co | 47 80 | |
| | | " A Ponce | 183 10 | |
| | 4 | " Horton & Rikeman | 82 50 | |
| | | " J S Rogers | 479 98 | |
| | | " Silber | 103 89 | |
| | 7 | " C H Camfield | 28 75 | |
| | | " S Palmer & Son | 83 03 | 9383.37 |
| | 10 | " Aikin & Burns | 52 91 | |
| | | " W T Williams | 31 82 | |
| | 15 | " M J Solomons | 310 76 | |
| | | " A A Solomons | 137 29 | 9916.15 |
| | 24 | " E H Hogan | 105 " | |
| | 25 | " R Cogdell | 14 04 | |
| March | 1 | " De Witte & Morgan | 166 33 | |
| | | " R & J Lacklison | 11 45 | |
| | 6 | " Mitchel & Pease | 350 71 | |
| | | " T P Pease | 145 65 | |
| | | By Habersham a/c to date | | $11236.25 |
| | | To Balance due R H & Son | $ 309 51 | |

[This page was torn out of the Journal.]

Dr/ H. F Grant in a/c with

| 1854 | | | | |
|---|---|---|---|---|
| March 29 | To | Balance of a/c | $ 309 51 | |
| Augst 28 | " | Lockwood & Johnston | 200 " | |
| Oct 8 | " | Joseph H Goodbread Tax collector | 130 69 | |
| 30 | " | C Spalding favr of Darien | 25 " | |
| | | | | 665.20 |
| | " | Check valve . . . . . . . . | 7 50 | |
| Decr 12 | " | James Myers at 30 days | 96 " | |
| | " | J W Myers " 30 " | 250 00 | |
| | " | Cash sent me | 50 " | |
| Jany 15 | " | Jacob Barrett . . . . . . . . | 350 | 746.02 |
| | " | 100 bushels Corn | 123 " | |
| 22 | " | S. Palmer & Son | 117 05 | |
| | " | A Ponce | 106 50 | |
| 29 | " | Claghorn & Cunningham | 699 38 | |
| | " | A A Solomons & Co | 137 63 | |
| Feb 6 | " | Dr Holmes | 105 " | 534.56 |
| | " | W H May & Co | 64 65 | |
| | " | N B Knapp | 44 49 | |
| | " | Coln Williams | 25 50 | |
| 11 | " | A A De Lorme | 44 57 | |
| | " | Mitchel & Pease | 555 18 | |
| | " | Rogers & Laason | 290 67 | 1025.06 |
| 28 | " | J S F Heald . . . . . . . . | 18 00 | 2970.84 |
| March 6 | " | E H Hogan | 105 " | |
| | " | J F Meeker | 140 | |
| 15 | " | Kate Lewers | 100 " | |
| 17 | " | G S Nichols & Co . . . . . . | 35 | |
| 20 | " | Hamilton Couper | 9 68 | |
| | " | Parkhurst & Adams | 8 35 | |
| 22 | " | A A De Lorme | 15 | |
| | " | Freight on 3093 bushel Rice | 154 65 | |
| 26 | " | J. W Morrell & Co | 7 " | |
| April 20 | " | M E Grant | 50 " | |

## R Habersham & Son contra Cr/

1854

| | | | |
|---|---|---|---|
| April 11 | By | dfts on New York protested | $ 2500 00 |
| Decr 29 | " | 3045 bushels Rice less freight | 3015 68 |
| Mar 13 | " | Check on Marine Bank | $ 3000 " |

## Dr/ H. F. GRANT IN A/C WITH

|  | | |  |  | |
|---|---|---|---|---|---|
| 1855 | | | | | |
| May | 10 | To | dft Mrs Du Pre | $ 202 50 | |
| | | " | Browning & Leman | 47 59 | |
| | | " | Orcutt & Hickey | 19 50 | |
| | 17 | " | Wm M Tunno | 98 37 | |
| June | | " | My Note for 3000 & Interest . . | 3105 25 | |
| | 27 | " | Wm M Tunno | 155 50 | |
| Augst | 5 | " | J W Moore | 22 " | |
| | | " | 1 Qr Cask Wine | 68 75 | |
| 1856 | | | | | |
| Decr | 12 | " | Willis Hall preacher | $ 30 00 | |
| 1857 | | | | | |
| Jany | 9 | " | Cash | 150 | |
| | | " | 200 bu Corn | 171 95 | |
| | | | 1 tons Coal 9.00 & Expences 2.02 | 11 02 | |
| | | " | Freight Northern Belle 3367 Bushels Rice | 168 35 | |
| | 30 | " | J W Morrell | 170 50 | |
| | | " | A A Solomons & Co . . . . | 86 31 | |
| | | " | Bill of Oats, Rice flour | | |
| | | " | Peas & Salt | 133 51 | |
| Feb | 2 | " | T P Pease | 98 59 | |
| | | " | H P Horton | 262 93 | |
| | | " | M Powell & Co Ice | 69 14 | 1352.40 |
| | 9 | " | M Cullinan | 12 " | |
| | | " | De Witte & Morgan | 847 64 | |
| | 16 | " | W T Williams | 43 00 | |
| | | " | H Lathrop & Co | 52 11 | |
| | 20 | " | Est John Poole | 14 68 | |
| March | 3 | " | F R Goulding | 150 | |
| | 10 | " | Claghorn & Cuningham | 1106 82 | |
| | | " | To Amount brought up | $ 3578 65 | |
| | 17 | " | Mitchel & Pease | 465 48 | |
| | | " | A A De Lorme | 15 75 | |

## R. Habersham & Son contra Cr/

1855

| | | | | |
|---|---|---|---|---|
| May 3d | By | Balance due me | $ 1461 00 | |
| June 14 | " | Cash from Law & Bartow on a/c of Canal . . . . . . | 2256 34 | |

1856

| | | | | |
|---|---|---|---|---|
| Nov 28 | By | 3468 —— Bushels Rough Rice by Northern Belle . . . . . | 3365 31 | |

1857

| | | | | |
|---|---|---|---|---|
| Jany 7 | " | 3320 Bushels Rice by Cotton Plant | 3683 06 | |
| April 27 | " | 1067 Bushels Rice by the Elias Reed . . . . . . . . | 1164 25 | 8212.62 |

[Dr *cont.*, March 1857]

| | | | | |
|---|---|---|---|---|
| | " | Collins & Shine . . . . . . | 129 78 | |
| | " | Aikin & Burns | 31 25 | |
| | " | Butler & Frierson | 223 32 | 4444.13 |
| 24 | " | Mrs E H Hogan | 1105 00 | |
| | " | Freight on 3371 bu Rice by Cotton plant | 168 55 | 5715.68 |
| April 6 | " | T M Forman 200 bu Seed Rice | 200 | |
| | " | ¼ Cask Sherry Wine . . . . | 71 59 | |
| June 11 | " | M A & C Well | 55 99 | |
| | | N. L & Rogers | 431 94 | |
| 18 | | M Pease & Co | 50 " | 809.52 |
| | | | | 6527.18 |

8212.62
6527 18

1685.44

## Dr/ H. F. Grant in a/c with

| | | | | | |
|---|---|---|---|---|---|
| 1857 | | | | | |
| July | 6 | To | M E Grant | $ 100 00 | |
| | 13 | " | T P Pease | 50 " | |
| Augst | 5 | " | J Bryan & Son = Champagne | 21 " | |
| | 22 | " | H F Grant Jr & Sisters | 850 | |
| | 28 | " | C H Campfield | 27 25 | |
| Sept | 22 | " | T. P Pease. . . . . . . . . | 50 " | |
| | | " | 2 doz bottles Brandy | 50 54 | 1148.79 |
| | 20 | " | J H Goodbread Tax collector | 127 53 | |
| | 28 | " | M C B Wright Execution | 201 43 | |
| | | " | J M Burnett Road fine | 57 " | |
| Oct | 19 | " | H. F. Grant Jr | 100 | |
| Decr | 7 | " | E. Parsons & Son | 21 63 | |
| | 11 | " | L Veulesquez . . . . . . . | 25 00 | |
| | 12 | " | A T Burke for J J Morgan | 25 " | 557.59 |
| 1858 | | | | | |
| Jany | 11 | | Wm Pierce for 50 bu Corn | 37 50 | |
| | 18 | | E Parsons & Son | 4 41 | |
| | 25 | | R & J Lacklison & Co | 155 39 | |
| Feb | 4 | | W. T Williams . . . . . . . . | 73 28 | |
| | | " | Myself | 400 " | 730.58 |
| | 24 | " | W H Wiltberger & Co | 60 " | |
| March | 2 | " | Claghorn & Cunningham | 1211 81 | |
| | 3 | " | E P Brown . . . . . . . . | 70 00 | |
| | 10 | " | T. P Pease | 26 87 | |
| | | " | A A Solomons & Co | 101 84 | |
| | 19 | " | H P Horton | 132 29 | 2542.61 |
| April | 1 | " | Henry Lathrop & Co . . . . | 75 15 | 4979.57 |
| | | " | Wm H Guyon | 45 54 | |
| | 17 | " | Mrs Sarah Grant . . . . . . | 75 00 | |
| | | " | R Cogdell & Co . . . . . . | 16 31 | |
| | 26 | " | Wm F. Day for Monemia | 150 | |
| May | 3 | " | Rev E. P Brown for myself | 80 | |
| | 8 | To | Amount brought up . . . . | 5346 42 | |
| | | " | S. Palmer & Son | $ 20 25 | |
| | 13 | " | A. A De Lorme | 26 19 | |

## R Habersham & Son contra Cr/

1857

| | | |
|---|---|---|
| June 23 | By Balance of a/c rendered | $1614 37 |
| July " | " Overcharge on freight of Corn | 10 " |
| Decr 8 | By 3270 Bushels Rice by Elias Reed | 2418 23 |
| April 21 | By 2769 Bushels Rice by E. Reed | 2333 97 |

4042.60

## D$^{r}$/ Hugh F. Grant in a/c with

| | | | | |
|---|---|---|---|---|
| 1858 | | | | |
| June 14 | To | Paid Myself | $ 1000 00 | |
| | " | J. B Gordon | 261 68 | |
| | " | J. G Howard M D | 50 " | |
| Sept 23 | " | Battey, Hickman & Co | 418 29 | |
| Nov | " | Glover Agt | 520 | 2249.97 |
| Decr 5 | " | D[r] H. A Grant for my Mother | 200 .. | 200 |
| 1859 | | | | |
| Jay 13 | " | M Powell & Co . . . . . . . | 17 38 | |
| 22 | " | Mrs M Thomson of Philad | 316 29 | |
| 28 | " | John M Cooper & Co | 42 40 | |
| | " | D[r] C W West | 12 50 | |
| | " | M[me] C Gradet | 8 23 | |
| | " | W[m] T Williams | 20 93 | 417.73 |
| Feb | | Lime | | |
| 8 | " | Fire Clay. . . . . . . . . . | | |
| 9 | " | S Palmer & Son. . . . . . . | 134 34 | |
| 11 | " | H F. Grant Jr | 150 " | |
| 15 | " | N B Knapp. . . . . . . . . | 43 60 | |
| 16 | " | Collins & Shine | 217 28 | 545.22 |
| Mar 8 | " | 350 Bu Seed Rice @ 105¢ | 367 50 | |
| April 25 | " | W[m] F. Day for Monemia Wilson | 150 " | |
| May 19 | " | H. Allen Grant . . . . . . . | 17 " | 534.50 |
| 25 | " | Myself Cash | 300 " | |
| June 25 | " | C Wendell for Washington Union | 30 " | |
| 29 | " | A Galloway | 3 75 | |
| July 21 | " | T A Hillier . . . . . . . . . | 20 25 | |
| 27 | " | A A Solomons & Co for Paint. . | 30 95 | |
| Aug 10 | " | S Palmer & Son | 15 60 | |

R Habersham & Sons contra Cr/

| 1858 | | |
|---|---|---|
| May 22 | By balance of a/c | $ 1621 21 |
| | " Sales of Rice | 2334 91 |
| | | $ 3956 12 |

## Dr/ H F. Grant in a/c with

| | | | | | |
|---|---|---|---|---|---|
| 1859 | | | | | |
| Augst 31 | To | balance of a/c rendered | $ 670 11 | | |
| | " | Road commissioners . . . . | 76 80 | | |
| Nov 17 | " | M. P King, Iron Railing . . . | 248 70 | | |
| 23 | " | McKee & Bennett | 293 35 | | |
| 28 | " | Geo Oakley . . . . . . . . | 500 " | 1780.96 | |
| 1860 | | | | | |
| Jay 1 | By | Cash sent me to New York | 200 " | | |
| | " | Bbls Rice sent North | | | |
| 27 | " | Mitchel, Pease & Co . . . . | 254 92 | | |
| Feb 1 | " | R & J Lacklison & Co | 4004 35 | | |
| 2 | " | Claghorn & Cuningham | 1077 45 | 5536.72 | |
| 14 | " | M Powell & Co . . . . . . | 75 78 | | |
| 17 | " | J J Morgan . . . . . . . . | 264 69 | | |
| 20 | " | A Galloway | 4 50 | | |
| 23 | " | Dr Curtis . . . . . . . . . . | 40 | | |
| Mach 1 | " | Capt James Freeborn | 100 | | |
| | " | King & Waring | 51 83 | | |
| 20 | " | W C Jeffries | 109 57 | | |
| 27 | " | Revd E P Brown | 75 00 | 721.37 | |
| | " | 300 Bushels Seed Rice . . . . | | | |
| | " | Freight on 7665 bu. @ 5¢ | 383 20 | | |

R HABERSHAM & SON CONTRA $C^r$/[9]

Nov 20 By 3886 Bushels Rice

1860

Feb 1 By My Note at 24 Mon
3 " 3778 — Bushels Rice
" 2400 " "

[9] This page is torn so that only the information given above remains.

## Dr/ H. F. Grant in a/c with

| Date | Day | | Item | Amount | Total |
|---|---|---|---|---|---|
| 1852 | | | | | |
| June | 1 | To | My Note in favr H. B Gould | $ 200 " | |
| | | " | Interest on the same . . . . | | |
| | | " | Cash paid for Horse | 150 | |
| | | " | Expences on the same . . . . | | |
| Decr | 1 | " | Lockwood & Johnston | 690 50 | |
| 1853 | | | | | |
| Jany | | " | My Self . . . . . . . . . . . | 287 16 | |
| | | " | 300 Bushels of Corn. . . . . | | |
| | | | 1½ Tons Coal & Expences | 218 79 | |
| Mar | 15 | " | Cash | 50 " | |
| | 18 | " | 500 Bushels of Corn | 340 03 | |
| April | 18 | " | To Cash | 45 72 | |
| | | " | Advertizing place | 8 00 | |
| | | | | | |
| 1853 | | | | | |
| Augst | 22 | To | 50 bushels Corn | $ 45 60 | |
| Sept | | " | 15 Barrels of Lime | 24 07 | |
| | 10 | " | 100 Envellopes | 3 20 | |
| | | | Postage on same | 48 | |
| 1854 | | | | | |
| Jany | 15 | | Cash | 125 " | |
| | | | 1 Ton Guano | 42 | |
| | | | 33 Stamps | 1 " | |
| Mar | 3 | " | S. Ford | 89 84 | |
| | 6 | " | T P Pease | 100 " | |
| | 11 | " | A A Solomons & Co | 134 07 | |
| | | " | L W Wall | 8 | |
| | 16 | " | J J Morgan | 27 " | 600.26 |
| | | " | 600 bushels Corn @ 90¢ | 540 16 | |
| | | | 10200 Brick | 119 | |
| | | | 10 bbls Lime & Expences on Cargo | 30 13 | |
| | 22 | " | two dfts S. Ford $85 & $64.18 | $ 149 18 | |
| | 23 | " | J W Myers | 26 " | |
| | | " | H A Grant . . . . . . . . . | 50 | 1514.73 |
| | 27 | " | E P Brown | 35 | $ 1549.73 |

## N A Hardee & Co contra Cr/

| | | | |
|---|---|---|---|
| 1852 | | | |
| Oct 30 | By | 1959 Bushels Rough Rice making 69 Casks | $ 1357 43 |
| April 3 | By | 4 Bags & 2 pockets cotton | 662 54 |

BALLANCED

| | | | |
|---|---|---|---|
| 1854 | | | |
| Feb 28 | " | Cash from Mr Fiske | $ 2000 00 |
| March 3 | " | dft on Ravanel & Co | 1000 " |
| 16 | " | Postells dft on Barton & Velliger | 1806 37 |
| | | | 4806 37 |

## Dr/ H. F Grant in a/c with

| Date | | | Item | Amount | | Total |
|---|---|---|---|---|---|---|
| 1854 | | | | | | |
| March | 27 | To | Amount brt over. . . . . . . | $ 1549 | 73 | |
| April | 15 | " | 50 Shares Exchange Bank first Installment of 25 per cent | 1250 | " | |
| | 22 | " | Charles Stevens . . . . . . . . | 143 | 46 | |
| | 27 | " | Paid Myself | 200 | " | |
| May | | " | J F Meeker | 140 | " | |
| | 22 | " | Boards, Sashes &c &c . . . . | 46 | 81 | |
| | 26 | " | Paints, brushes, pallets &c | 13 | 19 | |
| June | 6 | " | Mrs F Grant | 100 | " | |
| | 29 | " | 100 bushels Corn | 95 | " | |
| | " | " | Sashes | 17 | 05 | |
| July | 8 | " | Cash sent me . . . . . . . . . . | 30 | " | |
| | 9 | " | Dr Royal | 57 | | |
| | | " | T M Forman | 170 | | |
| | 20 | " | Edts Georgian 2 yrs . . . . . | 10 | | |
| Sept | 1 | " | M C B Wright Road fine | 117 | " | |
| | 21 | " | J W Moore | 5 | 37½ | |
| | 28 | " | W H Myers for Wheels | 46 | " | |
| | | " | Bishop Elliott for Supper in Savanah | 50 | " | |
| Oct | 4 | " | R Grant | 17 | " | 4057.61 |
| Nov | 10 | | S Ford | 125 | " | |
| Dec | | | Thowburn & Co for trees | | | |
| Dec | 20 | " | Mitchel & Pease | 30 | " | |
| 1855 | | | | | | |
| Jany | 12 | " | E P Brown | 105 | " | |
| | 17 | " | D H B Troup | 100 | " | |
| | 22 | " | Self | 400 | " | |
| | 29 | " | " | 240 | | |
| Feb | 10 | " | Robinson & Camp | 91 | 75 | |
| | | " | T P Pease | 74 | 71 | |
| | | " | Boards Lime & Laths | | | |
| | 23 | " | Aikin & Burns | 74 | 34 | |
| | | " | T P Pease | 97 | " | |
| | 20 | " | 56¼ Bushels Corn | 68 | 89 | 5365.40 |

N A. HARDEE & CO. CONTRA Cr/

| 1854 | | | | |
|---|---|---|---|---|
| March 27 | By Balance brought over | $ 4806 37 | |
| | " 9 Bags S. I. Cotton. . . . . . | 763 30 | |
| April 6 | " J H Coupers check B[ank] S[tate] G[eorgia] | 433 79 | |
| May 2 | " Cash deposited | 500 " | |
| | " Cash from H S [sic] Fiske | 339 00 | |
| 22 | " Dft on A Low & Co for | 98 " | |
| June 21 | " J H Coupers dft on R Mure | 295 90 | 7236.36 |
| | " 1st Installment on 50 Shares of Exchange Bank | 1250 00 | |

## Dr/ H. F Grant in a/c with

| | | | | | |
|---|---|---|---|---|---|
| 1855 | | | | | |
| April 20 | " | C Stevens for freight | $ 54 50 | | |
| May 10 | " | D B Nichols | 28 75 | | |
| | " | 500 Bushels of Corn | 625 " | | |
| 12 | " | Lockwood & Johnston | 84 50 | | |
| June 6 | " | G B Mitchell | 233 " | | |
| 9 | " | Chaffer & Co | 29 70 | | |
| 14 | " | F Silber . . . . . . . . . . . | 7 38 | | |
| | " | Express to Marietta | 2 " | | |
| 16 | " | C H. Campfield | 69 " | 1133.83 | |
| July 30 | " | J. J Morgan. . . . . . . . . . | 60 27 | | |
| Augst 10 | " | My Self | 100 " | | |
| 18 | " | " " | 50 | | |
| | " | F R Goulding | 100 | 1444.08 | |
| 20 | " | M C B Wright Taxes . . . . | 100 | | |
| Sept | " | C C Poole | 85 90 | | |
| Oct 8 | " | J W Myers | 10 " | | |
| 15 | " | Collins & Shine . . . . . . . | 24 41 | | |
| | " | Bill by Northern Belle | 57 42 | | |
| 17 | " | By Cash Myself | 100 | | |
| 19 | " | W H Wiltberger & Co | 50 | | |
| 25 | " | T. T Long | 110 " | | |
| Nov 14 | " | Edward B. Moylan | 46 " | | |
| | " | Bill castings | 68 75 | | |
| Decr 10 | " | A J Bucknor | 65 " | 2161.06 | |
| | " | 1 bbl Cement | 2 46 | | |
| 17 | " | 200 Bushels Corn 95¢ | | | |
| | | 24 Bushel Oats 75¢ | | | |
| | | & Expences | 213 38 | | |
| 25 | " | A A De Lorme | 17 84 | | |
| 31 | " | T P Pease | 100 " | | |
| 1856 | | | | | |
| Jany 15 | " | E C P Dart | 135 " | | |
| | " | S Palmer & Son | 153 39 | | |
| | | C H Camfield | 54 08 | | |
| | " | Go S Nichols & Co | 109 25 | 785.40 | |
| | | | | 2946.46 | |

N A HARDEE & CO   CONTRA   Cr/

| | | |
|---|---|---|
| 1855 | | |
| March 12 | By balance of a/c due me | $ 2834 16 |
| | " Overcharge on Express Box | 4 00 |
| 1856 | | |
| Jany 3 | By Cash deposted [sic] | 500 |
| | | 3338 16 |
| | | 2946 46 |
| | | $ 391 70 |

## Dr/ H. F Grant in a/c with

| 1856 | | | | | |
|---|---|---|---|---|---|
| Jany 21 | To | Mrs Frew | 9 | " | |
| 23 | " | John Cant | 40 | | |
| 28 & 29 | | E P Brown | 50 | | |
| 29 | " | Collins & Shine | 23 | 20 | |
| | " | Dr Holmes | 15 | | |
| Feb 1 | " | De Witte & Morgan | 616 | 58 | |
| | " | Aikin & Burns | 13 | 25 | |
| | " | D A Gardner | 20 | 62 | |
| | " | W T Williams | 23 | 76 | |
| | " | Rokenbaugh & Ladson | 8 | 06 | |
| | " | Wm H Guion | 244 | 50 | |
| 3 | " | D H B Troup professionally | 100 | " | |
| 5 | " | Claghorn & Cunningham | 862 | 14 | |
| 6 | " | Mitchel & Pease | 371 | 49 | |
| | " | A A Solomons & Co | 155 | 67 | |
| | " | T. P Pease . . . . . . . . . | 62 | 74 | |
| | " | J W Morrell & Co . . . . . . | 173 | 68 | 2789.63 |
| | " | J. F S Heald | 4 | 50 | |
| 14 | " | Bill by Northern Belle | 513 | 55 | |
| 18 | " | Bill of Fruit | 2 | 17 | |
| 21 | " | A Ponce | 51 | 27 | |
| | " | Commission on 4000 bu Rice | 108 | | |
| | " | Freight by Northern Belle | | | |
| Mar 3 | " | John Cant | 50 | " | 3519.12 |
| 4 | " | Lockwood & Johnston | 350 | " | |
| 10 | " | Horton & Rikeman | 145 | 05 | |
| | " | Myself | 400 | | |
| | " | W H May & Co | 91 | 77 | |
| | " | Valesquez . . . . . . . . . . | 29 | 75 | |
| 13 | " | Mr F R Goulding | 100 | | |
| | " | Mes E H Hogan | 105 | | |
| | " | C C Poole . . . . . . . . . | 48 | 20 | 4788.89 |

N A Hardee & Co contra Cr/

1856

| | | | |
|---|---|---|---|
| Jany 15 | By | Amt brought over | $ 391 70 |
| 29 | " | Deposite [sic] from Mr Fiske | 6343 " |
| Feb 22 | " | deposite [sic] from Mr S H Fiske | 1000 " |
| Apr | " | " " Do Do | 708 56 |

## Dr/ H. F GRANT WITH

| [1856] | | | | | |
|---|---|---|---|---|---|
| March 18 | To | Amt brt forward | 4788 89 | | |
| | " | Paid Mrs Grant | $ 100 00 | | |
| 24 | " | W H Wiltberger & Co | 149 60 | | |
| | " | Robinson & Camp. . . . . . | 56 37 | | |
| Apr 1 | " | Wm Morgan . . . . . . . . . | 120 | | |
| | " | Bill Lime, Laths &c | 58 62 | | |
| 3 | " | G. C Dent . . . . . . . . . . | 36 50 | 5309.98 | |
| 18 | " | John Cant | 30 " | | |
| | " | J Q A Butler | 200 | | |
| 24 | " | D H B Troup Seed Rice | 234 | | |
| May 2 | " | 4 Bbls Lime | 6 96 | | |
| 6 | " | Mrs Freeland . . . . . . . . . | 42 95 | | |
| 14 | " | J Q A Butler . . . . . . . . . | 122 87 | | |
| 16 | " | D H B Troup | 200 | | |
| 19 | " | My order | 80 | | |
| | " | C C Poole | 102 99 | | |
| | " | Lockwood & Johnston | 400 | | |

| 1856 | | | | |
|---|---|---|---|---|
| June | " | Mrs Frew | $ 30 67 | |
| | " | S W Taylor adm Lowry | 400 " | |
| 6 | " | Wm F Day for Monemea | 140 " | |
| 9 | " | G C Dent | 55 " | |
| | " | Wm M Tunno | 15 39 | |
| 10 | " | Butler & Frierson . . . . . . | 196 59 | |
| 12 | " | B M Cargyle M D | 20 " | |
| | " | Nevitt Lathrop & Rogers | 422 36 | |
| | " | 2 Bbls Lime. . . . . . . . . . | 4 27 | |
| 17 | " | H. F. Grant Jr | 12 " | 1284.28 |
| 25 | " | W W Hazzard . . . . . . . . | 75 " | |
| | " | E P Brown | 25 | |
| July 2 | " | 200 Bushels Corn & Expense | 138 06 | |
| | " | Capt Stevens $25 Myself $25 | 50 | |
| | | | | $ 1584.34 |

## N A Hardee & Co contra Cr/

| | | |
|---|---|---|
| 1856 | | |
| | By Amt brought forward. . . . . . . . . | $ 8443 26 |
| April 17 | " S H Fiske deposite [sic] . . . . . . | 708 56 |

---

| | | |
|---|---|---|
| 1856 | | |
| June 1 | By Balance due me | 1780 13 |

## Dr/ H. F Grant in a/c with

|  | | | | | |
|---|---|---|---|---|---|
| 1856 | | | | | |
| July 10 | To | Amount brt over | $ 1584 | 34 | |
| 4 | " | Cash sent me | 50 | " | |
| 10 | " | A A DeLorme | 3 | 37 | |
| 19 | " | R B Hilton & Co . . . . . . | 3 | | |
| 22 | " | Lockwood & Johnston . . . . | 729 | 13 | |
| | " | Horace Morse | 6 | " | |
| | " | H. F. Grant Jr | 15 | | |
| Augst 25 | " | T P Pease . . . . . . . . . | 61 | 23 | |
| | " | Road commissioners . . . . . | 57 | " | |
| Sept 25 | " | H. F Grant Jr . . . . . . . | 35 | | |
| Oct 10 | " | M C B Wright | 19 | 73 | |
| 30 | " | Revd F R Goulding | 137 | 77 | |
| Nov 8 | " | 200 Bushels Corn . . . . . . | 190 | 32 | |
| | " | 50 " Rice flour . . . . | | | |
| 19 | " | Mitchel & Pease | 50 | " | |
| | " | Thomas Barns | 7 | 62 | |
| 1857 | | | | | |
| Jany 1 | To | Willis Hall | 25 | " | |
| | " | W L Morgan Beef | 16 | | |
| 14 | " | Rev E P Brown | 71 | 80 | |
| | " | W Warner | 145 | — | |
| | " | S. Palmer & Son . . . . . . | 115 | 35 | |
| 30 | " | G S Nichols & Co . . . . . . | 201 | 50 | |
| | " | Dr James Holmes | 30 | – | 3680.17 |
| 16 | " | E P Brown . . . . . . . . . | 35 | | |
| | " | H. F Grant Jr | 610 | | |
| 27 | " | Corn by Elias Reed | 105 | 99 | |
| March 30 | " | H F Grant Jr | 50 | | |
| | " | Wm F. Day for Monemia Wilson | 140 | | 4621.16 |
| April 6 | " | James P Johnston for M P Johnston | 150 | | |
| | " | J Rokenbaugh | 12 | 50 | |
| 8 | " | 500 bushels Corn by Elias Reed | 430 | 20 | |
| 23 | " | Myself | 200 | | |
| 25 | " | W. H Wiltberger & Co | 100 | | 5513.86 |
| 28 | " | T P Pease | 35 | 38 | |

## N A Hardee & Co contra Cr/

1856

| | | | | |
|---|---|---|---|---|
| June | 1 | By Balance of a/c | $ 1780 13 | |
| July | 4 | " Check on New York | 50 00 | |
| Nov | 8 | By 3247 Bushels Rough Rice | 2439 95 | |
| March | 8 | " 2850 Bushels Rice 95¢ | 2497 31 | 6767.39 |
| April | 23 | " By Check on Hartford Bank | 100 " | |

[ Dr *cont.*, April 1857 ]

| | | |
|---|---|---|
| " D H B Troup . . . . . . . . . | 102 50 | 5651.74 |
| " H. F. Grant Jr | 130 00 | |
| " 5 Gallons Whiskey | 18 62 | |
| " J Cromley for Boots | 6 50 | |
| | | 305.12 |
| | | 5956.86 |

## Dr/ H. F. Grant in a/c with

1857

| Month | Day | | Item | Amount | Total |
|---|---|---|---|---|---|
| June | 16 | To | F R Goulding- | $ 150 " | |
| July | 13 | " | Miss Gardner | 10 " | |
| Augst | 1 | " | Alexander Blue for Whiskey . . | 61 90 | |
| | | " | Savh Georgian | 4 " | |
| | 10 | " | 150 Bu Corn $1.15¢ | 185 32 | 411.22 |
| Oct | | | 3 Bushels Hair & expences | | |
| Nov | 16 | | 100 bu Corn & 50 bu flour & the expences | 115 78 | |
| | 24 | " | Paid me in person | 400 " | |

1858

| Month | Day | | Item | Amount | Total |
|---|---|---|---|---|---|
| Jany | 30 | " | 100 bushes Corn & expences | 84 36 | |
| Feb | 4 | " | S. Palmer & Son | 161 54 | |
| | | " | G H Nichols | 177 57 | |
| | | " | C H Rikeman | 48 75 | |
| | 8 | " | Dr Holmes | 32 00 | 1020.00 |
| | | " | J Cromley . . . . . . . . . | 20 | |
| Mah | 1 | " | De Witt & Morgan | 1025 23 | |
| | | " | Mss Thompson Phil . . . . | 64 91 | |
| | 2 | " | M. Pease & Co | 641 56. | 1751.70 |
| | | " | M Powell & Co Ice . . . . | 68 85 | |
| | | " | W S Sawyer & Co. . . . . . | 16 78 | |
| Feb | 19 | " | Bill Rice flour &c | 13 03 | |
| Mah | 10 | " | Butler & Frierson | 157 52 | 256.18 |
| | | " | Robinson & Camp | 82 10 | |
| | | " | S A Tennson . . . . . . . . | 20 10 | |
| | 15 | " | $345\frac{1}{4}$, Bushels Corn 75¢ 50 bu Rice flour $37\frac{1}{2}$¢ & Expence | 285 91 | |
| | 20 | " | J J Morgan Beef . . . . . . | 35 | 423.11 |
| | 30 | " | H. F. Grant Jr | 30 | 3862.21 |
| April | 1 | " | Nevitt, Lathrop & Rogers | 447 45 | |
| | 2 | | $607\frac{1}{2}$ Bu Corn 80¢ | 497 41 | |
| | 19 | | Dr H A Grant | 591 | |
| May | 5 | " | McKee & Bennett | 41 36 | |
| | | " | J Le Grovenstine | 32 42 | $5472.85 |

## N A Hardee & Co contra Cr/

1857

| | | | |
|---|---|---|---|
| June 15 | By | Balance of a/c rendered | $ 275 95 |
| Nov 19 | " | 4075 Bushels Rice by E. Reed | 2143 36 |
| Mar 23 | " | 3472 Bushels Rice by E.[lias] R[eed] | 2534 60 |
| | " | 3 Casks Middling Rice | 35 33 |
| May | | 696 Bushels Sheet Rice @ 75¢ | $ 474 15 |

## Dr/ H. F. GRANT IN A/C WITH

1858

| Date | | Item | | Amount | Total |
|---|---|---|---|---|---|
| May 20 | To | balance from old a/c | $ | 51 73 | |
| 24 | " | Mitchel, Pease & Co | | 267 94 | |
| June 1 | " | E. P Brown | | 50 | |
| 13 | " | Capt Everglade | | 62 " | |
| 14 | " | Myself | | 150 " | |
| July 23 | " | M J Buckner | | 93 " | |
| 21 | " | Bill of Goods | | 22 07 | |
| Augst 11 | " | J J Morgan | | 100 — | |
| Sept 23 | " | Battey, Hickman & Co | | 320 " | |
| Nov 4 | " | W. H Battey | | 37 50 | |
| 11 | " | Myself | | 200 | 1354.24 |
| | " | 200 Bushels Corn | | 190 24 | 190.24 |
| | " | 1 Flute & Note Book | | 4 50 | |
| | " | SubScription to Republican try weekly . . . . . . . . . . . | | 4 " | |
| Dec 24 | " | H. F Grant Jr | | 25 00 | |
| 31 | " | M. C B Wright for Taxes | | 122 76 | |

1859

| Date | | Item | | Amount | Total |
|---|---|---|---|---|---|
| Jany 13 | " | M Molina . . . . . . . . . | | 10 00 | |
| 15 | " | Paid R & J Lacklison | | 259 83 | 426.19 |
| | " | 6000 Brick | | 60 " | |
| | " | 10 Bbls Lime | | 10 " | |
| | " | 1 Wind fan | | 42 " | |
| Feb | | Charges on *do* | | 11 20 | |
| 14 | " | J J Morgan | | 20 " | |
| | " | C. Grant note in Bank | | 100 — | |
| 15 | " | W H May . . . . . . . . . | | 113 96 | 357.16 |
| March 3 | " | H F. Grant Jr | | 50 " | |
| 8 | " | 8000 Brick & 12 Bls Lime | | 95 00 | |
| April 1 | " | M J. Buckner | | 229 25 | |
| | " | Geo S Nichols & Co | | 258 | |
| 6 | " | Revd E P Brown . . . . . . | | 75 4 | 487.25 |
| 7 | " | E M Blount Flats | | 79 | |
| 11 | " | Isaac M Aikin for Mule | | 104 | |
| | " | James M Brown Mason | | 65 | 248 |
| 13 | " | De Witte & Morgan | $ | 313 32 | |

## N A Hardee & Co contra Cr/

| | | |
|---|---|---|
| 1858 | | |
| Decr 14 | By 3930 Bushels Rice from Grantly | $2562 36 |
| 1859 | | |
| April 23 | By 3610 Bushels Rice from Grantly | 2811 29 |
| | | 5373 65 |

[ Dr *cont.*, April 1859 ]

| | | | | |
|---|---|---|---|---|
| | " | A A Solomons & Co | 166 66 | |
| | " | Claghorn & Cuningham | 1102 00 | |
| 14 | " | 811 Bushes Corn 90¢ & Storage 40 Bbls Lime | 815 00 | |
| 19 | " | H. P Horton | 56 65 | |
| | " | Nevitt Lathrop & Rogers | 343 36 | |
| 23 | " | John J Morgan | 300 " | |
| | " | Dr James Holmes | 34 " | |
| | " | R B Donnelly | 100 " | 3230.99 |

## Dr/ H. F Grant in a/c with N. A. Hardee & Co.

| Date | | Item | | Amount | Total |
|---|---|---|---|---|---|
| 1859 | | | | | |
| May 20 | To | Amount brt from old a/c | | $1455 11 | |
| 23 | " | Woodruff & Anderson for Lumber | | 307 30 | |
| 28 | " | Wm Carson for Lumber | | 332 00 | |
| June 10 | " | Horace Barnard | | 50 00 | |
| July 22 | " | Bill by Northern Belle | | 240 82 | |
| Augst 17 | " | H. F. Grant Jr | | 75 00 | |
| Sept 4 | " | Dr Leffler | | 24 00 | |
| 21 | " | R B Donnolly . . . . . . . . . | | 241 12 | |
| | " | Burr Winton | | 80 " | |
| 25 | " | H. F Grant Jr . . . . . . . . | | 50 | |
| | " | T C Downie . . . . . . . . . | | 56 " | |
| | " | Lewis Dupree Tax collector | | 122 70 | |
| Oct 28 | " | John A Carpenter | | 32 00 | |
| | " | 1 Bll Plaster paris | | | |
| 27 | | Invoice of Flooring boards &c | | 115 80 | |
| Nov 17 | " | Morris Whithers, Mason | | 310 " | 3491.88 |
| | " | 300 Bu Corn . . . . . . . . . | | | |
| | " | Fav of R S Pritchard for Beef | | 25 " | |
| | " | " " Thomas Seeborn for Corn | | 8 25 | |
| 1860 | | for Corn. . . . . . . . . | | 11 25 | |
| Feb 14 | " | 734 Bushels of Corn & Expences | | 802 14 | |
| 1 | " | G S Nichols & Co | | 62 50 | |
| | " | M J Buckner | | 206 90 | |
| | " | S Palmer & Son | | 443 36 | |
| | " | J M Cooper & Co | | 34 46 | |
| | " | W A Price | $5625.57 | 201 47 | 948.69 |
| 10 | " | A A Solomons | | 238 37 | |
| | " | J Hasbrouck | | 127 61 | |
| 15 | " | E C P Dart | | 50 " | |
| 17 | " | T T Willmott | | 69 25 | |
| | " | D Y Shine | $6852.70 | 825 45 | 1310.68 |
| 20 | " | De Witte & Morgan | | 590 69 | |
| | " | Nevitt, Lathrop & Rogers | | 651 88 | |

[This page was torn out of the Journal.]

## Dr/ H. F Grant in a/c with

1852

| | | | |
|---|---|---|---|
| March 23 | To | 300 Bushels of Corn | 210 78 |
| | " | paid for Bacon | 163 23 |
| April 1 | " | Paid J B Gordon | 52 00 |
| | " | 6 doz Ale . . . . . . . . . . . . . . . | 19 37 |
| | " | Sashes for Morgans house | 5 " |
| 24 | " | To Cash J K Teft | 200 |
| | | | 650 38 |
| June 20 | " | N A Hardee & Co | 288 42 |
| 30 | " | W Matthiessen | 62 50 |

1853

| | | | |
|---|---|---|---|
| Feb 1 | " | G E Keen | $ 114 39 |
| 28 | " | Mrs E H Hogan | 105 " |
| Mar 18 | " | D W Southerland | 50 " |
| | " | Mrs Grant & daughters | |
| April 25 | " | Mrs Du pre . . . . . . . . . . . . . | 171 03 |
| May 3 | " | " " | 24 00 |
| 10 | " | R Habersham & Son | 2029 76 |

## W M Tunno contra Cr/

1852

| | | | |
|---|---|---|---|
| March 23 | By | 874 Bushels Rough Rice @ 79¢ | 622 89 |
| 28 | " | T P Hugers draft on Ravanl & Co | 40 62½ |
| 29 | " | Dr Troups dft Legare, O Hear & Co | 40 62½ |
| April 24 | " | 305 Bushels Rice. . . . . . . . . . | 297 17 |
| | | | 1001 31 |
| | | BY BALANCE | 350 93 |

SETTLED H. F. GRANT

---

1853

| | | | |
|---|---|---|---|
| Jany 28 | By | 2625 = Bushels R Rice | $ 2294 10 |
| Mar 28 | " | T. P Hugers draft for | 500 |
| | " | Draft on Lockwood & Johnston | 14 75 |

## Dr/ H. F Grant in a/c Tunno Pinckney & Co

| 1854 | | | |
|---|---|---|---|
| Jany | 9 | To 200 Bushels of Corn & Expences | $ 184 50 |
| April | 6 | To dft in favr D H B Troup | 150 " |
| | " | G B Walsh agt for McC & Norton | 77 83 |
| | " | Robinson & Camp | 110 50 |
| | | BALLANCED | 2150.18 |

H. F Grant in a/c Tunno Pinckney & Co
contra $C^r$/

1854

| | | |
|---|---|---|
| Feb | 7 By 2370 bushels Rice | $ 2150 18 |

SETTLED IN FULL H. F. GRANT

# Slave Lists

## List of Negroes Belonging to Elizafield Plantation

### *Property of Hugh Fraser Grant*

KEY: *x equals old*
*o equals young*

| January 1834 | *Prime 1834* | *Rate 1839* |
|---|---|---|
| 1 Driver John | 1 | 1 |
| 2 Nelly | x½ | ½ |
| 3 O. Cinda Died 26 April 1834 | x½ | |
| 4 M. John | 1 | 1 |
| 5 Matilla | 1 | 1 |
| 6 Looky | | ½o |
| 7 Rebecca born Sept 1836 Obt 1 Sept 1840 | | |
| Lydia born Oct 1839 | | |
| 8 Mingo Sold | 1 | 1 |
| 9 Bobbett | 1 | 1 |
| 10 Stephen | 1 | 1 |
| 11 Judy | 1 | 1 |
| 12 Jack | ½o | 1 |
| 13 Hannah | | |
| 14 Cinda | | |
| 15 April | 1 | 1 |
| 16 Sue | 1 | 1 |
| 17 Jackson | | |
| Jacob | | |
| 18 Toby Died 1 Feb 1842 | 1 | 1 |
| 19 Jeany | 1 | 1 |
| 20 Amey. Jeany born June 1841 died Sept 18, 1841 | ½o | 1 |
| 21 Delia | ¼o | ¾ |
| 22 Jupeter Died 18 May 1838 | x½ | |
| 23 Bella | x½ | ½ |
| 24 Prince | 1 | 1 |

| | *Prime 1834* | *Rate 1839* |
|---|---|---|
| 25 Sary | 1 | 1 |
| 26 Dinah Born 6 Nov 1838 | | |
| Jupeter Born 3 May 1841 Dead | | |
| 27 Alick Sold | 1 | 1 |
| 28 Ben Sold | 1 | 1 |
| 29 Susy & child Jacob Born 20 July 1847 | 1 | 1 |
| 30 Richard | | $\frac{1}{2}$ |
| 31 Maryann. Died 21 Dec 1838 | | |
| 32 Abraham | | |
| 33 Molly Died June 1836 | | |
| 34 Caesar | 1 | 1 |
| 35 Biney | 1 | 1 |
| 36 Molly | | |
| 37 J Stake | 1 | 1 |
| 38 Bess | 1 | 1 |
| 39 Charles | | $\frac{1}{2}$ |
| 40 Mary Margaret Died April 1840 | | |
| 41 Winter Died 27 April 1835 | 1 | |
| 42 Nancy | 1 | 1 |
| 43 Jim | 1 | 1 |
| 44 Mirah | 1 | 1 |
| 45 Venus Died Sept 1836 | 1 | |
| 46 March | $\frac{1}{2}$o | 1 |
| 47 Hardtimes | | $\frac{1}{2}$ |
| 48 T. Abraham | 1 | 1 |
| 59 Phillis Sold | 1 | 1 |
| 50 Flora Sold | $\frac{1}{4}$o | 1 |
| Affey Born May 1842 Sold | | |
| 51 Fortune | 1 | 1 |
| 52 Phoebe | 1 | 1 |
| 53 Ned Sold Nov 1843 Dead | $\frac{1}{2}$o | 1 |
| 54 Harry | $\frac{1}{4}$o | 1 |
| 55 Kate | | |
| 56 Hannah | | |
| 57 Adell | | |
| 58 Sampson Died 26 April 1836 | 1 | |
| 59 Sophy Died July 1842 | x$\frac{1}{2}$ | $\frac{1}{4}$ |
| 60 George | | $\frac{1}{2}$ |

| | *Prime 1834* | *Rate 1839* |
|---|---|---|
| 61 Julys Betty | 1 | 1 |
| 62 Elsy | | |
| Died 1836 | | |
| 63 Phoebe | | |
| Joe | | |
| 64 Jack Died 12 Decr 1841 | 1 | 1 |
| 65 Nanny Died 18 Nov 1843 | x$\frac{1}{2}$ | $\frac{1}{2}$ |
| 66 O Scipio Dead | | |
| 67 Grace Died 6 April 1840 | | |
| 68 Y Scipio | 1 | 1 |
| 69 Dido | 1 | 1 |
| 70 Clora | 1 | 1 |
| 71 Harry | 1 | 1 |
| 72 Jeany | 1 | 1 |
| 73 May | $\frac{1}{4}$o | 1 |
| 74 Cumsey | | $\frac{1}{2}$o |
| Kate | | |
| George Born 27 Augst 1847 | | |
| 122 [1] Duncan | $\frac{1}{2}$o | 1 |
| Purchased January 1839 | Prime | |
| Cost $3,000. | 1839 | |
| 123 Rina | 1 | 1 |
| 124 Margaret, Eve Born 1 July 1839 | 1 | 1 |
| " Died Oct — 1839 | | |
| 125 Sissy or Cate | $\frac{1}{2}$o | $\frac{1}{2}$ |
| 126 Phoebe | | |
| 127 Frederick | | |
| 128 Prince | | |
| Purchased January 1841 | | |
| 129 Jim | 1 | |
| 130 Charlotte | 1 | |
| 131 Chanty | | |
| 132 Caesar } Sold for $3,150 | | |
| 133 Lydia | | 3150 |
| 134 Clarissa | | 1760 |
| Jacob Cost $1,760. | | —— |
| | | $ 1390 [profit] |

[1] Three pages listing slaves numbered 75 to 121 inclusive are missing.

## Births from 1838 to 1845

| Date | Name | | Name of the Mother |
|---|---|---|---|
| June 1839 | Eve (died) | | Margaret |
| July " | Sam | | Haigar |
| Sept " | Mary Ann | | Nanny |
| Oct 15 | Lydia | | Matilla |
| 1840 | | | |
| January 1 | Joe | | Betty |
| April 29 | Satilla | | Mirah |
| 1841 | | | |
| May 3 | Jupeter (died) | | Sary |
| June 15 | Jeany | | Amey |
| 1842 | | | |
| Jany 7 | Amos | | Haigar |
| Feb 1 | Beck | | Dido |
| May 4 | Affey | | Flora |
| July 17 | Bella (died) | | Nanny |
| Aug 26 | Daniel | | Mira |
| " 28 | Died 3 Sept 1842 | | Nann |
| Sept 6 | Jacob | | Charlotte |
| " 28 | Toney | | Sue |
| Oct 17 | Dinah Bella (died) | | Sary |
| 1843 | | | |
| Oct 16 | Renty | | Nann |
| 1844 | | | |
| March | Jacob | | Susy |
| Augst 20 } | Died from | | Sue |
| " 30 } | whooping | | Nanny |
| Sept 1 } | cough | | Dido |
| Oct 7 | Andrew Died from Cough | | Mira |
| Jany 1845 | William | | Margaret |
| March 8 | Kate or Sissy | | Cumsey |
| " 20 | Bella | | Catherine |
| July 4 | Present | | Amey |
| Augst 25 | Rina (died) | | Sary |
| Sept 11 | Rina | Rina | Kate |

## Partial List of Negroes—about 1848[2]

D Prince
Nancy
George Ann
Mary Ann
Mathew
Simon born 22 Oct 1848
David born 15 May 1852
London
Sary
Dinah
Bella
Sary — Pussy Boy born 25 Augst 1850
Richard
Hardtimes
Susy
Venus dead 1849
Gabrael born Augst 1851
Pown or Abram
Caesar
Biney
Molly
Cuffy Child
J Stake
Bess
Abraham
Nancy
Mira
March
Amaretta
Rose 53[3]
Jacob Dead
Fortune
Phoebe
Kate Tyra dead

Hannah
Juno born 1848
Catherine
Bella
Cretia
Sabrinna
Andrew
Mira
Kate
Satella
Daniel
Ella
Amelia
Luce born 3 Sept 1851
O. Grace
Emperor
Haigar
Hannibal
Abbey
Phillis
London
Sam
Amos
Lot
Nancy, Joe born 1851 dead 1852
O Dinah died 15 Augst 1848
Pussy
Chance
Cyrus
William
Bruster
Nelly
Patty
Mark born July 1848

[2] The page heading in the manuscript Journal indicates that this is a continuation of a list of slaves, the first page of which was torn out.

[3] Markings on the page suggest that this figure indicates total Negroes listed to this point.

O Rina
Margaret
William
March
John born 29 Oct 1850
Kate

July dead 1849
Celia
Phoebe Jeany born 1 Sept 1852
Frederck
Prince

## 1st Sept 1851 Negroes at Elizafield

M John, Matilla, Lydia
Looky, Perida
Judy
Jack, Cumsey, Sissy, Charles, Lucy
Frederck, Sarah, Hannah
Richard, Hannah, John, Caroline
April, Bella, John
Robert, Phoebe, James
Duncan, Sue, Toney, Clarinda, Jacob
Jeany, James
Delia, John, Butler, Fanny
D Scipio, Amey, Betsey, Beck, Martha
Jefferson
Clora
Jackson, Adell, Caroline
O Bella
D Prince, Nancy, George Ann, Mary Ann
Mather, Simon, David
London died 2d April 1855 Sary, Dinah, Bella Pussy, Molle
Hardtimes, Susy, Jacob, child
Pown, Hannah, Juno
Caesar, Biney
Molly, Cuffy, Pumus

J. Stake, Bess
Abram & Nancy
Mira
March, Amaretta Rose
Fortune
Phoebe
Kate
George, Venus
Caesar, Abbey
Natt, Betty, Joe
Bobbett
O. Harry, Jeany
Bruster, Mary
Mark, Kate, Celia, Grace
Y Harry, Catherine, Bella, Cretia
Sabrinna, Sylvia, Ned born March 1855
L. Dinah, Anthony
Andrew, Mira, Kate, Stella, Daniel
Ella, Amelia, child
O Grace
Emperor, Haigar, Phillis, London
Sam, Amos, Lot, Nancy
Hannibal, Patty, Mark, Lydia
Pussy, Cyrus, William
86[4]
Chance, Looky, Penda

[4] This figure also probably refers to total Negroes to this point.

| | |
|---|---|
| Nelly died April 1855 Consumption | Margaret, William, March, John, Elizabeth |
| Rina | Prince, George Ann |

## List of Negroes 1 April 1855

| *Rate* | | *Rate* | |
|---|---|---|---|
| 1 | Driver Prince dead 1862 | 1 | April dead 1862 |
| 1 | Nancy | 1 | Bella |
| 1 | Mary Ann | 1 | John |
| | Mathew | 1 | Robert |
| | Simon | 1 | Phoebe |
| | Elvira | | James |
| | | | April |
| 1 | D. Scipio | | |
| 1 | Amey | 1 | Duncan |
| | Betsey | 1 | Sue |
| | Rebecca | ½ | Toney |
| | Martha | | Clarinda |
| | | | Jacob |
| 1 | Matilla | | |
| 1 | Judy | 1 | N Jeany dead 1862 |
| 1 | Jack | 1 | Delia |
| 1 | Cumsey | | Butler dead 1860 |
| | Sissy | | Fanny born 1853 |
| | Charles | | George |
| | Lucy | 1 | Clora |
| | Jack | | |
| | Thomas | 1 | Jackson |
| | | 1 | Adele |
| 1 | Frederick | | Harrett born 1853 |
| 1 | Sarah | | Lear |
| | Hannah born 1854 | | Roger, Will |
| | Lydia | | London died 2[d] April 1855 |
| 1 | Phillis | 1 | Sary |
| 1 | Richard, | 1 | Dinah |
| | John | | Bella |
| | Caroline | | Pussy |

| Rate | | Rate | |
|---|---|---|---|
| | London | 1 | Mark |
| | | 1 | Kate |
| 1 | Hardtimes | | Celia |
| 1 | Susy | | Grace |
| | Gabrael | | Augustus 80[5] |
| | Aaron | | Maretta |
| | Rose | | |
| | | 1 | Y Harry |
| 1 | Pown | 1 | Catharine |
| | Juno | | Bella or Dore |
| 1 | Caesar | | Cretia |
| 1 | Biney | | Sabrinna |
| 1 | Molly | | Sylvia |
| | Cuffy | | Ned born 1855 died 1856 |
| | Girl | | |
| | | 1 | L Dinah Died Pneumonia 17 March 1856 |
| ½ | J Stake | 1 | Anthony |
| ½ | Bess | 1 | Andrew |
| 1 | Abraham | 1 | Mira |
| 1 | Nancy | 1 | Stella (child) |
| 1 | Mira | ½ | Daniel |
| 1 | March died 1858 | | Ella |
| 1 | Amaretta | | Amelia |
| 1 | Rose | | Hasford born 1853 |
| | | | Comodore |
| 1 | Fortune | | |
| 1 | Phoebe | ½ | O Grace |
| 1 | Venus | 1 | Emperor |
| 1 | Caesar | 1 | Haigar dead 1862 |
| 1 | Abbey | 1 | London |
| | Natt dead 1855 | | Sam |
| | Betty dead 1855 | | Amos |
| ½ | Joe | | Lot |
| | | | Nancy |
| 1 | Bobbett dead 1862 | | |
| | O. Harry dead 1857 | | |
| ½ | Jeany | 1 | Hannibal |
| 1 | Buster | 1 | Patty |
| 1 | Mary | | Mark |

[5] Possible count of slaves.

*Rate*

York

1 Pussy
1 Cyrus
1 Kate
Duncan

1 William

1 Chance
1 Looky

*Rate*

Penda
Pussy

Nella dead 1855

1 Rina sold
1 Margaret
William
March
John & Daniel
Elizabeth dead 1855

# Crop Summaries

## Crop of 1836

8860 Bushels from 145 Acres 61½ Bu per Acre

## Crops of Rice & Cotton of 1841

| | | | NETT SALES |
|---|---|---|---|
| Nov 1 | 10 | 673 Bushels to Butlers Mill making 19 Whole barrels, 33 Bu small bu Flour . . | 214.28 |
| Decr | 9 | Sent to R Habersham & Son of Savannah 2395 Bushels | 1003.59 |
| Jany | 16 | Sent to Robertson & Blacklock of Charleston 2000 Bushels | 721.09 |
| | | | 1,938.96 |

## Crop of 1842

| | | | Gross | |
|---|---|---|---|---|
| Nov | 18 | 1847 Bushels to Mitchell & Mure | $1223.74 | $896.18 |
| Decr | 16 | 2155 " " " " | | 777.84 |
| | 29 | 2050 " " " " | | 855.05 |
| Feb | 1 | 1650 " " " " | | 690.83 |
| | " | 7½ Bags Sea Island Cotton, @ 15¼¢ | | 355.13 |
| April | 7 | 1895 Bushels to R. Hogan New York | | 1100.00 |
| | | | | $ 4,676.03 |

## Crop of 1943

| | |
|---|---|
| 600 Bu Corn @ 60¢ | 360 |
| 200 " Pease @ 60¢ | 120 |
| 2758 Bushels Rice @ | 1475.70 |
| 674 Butlers Mill | 450 |
| 2466 Bushels Rice @ | 1287.06 |
| 2669 Bushels Rice @ | 1717.82 |
| 1000 Bushels for provisions @ 40¢ | 400.00 |
| 1000 " " Seed @ 70¢ | 700.00 |
| | $ 6450.58 |

## Nett Crop of 1844

| | | Gross | Nett |
|---|---|---|---|
| | 6 Negroes born . . . . @ $300 | | $1,800 |
| Oct 31 | Shipped to Messr R. Habersham & Son of Savannah 900 Bushels Rice making 31 Casks whole @ $2 11/16 | | |
| | 2 Casks Light $2 3/8 | 596.91 | 500.86 |
| Decr 5 | 2290 Bushels Rough Rice Sent to Mitchell and Mure Charleston made 105 Casks Whole @ $2 3/4 | | |
| | & 5 " Light @ $1.93 3/4 | 1839.09 | 1432.99 |
| 5 | 3 Bags Sea Island Cotton to Mitchell & Mure @ 14¢ | 106.40 | 100.46 |
| Jany | 4 Bags Cotton to R Habersham & Son @ 15¢ | 150.00 | 143.80 |
| March 1 | 6960 Bushels to R Habersham & Son Savannah. . . . . . . . | 6364.81 | 5568.17 |
| | 350 Bu Corn @ 60¢ | | 210.00 |
| | 1000 " Potatoes @ 20¢ | | 200.00 |
| | 675 " for Seed @ 90¢ | | 607.50 |
| May 1 | 1017 Bushels Rice to Habersham & Son | | 777.79 |
| June 8 | 1½ Bags Sea Island Cotton | | 67.00 |
| | | | $ 11,438.67 |

## Crop of 1845

| | | Gross | Nett |
|---|---|---|---|
| Sept 25 | 1634 Bushels Rice R Habersham & Son @ $4 5/8 | 1868.37 | $1757.42 |
| Oct 9 | 1700 " " " | 1912.84 | 1788.17 |
| Nov 28 | 3000 " " " | | 2799.94 |
| Decr 9 | 1400 " " " | | 1296. |
| Feb | 2568 " " @ 87½ | | 2165.93 |
| | 1500 | | 1187.20 |
| | | | $10992.96 |

## Crop of 1855 Elizafield

1855

Decr 14 Sold 4000 Bushels of Rough Rice to S H Fiske @ 107¢ per bushel . . . . . . . . . . . $4280

Sold 1795 bushels Rough Rice to S H Fiske @ 107¢ per bushel . . . . . . . . . . . 1920.65

1856

Jany 21 Sold 2900 bushels Rough Rice to S H Fiske @ $1.07 per bushel 3103.00

Nett Crop of Elizafield $ 9,303.65

## Crop of 1855 of Grantly

Jany 29 Sold S H Fiske 3000 bushels Rice at 108¢ 3240.

Feb " Sold S H Fiske 1000 bushels at $1.08 per Bushel 1080

Sold S H Fiske 1500 bushels Rice at $108¢ per bushel 1620

Nett Sales of Grantly $5,940

Nett Crop of 1855 Rice $15,343.65

## Sales of Rice from Crop of 1856

1856

Nov 8 Shipped this day by Northern Belle to Mess N A Hardee & Co of Savh 3265 Bushels Grantly Rice

Nett Sales *Grantly Rice* $2439 95

2400 bu Grantly
865 Elizafield

3265

Nov 28th Shipped this date by Northern Belle to Messr R Habersham & Son ——

3386 — Bushels *Elizafield Rice*

Nett Sales . . . . . $3365 31

[November 1856]

|  |  |  |
|---|---|---|
| | Shipped this date by Cotton plant to Messr R Habersham & Son<br>3370 —— Bushels Elizafield Rice<br>Nett Sales . . . . . | 3683 06 |
| March 9 | Shipped this date by Elias Reed to N A Hardee & Co 2850 bushels of Grantly Rice —— Nett Sales . . . . | 2497.31 |
| April | Shipped this date by Elias Reed to R Habersham & Son<br>700 Bushels prime Rice<br>400 Do Margin Rice Elizafield Rice<br>——<br>1100<br>Nett Sales . . . . . | 1164 25 |
| 1857 | | |
| Nov 18 | Shipped by Elias Reed to Mess N A Hardee & Co<br>4070 of *Grantly Rice* Nett Sale | 2143.36 |
| Decr 8 | Shipped by Elias Reed to Messr R Habersham & Son<br>3270 Bushels of *Elizafield Rice* Nett Sales | 2143.36 |
| March 28 | " Shippd 3472 Bu Grantly to N A H | 2534 60 |
| April | " Shipd 696 Bu Elizafield to R H & Son | 474 15 |
| " " | " Shipd 2769 B Elizafield Ric R Hab & Son | 2333 97 |

## Nett Sales of Rice for 1855 = 6 = 7 = 8

|  |  |  |
|---|---|---|
| 1855 | Elizafield Nett Sales 220 Acres | $9303 65 |
| " | Grantley Crop Nett Sales. 120 Acres | 5940 |
| | | $ 15343 65 |
| 1856 | Elizafield Crop Nett Sales 230 Acres | 8763 37 |
| | Grantly " " " 125 " | 5249 31 |
| | | 14012 68 |

| | | |
|---|---|---|
| 1857 | Grantly Crop Nett Sales 125 Acres | $ 4677 96 |
| | Elizafield " " " 220 Acres | 5226 35 |
| | | $ 9,904 31 |
| 1858 | Grantly Crop Nett Sales 120 Acres | 5373.65 |
| | Elizafield " " " 230 Acres | 2334 91 plus 840.85[1] |
| | N.B. Nearly all of Elizafield Crop destroyed by fire | $7708.56 |

[1] The item listed above as "plus 840.85" was entered in pencil after the original entries. This may represent an additional amount recovered from the crop damaged by fire.

# Accounts with Overseers

## Dr/ B Talbott to H. F Grant

| Date | | Item | Amount | Total |
|---|---|---|---|---|
| 1842 | | | | |
| Augst 29 | To | Cash | $ 2 00 | |
| Sept 15 | " | One double barrell Gun | 25 00 | |
| Oct 28 | " | 4 lbs Coffee | 67 | |
| | " | 2 bars of Soap | 50 | |
| | | 3 pr Worsted socks @ 37½ | 1 12½ | |
| Nov | | Bill @ Mr Pease | 12 92 | |
| | | Paid Mrs Blount for making Clothing | 3 50 | |
| 29 | | 5 yds Homespun @ 8½ | 44 | |
| | | 5 " Cloth @ 48 | 2 40 | |
| | | 3 " Sattinett. 45 | 1 35 | |
| Dec 12 | | 1 pr Gloves | 1 00 | |
| | | | | 49.90 |
| " | | 1 pr Boots | 3 50 | |
| 1843 | | | | |
| Jany 1 | | 1 Ham $1.50 Knife $1.50 | 3 00 | |
| 18 | | 9 Shot & Box Caps | 1 20 | |
| 25 | | 2½ gals Molasses @ 26 | 70 | |
| Feb 1 | " | 2 Barrels of Potatoes | 2 37 | |
| " | " | 1 keg Butter 85 lb 18 cents | 15 30 | |
| | " | ½ barrel pork | 5 " | |
| | " | 4½ Gals Molasses | 1 25 | 32.32 |
| | | Capt Hammond's bill | | |
| 4 | | 1 pr Botts [sic] | 3 50 | |
| | | One Bay Mare | 40 00 | |
| | | 2 Shirts @ 50 | 1 00 | |
| | | 1 lb Tobacco | 0 12½ | |
| | | Plates & Crockery bought from Mr Skinner | 10 00 | 54.63 |
| March 2 | | Bill at Pease & Smiths | | |
| 3 | | 4 lbs Tobacco 12½ C | 00 50 | |

[March 1843]

| Date | | Item | Amount | Total |
|---|---|---|---|---|
| | 8 | 1 Box caps | 37½ | |
| | 10 | 13 lbs Shot @ 10¢ | 1 30 | |
| April | 8 | Cash Capt Hammond | 1 25 | |
| | 10 | 4 lb Shot 50¢ 2 Box Matches @ 12½¢ | " 62½ | |
| " | ' | 2 lb Tobacco 50¢ | " 50 | |
| | " | 33 yds Homespun @ 8¢ | 2 64 | |
| | | | | 7.19 |
| | | Amount brought up | | 144.04 |
| April | 12 | To Cash | 3 00 | |
| | 25 | " 30 yds Cotton Osnabergs @ 9¢ | 2 70 | |
| May | 20 | " Paid Mrs Blount | 1 75 | |
| | 25 | " Cash | 5 00 | |
| June | 15 | " To Cash paid M John | 50 | |
| July | 10 | " " " " Jeany | 1 00 | 13.95 |
| Augst | 1 | " My Note for | 100 00 | |
| " | " | Cash | 1 80 | |
| | 15 | " Cash | 1 " | |
| | | Tobacco 2 lb | " 25 | |
| Sept | 19 | " Cash | 1 50 | |
| " | " | " 333 Segars | 2 50 | |
| Oct | 27 | " Cash | 2 " | |
| Nov | 7 | To Taxes | 80 | |
| | 11 | " One Hog — 105 lbs @ 2½¢ | 1 62½ | |
| | 25 | " paid M John | 0 75 | |
| | 29 | " Cash | 4 00 | |
| | | L M Smiths a/c | 54 59 | 170.81 |
| | | | | $414.78 |
| | | Rokenbaughs a/c. . . . . . . . | 58 91 | |
| | | Corn, Pork & Tobacco | 17 07 | |
| | | Florida excursion | 3 75 | |

---

1 Jany 1844,

Settled up to this date

HUGH FRASER GRANT

$1.34 BENJMIN TALBOT

1844

|  | |  |  |
|---|---|---|---|
| Feb | 9 | 13 lbs Brown Sugar 9½ | 1 24 |
| | | 1 Shad @ 18¾ | 18¾ |

[February 1844]

| | | | | |
|---|---|---|---|---|
| | 24 | " | 3 Pr Socks at Collins & Co & 25¢ | 75 |
| | | " | 3 boxes Matches @ 6¢ | $18\frac{3}{4}$ |
| | | " | 1 box caps @ $37\frac{1}{2}$ | $37\frac{1}{2}$ |
| March | | " | 1 Barrel Pork $12 freight 50¢ | 12 50 |
| | 7 | " | 16 lbs Pork @ 6¢ | 96 |
| | 9 | " | 1 Pad Lock @ $62\frac{1}{2}$ | $62\frac{1}{2}$ |
| | 20 | " | Cash. | 13 00 |
| | | " | Capt Hammonds bill/ less ½ barrel potates [sic] | 12 50 |
| April | 10 | " | 5 lbs Sugar @ $9\frac{1}{2}$¢ | 48 |
| " | " | " | 5 yds Linseys @ 20¢ | 1 00 |
| May | 3 | " | Cash | 10 00 |
| 1844 | | | | |
| June | 1 | " | 6 yds Osnabergs @ $12\frac{1}{2}$ | " 75 |
| | 1 | " | Georgian Office | 1 00 |

## John J Morgan in a/c with H F. Grant Dr

| | | | | |
|---|---|---|---|---|
| 1859 | | | | |
| Jany | | To | Cash | 20 00 |
| Feb | | " | a/c at Mitchel & Pease for Grocaries [sic] | 26 97 |
| March | | " | a/c " Claghorn & Cuningham | $ 91.43 |
| April | 16 | " | 1 piece bleached Shirting $12\frac{1}{2}$¢ | 4 75 |
| | | " | 14 yds brown linnen Drill | 5 25 |
| | | " | 14 yds brown linnen Drill | 5 25 |
| | | " | 12 " Flax Osnabergs . . . . | 1 50 |
| | | " | 4 " Table Cloths | 3 50 |
| | | " | 4 doz pearl Shirt buttons | 50 |
| | | " | 25 Spools thread | 1 00 |
| | | | 1 doz Cups & Saucers | 1.70 |
| | | | 1 " Soup plates . . . . . . . . | 1.50 |
| | | | 2 " Vegetable dishes | 1.50 |
| | | | ½ doz knives & forks | |
| April | | | 1 Carver & fork | |
| | 14 | | Bill from DeWitte & Morgan | $ 16 75 |
| May | 20 | " | Cash Loaned & interest | 96 36 |
| Sept | 6 | " | C[laghorn] & Cuningh[am]s Bill Grocarers | 13 40 |

[November 1859]

| | | | |
|---|---|---|---|
| Nov 1 | " | 1 Bag Flour | 6. |
| | " | Taxes | 2 90 |
| | " | Repairing Watch . . . . . . | 5 50 |
| | " | Cash from Fraser | 7 50 |

## Dr Thos Skinner in a/c with H. F Grant

1842

| | | | |
|---|---|---|---|
| Jany | " | To one Pad Lock from Rokenbaugs | $ 1 25 |
| 20 | " | One Double barrel Gun | 25 00 |
| Feb | " | 100 lb Bacon @ 8¢ | 8 00 |
| 24 | " | one pair Boots from Rokenbaugs | 3 00 |
| " | " | ½ Bottle varnish " | 62½ |
| March 19 | " | 1 piece Paullion Rokenbaughs | 3 50 |
| | " | 5 yds Homespun " | 75 |
| 23 | " | 1 pr Smoothing Irons | " 87½ |
| " | " | 1 lb (Powder?) Hudnalls | " 50 |
| | " | ½ keg Lard " 10 cts | 2 50 |
| April 15 | | ½ doz pints porter @ *$2.50 pr doz* | 1 25 |
| 19 | | ½ doz " " " | 125 |
| May 5 | | One Saddle & Bridle | 7 00 |
| " | | 100 lbs Hams | 7 50 |
| " | " | Cash | 2 50 |
| " | " | Butter | 2 04 |
| June 11 | " | 1 pr Boots Rokenbaugh | 3 00 |
| " | " | 4 lb Buck Shot Do | 50 |
| 13 | " | 50 lbs Sugar Reas & Sartell | |
| " | " | 20 lbs Coffee " | 8 05 |
| Augst 4 | " | To Cash | 500 |
| 11 | " | 1 Pair Boots Alick Turner | 2 50 |
| " | " | your order in favor of Mr C. Putnam for Cow | 10 00 |
| | | Rice Sold & Pork | |
| 27 | " | Cash | 137.11 |

CONTRA

Cr

By 8 Months wages @ $29.17 per Month $233.36

Augst 29 Discharged Mr Skinner for Non attendence to Business

## Accounts with Relatives and Neighbors

*Debtors Cha[s] Grant in a/c with H. F Grant*

| | | |
|---|---|---|
| 1842 | | |
| April 16 | To 56 yds osnabergs @ 11 | $ 6 16 |
| May | " draft in favor of R Grant on a/c of Cows accepted & paid . . . | 60 00 |
| | To 1 Plough | 4 50 |
| | " 4 foot Jins @ $5 | 20 00 |
| 1843 | " 35 bushels Rice flour 16c | 5 60 |
| | " 10 Gals Molasses @ 26. Cents | 260 |
| May 5 | " To Cash Loaned in Savannah | 105 00 |
| June 12 | " 1½ gr Boxes Segars @ | 8 25 |
| Oct 19 | 2 pr Boots @ $3.50 | 7 00 |

*Chas Grant in a/c with H. F Grant Contra C[r]*

| | | |
|---|---|---|
| 1843 | | |
| June 17 | By Cash | 105 00 |
| 1844 | | |
| Oct 1 | " 1 pr Mules | 150 00 |
| 1845 | | |
| May | 1 yoke Oxen | 30 00 |

---

*Debtor J. C Tunno in a/c with H. F G——*

| | | | |
|---|---|---|---|
| 1842 | | | |
| March 27 | To 9 Barrels of Lime | | |
| | | Settled | |
| | " ⅔ " Hair | | |
| 1843 | 1000 ft boards @ $16 | | 16 00 |
| | | Settled | |
| | 1000 Shingles @ $ 3 | | 3 00 |
| | To One Broun Horse | | 75 00 |

*J C Tunno in a/c with H. F G   Contra   Cr*

| | | | | |
|---|---|---|---|---|
| | | By 4 Mortice locks | Settled | |
| March | 1 | By 268 Bushels of Rice @ 75 | Settled | 163 50 |
| | | By 1 Keg white lead | | 12 00 |
| | | " 5 gals paint Oil 1.12 | | 5 62½ |

---

*Debtor Robt Grant*   Dr

| | |
|---|---|
| To 30 Gallons Molasses @ 26 c | 7 80 |
| " 1 pr Carriage Bridles | 5 00 |
| " Charleston Cousin | 5 " |
| " 3 doz Congress Water | 8 25 |
| " Taxes paid | 6 02 |
| " 7 yds Bombazin @ $2 | 14 00 |
| 1 yds brown Holland | 25 |
| 1 " " " | 25 |
| 1 Shawl | 5 50 |
| 1 pr Silk Stockings | 2 38 |
| 2 " kid Gloves | 1 50 |
| " Sewing Silk | 50 |
| " Paper Cambrick | 1 25 |
| " Mrs Blunt | 8 00 |
| " Paid her thrg R Hogan | 124 00 |

*Contra   CR*

| | | | |
|---|---|---|---|
| 1844 | | By Cash from Col Dubignon | $272-33 |
| May | 1 | " Cash from Dr Wests Note | 343 41 |
| June | 3 | " " " Col Dubignon | 600 00 |

---

1844   *Debtor James Holmes*

| | | |
|---|---|---|
| May | To one bay horse | $ 75 00 |
| | " 4 bundles of hay | 10 00 |

---

*Debtor Fanny E Troup to H. F. Grant*

1851

| | | | |
|---|---|---|---|
| April | 28th | To draft on R Habersham & Son | $500.00 |
| Nov | 1 | " Cash | 100. |

## Dr/ Hugh F. Grant in a/c with

| | | | | | |
|---|---|---|---|---|---|
| 1843 | | | | | |
| Nov 8 | To | balance due R Hogan this date | 196 78 | $196 78 |
| Dec 1 | " | 100 yds Paper binding . . . . . | | |
| | " | Cash paid Dr H. A Grant | 1284 00 | |
| | " | Weighing not charged in a/c | 10 | |
| 1844 | | | | |
| Feb | " | Paid Miss Davis | 30 00 | |
| March 18 | " | L M Smith | 81 47 | |
| 9 | " | 4 Pr Boots | 15 50 | |
| | " | 1500 Segars | 24 75 | |
| March 1 | | J. F Meeker | 350 | 1642 50 |
| April 23 | " | Cash paid Mrs Hogans Int | 140 00 | 490 |
| May 22 | " | " " J F Meeker | 300 | |
| | " | Saturday (Courier) | 25 | 325 |
| June 4 | " | Mrs Sarah Grant | 173 | |
| 7 | " | Dr H A Grant | 1530 00 | |
| July 31 | " | J. F. Meeker | 700 00 | 2403 |

## Dr/ H F Grant in a/c with

| | | | |
|---|---|---|---|
| 1845 | | | |
| March 7 | " | H. A Grant @ 10 days | $ 700 |
| | | J F Meeker for Miss Wilson | 250 |
| 11 | | Mrs S. Grant | 414 |
| 25 | | Mrs Hogan | 140 |
| May 17 | " | H A Grant at Sight | 2244 00 |
| 29 | " | Miss Eccleston | 120 00 |

## Robert Hogan Esqr[2] Contra Cr/

1843

| | | | | | |
|---|---|---|---|---|---|
| April | 7 | By | 1895 Bushels of Rough Rice | | |
| May | 9 | " | Cash from Mitchell & Mure | | 300 |
| June | 5 | " | Do Do | | 300 |
| | | | " " | | 250 |
| Dec | 7 | By | 100 Tierces of Rice Shipped by Mess Mitchell & Mure @ $2.62½ | Gross $1623 92 | Nett $1475 70 |

1844

| | | | | | |
|---|---|---|---|---|---|
| March | 18 | " | 118 Tierces of Rice. Shipped by Mess Mitchell & Mure | Gross $1943 37 | 1717 82 |
| June | 3 | " | Col Dubignons draft | | 600 00 |
| | 4 | " | Rob Habersham & Son " | | 1000 00 |

## Messrs Hogan & Finlay Contra Cr/

1845

| | | | | | |
|---|---|---|---|---|---|
| March | 7 | By | R Habersham & Son | Check | $ 1500 00 |
| May | 14 | " | R Habersham Son | Check | $ 2500 00 |

[2] Robert Hogan, a New York broker and merchant, was a brother-in-law of Hugh Fraser Grant.

## Dr/ Walter Button in a/c with (H. F Grant)

| | | | |
|---|---|---|---|
| 1841 | | To 14 Bushels Rice 80 | $ 11 20 |
| | | " Overpaid in last settlement | 15 00 |
| June | | " 6 Bu Rice 80 @ | 4 80 |
| | | " 20 Bu Corn 75 @ | 15 00 |
| | | " 5 " " " | 3 75 |
| July | | " 10 " " " | 7 50 |
| | | " 20 " " " | 15 00 |
| | | " 10 " " " | 7 50 |
| | | " 10 " " " | 7 50 |
| Augst | 9 | " 10 " " " | 7 50 |
| | " | " 5 Bu Rice 80 ¢ | 4 00 |
| | " | " 10 " Corn 75 ¢ | 7 50 |
| | " | " 5 " " " | 3 75 |
| 1842 | | " 10 " " Mrs Lamb " | 7 50 |
| Feb | | " 2 " Rice J. Gignilliatt 80 c | 1 60 |
| | 4 | " 5 " " Mr Blunt " | 4 00 |
| 1843 | | | |
| Feb | 13 | " Cash on Mitchell & Mure | 77 50 |
| March | | 1400 Brick $8. | 11 25 |
| | | 2342 lbs Fodder @ 75 ¢ | 17 56 |
| April | | 300 Brick | 2 40 |
| | | | $ 231.82 |

Cr. by CASH . . . . . . . . . . . . . . . . . . $ 231.82

By my note for $406. —— payable 1st Jany 1844

[1] This account is probably illustrative of the type of plantation operating credit which has been referred to previously as "community exchange of goods and services." See pages 44-45.

# Tax Returns

1845

105 Negroes
300 Acres Prime Rice Land
800 " Pine Land adjoining
90 " Second quality Hammock
600 " Pine Land adjoining

1848 Tax Return
106 Negros
300 Acres prime tide Swamp
1400 Acres pine Land
90 " Second Quality Hammock

1849 112 Negros
300 Acres tide Swamp
1400 " Pine Land
90 " 2d Hammock
2 4 Wheel Carriages

1850 119 Negroes
the rest as above

---

1854 26 District G[lynn] C[ounty]

| | |
|---|---|
| 1 poll | |
| 325 Acres prime quality Rice Land | |
| 1500 " Pine Land | $45,000 |
| 150 " 2d grade Hammock Land | |
| & Improvements | |
| 130 Slaves @ $400 | 52 000 |
| Furniture | 1,200 |
| All other property | 1 500 |
| | $99,700 |

Tax Return for 1855

| | |
|---|---|
| 1 Poll | |
| 420 Acres Rice Land } | |
| 800 " Pine Land adjoining } | $45,000.00 |
| 400 " & Improvements at Summer place | 1,000.00 |
| 125 Negros at $400 | 50,000. |
| Furniture & all other property | 2,700. |
| | 98,700.— |

1856

| | |
|---|---|
| 1 Poll | |
| 420 Acres Rice Land | |
| 800 " Pine adjng . . . | 45,000 |
| 400 Summer place | 1,500 |
| 126 Negroes at $400 | 50,400 |
| All other property | 2,700 |
| | 99,750 |

17 May 1856

# Land on Champneys Island

1839

| | | | | | |
|---|---|---|---|---|---|
| Nov | 25 | 15 | Hands | cleaning | land |
| " | 26 | 15½ | " | " | " |
| " | 27 | 18 | " | " | " |
| " | 28 | 23 | " | " | " |
| " | 29 | 32 | " | " | " |
| Decr | 2 | 13 | " | " | " |
| " | 3 | 13 | " | " | " |
| " | 4 | 19 | " | " | " |
| " | 5 | 19 | " | " | " |

Sold to D[r] J. Champneys Tunno

## Cattle and Poultry

May 1846 Account of Cattle

15 Cows
13 Calves
13 Yearlings
3 Steers
6 Oxen
1 Bull . . . . . . . . . . . . . . . . . . . . . 51 Head

Account of Cattle 1 Sept 1851

Oxen & their Names

Ben, John, Buck, Lemon, Woolly, Prince, Brandy, Bright, Darly, Harry, O Luke & two Stray Cows No. 11

Mary Ann, Mira, Charlotte, Julatta, Sabrinna, Phoebe, Lear, Cinda, Lynda, Sary, Kate, Stella, Mary, Nelly, Betsey, Agnes, Dido, Sissy, Susy, Strawberry, Delia No. 21

| | |
|---|---|
| Three year old Steers | 6 |
| Yearling Steers | 2 |
| Spring Calves | |
| Steers | 9 |
| Heiffers | 5 |
| | Head 54 |

Bull Stray

54 head & three strays

4 May 1840 Account of Poultry

Geese — 32
Turkeys — 23
Fowls — 25
Ducks — 9

RECT FOR CHOLERA MEDECINE

| | |
|---|---|
| Bruised Rheubarb | 6 oz. |
| " Cloves | 2 " |
| " Ginger | 4 " |
| Extract Catichu bruised | 3 " |
| Tinct Cinnamon | 1¼ oz |
| " Camphor | 2 " |
| " Laudanum | 4 " |
| Alcohol | ½ gallon |
| Water | ½ " |
| Simple Syrup | 2 pints |

Add the alcohol & water to all the bruised ingredients let stand for 8 to 10 days Stir the mixture every day, then strain and add the other articles

Dose: 1 table spoon full for an adult every 2 hours until the disease is checked 1 tea spoon full for 10 to 14 years & children in proportion

H. F GRANT

D[r] GRANTS CHOLERA MIXTURE

| | |
|---|---|
| Tinct (compound) Rheubarb | 2½ oz |
| " Camphor | 4 drachms |
| " Laudanum | 6 drachms |
| " Capsicum | 2 " |
| Chloric Aether | 4 " |

Make a Mixture

For Adults: Dose 1 to 3 tea spoons full in a little water every 20, 30 or 60 minutes if very severe or urgent if not very urgent once every 2 hours or three

FOR CHOLERA

1 pint of Brandy
1 oz Laudanum
1 oz Gum Camphor
½ oz Cayenne pepper
doze tea spoon full, until relieved . . .

THE CHOLERA.[1]

As there is a probability that the cholera may visit the country generally, during the summer, we annex two recipes to check it in its incipient stages. We say incipient, because, if not checked in time, there is no medium or power on earth to check it. The first recipe is obtained from Coroner Hilton, who used it with the greatest success in 1832, '34, and in '49. It was also largely used with the same success by our City Inspector, Mr. Downing. The recipe costs from six shillings to a dollar — and must be prepared by a regular chemist or apothecary.

RECIPE FOR THE PREMONITORY SYMPTOMS OF CHOLERA.

Tincture Opium, 3 drachms.
Tincture Capsicum, 2 drachms.
Tincture Rhubarb, Aromatic, 2 ounces.
Tincture Cardamon Compound, 1½ ounces.
Spirits Camphor 2 drachms.
Essence Cloves, ½ drachm.
Aqua Ammonia, 1 drachm.
Essence Peppermint, 1 ounce.
Chloric Aether, ½ ounce.

Mix together, and add, of Bi-Carbonate Potash, 1 drachm, dissolved in ½ ounce of water.

Take ½ to a tea-spoonful in two or three tablespoons of water. This may be repeated every half or two or three hours, as may be required.

[1] This remedy was reprinted from the New York *Express* by a local paper. H. F. Grant clipped this article and pasted it on the inside back cover of the Journal.

The following recipe is by Dr. Dillon, of Pearl-street:

Cumpound [sic] tincture of Cardemoms, 3 ounces.
Tincture of Opium, 2 drachms.
Tincture of Cayenne Pepper, 2 drachms.
Sulphuric Aether 3 drachms.
Cinnamon Water, 5 ounces.

One table-spoonful to be taken, mixed with two table-spoonfuls of water, with a little loaf sugar, every fifteen minutes, for three doses, which will generally be sufficient to check vomiting in the incipient state of cholera, or colera morbus; it may be resumed, and the three doses repeated in one hour after the first doses are administered.

The above recipe was successful in thirty cases out of thirty-two, since the commencement of the cholera. It costs from three to four shillings. — *N.Y. Express.*

FOR CLAP  Dr H A G[2]

Acetate Potash  1 oz to a pint of water
Dose ½ wine glass 3 or 4 times a day
Inject with Nitrate Silver

CONDITION POWDER FOR HORSES

| | |
|---|---|
| Pulverized Rosin . . . . . . . . | ½ lb |
| " Flour of Sulphur . . . . | ½ do |
| Cream Tartar . . . . . . . . . | ¼ do |
| Black Antimony . . . . . . . . | 2 oz |

Mix well and give *one* tea spoonful every night for three nights — discontinue, or repeat as may be necessary

COUGH MIXTURE

1 Table spoon Paragoric
1 do Spruss Squills
1 tea spoon each of Spt Nitre & antimonial wine
4 table spoons of Liquorice disolved about as thick as molasses

Dose
1 Tea spoon in water 3 or 4 times a day

[2] Dr. Harry Allen Grant of New York, brother of H. F. Grant.

FOR COUGH H A G

| | |
|---|---|
| Vinegar of Squills | 2 oz |
| Sweet Spirit nitre | 2 do |
| Paragoric | 2 do |
| Pul. Gum arabic | 1 oz |
| Sugar . . . . . . . . . . . . . | gr-s |

one tea spoon full occasionally

FOR CROUP (16 July 1848)

R

Castor oil — one oz
Vinegar Squills — one oz
Wine (ipecac) — one oz

Dose: one tea spoonful every 10 to 15 minut until it vomitses freely

— H. A. G. —

EPILEPTIC FITS

$\frac{1}{4}$ to $\frac{1}{2}$ gr Nitrate Silver 3 times a day & add Nitrate Bismuth 3 grs to each dose

CURE OF ITCH IN $\frac{1}{2}$ HOUR

Boil 1 part of quick lime with 2 parts of sublimated sulphur in ten parts of water, until the two parts are perfectly united, stirred with a piece of wood constantly, When well decocted [sic] decant the fluid in a well corked bottle, Wash clean with tepid water then rub well with the fluid for half hour.

FOR NEURALGIA

R

| | |
|---|---|
| Extract Canabis Indica | Fi |
| Ft. pill . . . . . . . . . . . . | XL |

Give ($\frac{1}{2}$) one half pill three or four times a day or until the pain is relieved = And increase it to one pill three or four times a day =

CURE FOR SALIVATION

15 grs Chlorate of Potash in one oz of water 3 times a day

SASSAFRAS BEER

5 Gils Molasses
3 lbs Sugar
3 pts Water
4 oz Tart Acid
Sassafras Root. Q. S.

[UNKNOWN]

R

Tincture Aconite

Give (10) ten drops in a little water three times a day =

## April 25th 1852 Exce!!

List of Measle Cases for April

Little Anthony, Y. Harry, Kate died on the 2d May 1852, Aet [aged] 26 years

Measles — L Hannah died 14 May aet [aged] 24 years Measles.

Mira, Kate, Stella, Daniel Ella, Amelia died

Cumsey — Susy, Sary, Judy, Hannah, died 6 June John Caroline died.

List of Measles April & May 1852

Y Harry Catharine, Sabrinna

List of those who had Measles in 1852

Anthony, Harry, Catharine, L Dinah, Bella, Betsey, Cretia, May Ann, Simon Julia, Ella Amelia, Beck Cumsey, Adell Rose, Pussy, Daniel Matthew, Martha, Charles, Jefferson, Laura, L Kate April, Mark, Stella, H Mira, George Ann Joe Lot William M — Susy John Jacob, Pown Robert, Sary, Phoebe, Butler, London Cissy, Panda, H John, Driver Prince, Milly, Cuffy Sam Caroline Amos Clarinda, Nancy, Pusy, William, Looky L Prince, Hardtimes, Torry, Duncan Jackson, Chance Richard, Alley, Phillis, Betsy, Patty, Gabrael, Hannibal, Nelly, Fredrick 71 Recovered 17 Others that died from its effects.

# Plantation Supplies Issued

Blankets given out January 1840

D. John, Fortune, Betty, O Harry, L Dinah, Amaretta, Emperor, Pussy, Y Bella, S Nelly, Stephen, Caesar, Abraham, Jim, Phillis, O. Jack, Lear, Sebrinna, Grace, O Dinah, Venus, London, Nanny, Cumsey, Mulatto John, Toby, J Stake, Y. Scipio, C. Bella, Charles, Rina, Margaret, Hannibal, Chance, Mark, Judey —

Blankets given out January 1841

O Nelly, Matilla, Lookey, L Jack, Bess, Susy, Richard, Prince Alick Ben, Sary, Dido, Clora, Ned, Mingo, Bobbett, March, Phoebe, L Harry, Julatta, Nann, Brister, Biney, Haigar, H Jeany, Mary, Nurse Jeany, Amey, Delia, April, Flora, Nancy, Sue, Patty, O Nanny, Mira, Duncan, Andrew, Mira, Natt, Sophy, George, Hardtimes, Cook Bella, Chive, P Cate, Jim & Charlotte

Blankets given out Nov 16th 1843

D. John, & Wife, Fortune, O Harry & Wife L Dinah, March & Amaretta, Emperor & Haigar, Y Bella, S Nelly, Stephen, & Hannah, Caesar & Biney, Abraham & Nancy, W Jim, April & Phillis, Brister & Lear, London & Sary, Prince & Nancy, M John & Matilla, Y Scipio & Dido, Rina, Mark, Margaret, R Phoebe, N Jeany — Duncan & Sue, Andrew & Mira, George, Charles, Hardtimes, Alick & Flora, Phoebe, Kate, Adell, Harry & Catharine, Natt & Betty Jim Caten, Pussy, John Stake, & Bess, Charlotte, Jack & Cumsey, Ben & Nann 60 [total] Frederic, Bobbett, O Grace, O Dinah, Susy — Mary, Patty, Clora, Richard, Molly P Hannah, Looky, Amey, Delia, Julatta, Mira, R Mingo Hannibal, Chance Sues child, Sarys ditto, Floras ditto, Haigar ditto, Miras child, Didos child.

Blankets given out 24 Jany 1853

Matilla, Cumsey, Nanny, Susy, Looky Sue, N Jeany, Amey, Delia George Ann Sary, S Dinah, Bess, Mira, Rose, F Phoebe, Adell, H Jeany, L Dinah, Catharine M Kate, Emperor, Haigar Phillis, London — Pussy, Patty, Rina, R Kate.

1 Blanket to Nannys child.

Axes. given out November 1839

Scipio, L Jack, Sabrinna, Julatta Bella Biney, Nelly, Phillis Dido Phoebe.

April 1840 London.

November 1853

Hannibal, William & L Prince

Spades given out Decr 1853

Chance

Hoes given out Nov 1853

Mira, Catharine, Nelly, M Kate, Cumsee, William, Hannibel

New Rice Hooks given out Augst 1842

Looky, Jack April Amey. Prince Sary Ben Mira, March Hardtimes, Phillis, Flora, Harry, Clora, Mary, Cumsey. Lear Julatta, Nann. Amaretta, Emperor. Brister Nelly Jim. Richard.

## Marine Bank Savh. in A/C with H. F. Grant

CREDIT IN BANK

| 1855 | |
|---|---|
| Decr 15 By deposite [sic] | 4280 00 |
| 26 " " | 1920 65 |
| | 6200 65 |

[WITHDRAWALS]

| 1856 | |
|---|---|
| Jany 3 To 1 Check for | $ 850 65 |
| 14 " Check for Jacob Barrett | 5350 |
| | $ 6200 65 |

## How to Grow Rice

PLANT THE USUAL WAY, water about Six days for Sprout flow, keep dry until the Rice is about Six inches high, then flow by covering up every thing so that no rice could be seen, the water about ten inches over the rice, keep it so for seven days, and then draw very slowly until the points of the Rice on the hills could be seen, then held it so for 24 hours. then lowered it gradually every day until the points of the Rice could be seen in the low places, from this time I keep it on for about twenty days stationary, at the end of 20 days begin to draw off very slowly about an inch or inch and a half in 24 hours, so as not to throw down any of the Rice. It will take from ten to 12 days to dry the field — I then keep it dry about 30 days, and picked the grass and gave a light hoeing, at the end of the 30 days dry growth put on the Harvest water, changing the water occasionally to keep it sweet. In a dry year it is as well to hoe during the dry growth, but not necessary, as there will be very little grass

H F. GRANT

## CANAL WORK

| 1854 | | |
|---|---|---|
| May | 9 | 6 Hands on work |
| " | 13 | 11 Hands on the Canal |

| | | |
|---|---|---|
| May | 9 | Scipio //// //// //// //// /// |
| " | " | Pown //// //// //// //// /// |
| " | " | March //// //// //// //// /// |
| " | " | Emperor //// //// //// //// /// |
| " | " | Frederick //// //// //// //// /// |
| " | " | Hannibal //// //// //// //// /// |
| " | 13 | Harry — //// //// //// //// |
| " | " | Abraham //// //// //// //// |
| " | " | Chance //// //// //// //// |
| " | " | Jackson //// //// //// //// |
| " | " | Cook //// //// //// //// |

$265.89 due me by Glearn

# Drafts of Letters and Speeches

*Address delivered by H F Grant Capt of the Glynn Rangers on presenting their Colours Decr 1849,*

Fellow Rangers, we meet here today as Soldiers, & in that name there is a peculiar and thrilling charm. It is the Synonime of Manly pride, of love of Country, of generous dashing Chivalry, of protection to all that Man holds dear in his cherished home. The wife of his bosom, the Children of his love, the girl of his heart and the friend of his fireside.

Such are the motives and feelings of Citizen soldiers that render them invincible.

We fellow Rangers are a portion of that arm of our country's guard, although our roll is small be not discouraged, the day of small things is not to be despised. David the King was the least of his fathers household. Benjamin was little Benjamin, yet among a thousand hills, there was none more honored than the little Hill of Hennan. Let us then act well our part for there the honor lies.

To day peace is in all our borders but tomorrow the Eagle may flutter from his repose and drums & trumpets sound to War. Let us then redeem the day of safety by preparation for the day of danger. let it be our mutual pledge to be ready it is our motto then let it be inscribed upon our honors as it is upon our banners ready.

Rangers in the stern discipline of the field in the history of all warlike nations, the colors of a Regiment were presented by the hand of the brave with the charge to defend it to the death. But it is our privilege to receive it from the hands of the fair. and when we remember the object of our association nothing could be more appropriate or in keeping with the spirit of our charter. Our first duty then is at home. let us be always on the alert for dangers within as well as without, to protect the hearth stone as well as the gate way the peace, honor & happiness of our families as well as the wrongs of our Country. Then whose voice so potent to fill our hearts & move our arms to do a Soldiers duty as that of Woman Sorely dependent confiding woman.

Your sparkling eyes and Manly forms give me your responce [sic], and as your Commanding officer when occasion shall require it I will seal it with my blood or redeem it in triumph.

Rangers this banner you are now to receive will be your ensign as long as you continue an organized corps, its devise is simple yet illustrative. The Phoenix presents you with a corps of Cavalry secured in the County of Glynn and at their post of duty

The devise [?] presents you with a ranger in his full uniform & equipments, his Sword pointing to his post & the speed of his charger shows his zeal & alacrity to fill it & his motto is ready

To the Cornet

Sir in the name of the Lady of your Commanding officer do I present you this stand of colours, Sir I commit it to worthy hands, feeling every confidence it will never be dishonored

H F Grant

Mr Editor

As a tax payer, I wish to call the attention of the Public to one or two items that draw heavily upon us without ever being a benefit to any except the few who are feeding from the Public crib. I allude first to the Alatamaha Steam boat speculation. Their [sic] are two old Steam boats that are in such a state of decay that a stick can be easily thrust through their bottoms without much effort. These boats are chartered by the Government at an expense of $120 per day to experiment upon. their [sic] has been employed a great many hands to work upon them & their has been purchased from 300 to 400 bales of Cotton to use upon them, and much of the Cotton is being wasted upon the River bank All this expenditure of Money is for what? Any one with the least experience would not hesitate to say that these ships could not bear the concussion of a single gun, their bottoms would not hold together. Another Item of expense is detaching a private soldier, who draws his pay regularly from the Government and receives Capts pay from the owners of a thing that he the Capt. affirms will never reach the mouth of the River. Would it not have been wiser on the part of those in power to have the boats inspected before the expenditure of near half a Million of dollars had been needlessly thrown away.

Dear Miller

Fraser informs me the Government is desirous of twenty hands to work on the fortifications about Savh & ct — That they offer $45 per Month for each man & to furnish them with food tools & Medical attend &c & the only expense I am to have is the Clothing. That you are to have them especially under your superintendence & for your care and attention you are to receive $5 per Month for each hand. All of which I am satisfied with & can furnish 15 or 16 Men upon their terms — At present 2 or 3 of the Men are hired out by the Month & as soon as their time is out can be sent on to you.

When Dr Troup & my hands were there some time since under the charge of Mr L——— [?], they were very badly fed. This Mr. L——— assured me was the case. If my Negroes go on now I wish them to be fed agreeable to the contract. Do you wish a driver to this gang and do they allow extra for him. Hope I may hear from you this evening whether they require Women as I can send on a few of them & what price for the women. I should suppose they will require one woman at least to Cook & wash your mess. Does the Government furnish transportation both ways — ?

(Draft of letter to local press)

If those in authority would look more to the interest of the Country, We the tax payers would be relieved of a considerable amount that now many find it difficult to meet Some Months since a Scheme was gotten up to fit out two old hulks of Steamers at Dr Torm [?] to capture or do some wonderful feat with the Yankey Gun boats in St Simons Sound. After an immense expenditure of Money & Labor & when the boats were nearly ready for their glorious descent a Board of Comm[issioner]s were sent to examine & report the condition of the Boats & &c And if I am correctly informed they reported adverse & the whole affair is laid up & condemned. Now Mr Editor would it not have been wiser to have made the inspection of the rotten hulks before so much Money had been thrown away upon them & The River Bank is now piled up with Cotton & much of it in a ruined condition, that had been purchased for the expedition. Whose business is it to have the Cotton saved & see that it is taken care of for the Government thousand of dollrs worth of it being wasted & getting worse & worse every day. And are the old hulks still in the pay of the Govt at the rate of $120 per day. If these matters were looked after it would save much to the Govt & relieve the

TAX PAYER

## LAST ENTRIES

Waresboro, Ware County 1861 Oct, 26,
Moved my family & part of the Negroes here out of the way of the Vandal Yankeys,

Oct 20, 1862 Visit to Savannah for two nights & one day

# MSS. INDEX[1]

| | Page |
|---|---|
| List of Negroes | 1 to 6 |
| Tax Returns | 9 |
| Culture of 23 Acre field | 13 |
| " 18 " | 14 |
| " 22 " | 16 |
| " 20 " | 18 |
| " 27 " | 20 |
| " 21 " | 22 |
| " 19 " | 24 |
| " Lower 20 " | 26 |
| " Upper 20 " | 28 |
| " 16 " | 30 |
| " 15 " | 32 |
| " 17 " | 34 |
| " 5 " | 36 |
| " 10 " | 38 |
| " High Land Crop | 42 |
| Sales of Crops, 1837, 1838, 1839, 1840 | 44 45 |
| Account Messrs Robertson & Thurston | 50 |
| Journal | 54 |
| Champneys Island | 11 |
| R Habersham & Son | 69 |
| Carterets Point farm | 73 |
| Rice Hooks | 60 |

[1] Prepared by H. F. Grant and listed a few pages from back cover.

# PART III

## Directory
## Notes on Sources
## Index

# DIRECTORY

THE "DIRECTORY" of persons and business firms listed in succeeding pages is designed to facilitate and expand the reader's understanding of the nature of the transactions listed in the accounts with the "factors of Elizafield" and the meaning of specific entries in the Elizafield Journal and elsewhere in the document. While a few of the people or establishments identified in this directory were not mentioned frequently by Mr. Grant, most of them appear time and again in the documentary account. Footnote identification of these repeated entries would clutter up the pages of the document to the point of confusion and redundancy. When examining separate entries, pages, or sections, the reader will find that constant reference to the information set forth in this alphabetical list will add considerably to his appreciation of the way of life of the owner of a Georgia rice plantation. The original record seldom gives any hint as to what the planter was buying or selling as he set down each entry. When, however, a glance at the "directory" reveals that the creditor or debtor named was a dentist, a milliner, a tax collector, a banker, or a dealer in ship chandlery and machinery, the nature of the proceeding becomes apparent.

Strict adherence to the canons of historical scholarship would require that the reader be provided with an exact citation as to the source or sources of the information identifying each person or firm. Since an attempt has been made to give pertinent information on upwards of 350 such persons or firms, it seems that any such slavish attachment to the mores of the profession would be of limited value and quite tiresome to the reader. Such an array of citations could not help but interfere with whatever train of thought or interest had been aroused by an examination of the entries of the planter. Therefore, it is hoped that the following general discussion of the modus operanda employed in compiling the directory information will satisfy the requirements of the trade.

The greater portion of identifying data was secured by a detailed study of the news items and advertisements contained in the files of various Georgia newspapers. These include the Brunswick *Advocate* for the years 1837-39, the Savannah *Republican* for the years 1840 to 1852, and the Savannah *Daily Georgian* for the years 1837 to 1854. Also the *Directories* of the City of Savannah for 1849, 1859, and 1871 were of great assistance in supplying information on business firms operating in that city. Conferences and correspondence with various residents of the Georgia coast, who have steeped themselves in the history of that region, were fruitful sources of valuable and significant information. Included in this list (in the order of their contributions to the problem) are: Mrs. Margaret Davis Cate of Brunswick and Sea Island, Georgia, Miss Bessie Lewis of Pine Harbor (near Darien), Georgia, Mr. Raiford J. Wood of Savannah, Georgia, and both Mrs. Marmaduke Floyd of Athens, Georgia, and the late Marmaduke Floyd of Savannah, Georgia.

Various descendants of the families which operated rice plantations in the Altamaha River basin have been helpful. The most notable of this group were Miss Miriam Dent and Miss Ophelia Dent who still reside at Hofwyl Plantation, their ancestral home. Several very valuable items were obtained from Mrs. F. D. Aiken of St. Simons Island, Georgia, who is a direct descendant of Hugh F. Grant of Elizafield. Finally, numerous isolated scraps of biographical and commercial information have been gleaned from the files of the *Georgia Historical Quarterly* and numerous monographs and compilations dealing with a wide variety of phases of life on the Georgia coast in the nineteenth century. Despite a search extending intermittently over more than a decade, some of the individuals referred to by Mr. Grant remain anonymous. It is hoped that these unknowns constitute no more than a small percentage of the significant names in the document. At any rate, enough identification has been achieved to make possible considerable added understanding of the economic and financial practices and problems of a Georgia rice planter.

AIKEN, ISAAC M. Liveryman and livestock dealer in near-by Darien.[1]

[1] Except when otherwise located, all places in this "Directory" are in the state of Georgia.

Aiken & Burns. Dealers in leather and dry goods in Savannah (1853).[2]

Alexander, H. D. W. Savannah bookkeeper.

Alston, John Ashe. Member of the famous Carolina rice-growing family, with a plantation at Pee Dee, South Carolina.

Alston, Thomas Pinckney & C. Members of the famous Charleston, South Carolina, rice-planting family. In 1840 they seem to have supplied Hugh Fraser Grant with loans of $7,543 and $7,778 in the form of personal bonds, which were accepted by Grant's Charleston factor, Robertson & Thurston.

Anderson, J. & Co. Savannah dry-goods dealers, who advertised ginghams, prints, silks, blankets, bagging, and cloths for Negroes.

Atwell, J. S. Operator of a clothing store in Brunswick.

Baker, E. Bright. Planter in near-by McIntosh County.

Bancroft, Joseph. Deputy Federal Marshal for District of Georgia (1844) and Brunswick agent for the Charleston Packet and Dispatch Line.

Barrett, Jacob. Owner of plantation on Champney's Island near Elizafield. This island was also known as Barrets Island.

Beals, J. A. Painter, whose business establishment was located at 34 Barnard Street, Savannah.

Blount, E. M. Near-by carpenter, millman, and builder of small boats.

Blue, Alex. Druggist in Darien, who also dealt in groceries.

Bond, Dr. E. H. Physician and planter in Glynn County.

Bond, T. S. Resident of Darien, father-in-law of Charles Grant.

Bowne, A. T. Savannah druggist.

Brown, [Rev.] Edmund P. Rector of Christ Church, St. Simons Island, and of St. David's parish on the mainland 1844-68. Mr. Brown and his wife were both originally from "the North." He began his ministry before being ordained but a year later was advanced to the priesthood by Bishop Stephen Elliott in Savannah.

Brown, James M. Local mason.

[2] This date and all such dates in parentheses which appear in subsequent entries in this "Directory," indicate the dates of the sources—newspapers or directories—on which the identifying data are based.

BRYAN & SON. Dealer in imported wines and liqueurs.

BRYAN, THOMAS FORMAN. Rice planter who owned Broughton Island in the estuary of the Altamaha River. He later changed his name to Thomas M. Forman. Some of his children used Bryan for the family name and others Forman. One of his daughters, Georgia Bryan Conrad, was the author of *Reminiscences of a Southern Woman.*

BULL & ANDREWS. Possibly a predecessor or successor company to the near-by firm of Bull Brothers, who were plumbers.

BULLOCH, WM. H. Publisher of the Savannah *Daily Georgian.*

BURKE, ARCHIBALD T. Citizen of Glynn County, who married Eugenia DuBignon of Jekyll Island in 1853 and later moved to Texas.

BURNETT, J. M. Glynn County planter, who held a variety of county offices such as Road Commissioner.

BURNETT, S. M. Planter and public official in Glynn County.

BUTLER, J. Q. A. Small planter, whose property was located near "The Parsonage," the ministerial home of the Rev. E. P. Brown who ministered to the families in the vicinity of Elizafield.

BUTLER ESTATE. Estate of old Major Pierce Butler, whose heirs were his grandchildren, John and Pierce Butler.

BUTLER, JOHN and PIERCE. Heirs of Butler estate. They were actually named John and Pierce Mease; however, they were grandchildren of old Major Pierce Butler and had their names changed legally to Butler in order to inherit under the will of the grandfather. Their father Dr. James Mease, was a Philadelphia physician.

BUTLERS MILL. Rice mill operated on Butler Island, rice plantation of Major Pierce Butler.

BUTTON, WALTER. Probably overseer of Elizafield or Evelyn 1841-43; possibly a local workman or yeoman farmer, who purchased grain and fodder for his livestock from Hugh Fraser Grant.

CARGYLE, BENJAMIN MONROE, M.D. Also spelled Cargile. Practiced medicine in Brunswick.

CARSON, WILLIAM. Savannah lumber dealer.

CATER, BENJAMIN FRANKLIN. Sometime proprietor of Kelwin Grove Plantation on St. Simons Island.

CHAFFER P Co. Savannah dealers in paints and experts in woodworking (1855).

CHAMPNEY, J. McIntosh County planter.

CHICK, T. C. Sheriff of McIntosh County (1841).

CLAGHORN & CUNINGHAM. Grocers and supply house, in Savannah or Darien, who also served as agents for the United States Mail Line which operated boats traveling up and down the Georgia coast from Savannah to St. Marys.

CLAGHORN & WOOD. *See* Wood, Claghorn & Co.

CLARK, ARCHIBALD. Superintendent of lights and buoys and Collector of the Port (1807-48) at St. Marys; was also an attorney and proprietor of "Traders Hill" plantation on the St. Marys River.

CLARK, [REV.] GEORGE H. The clergyman who presided at the wedding of Fanny Grant and Dr. D. H. B. Troup, April 28, 1851.

CLEVELAND, [REV.] B. One-time pastor of St. David's parish, Glynn County.

COBURN, MOSES. Savannah piano tuner and music teacher.

COHEN, SOLOMON. Partner in Cohen and Fosdick, Savannah dealers in bacon, mackerel, grapes, sugar, and hay. Also practiced law as attorney (1849).

COLLINS, S. L. & Co. General merchants in Darien, who occasionally dealt in small quantities of rice (1844).

COLLINS & SHINE. Operators of lumber mill in Darien.

COLLINS, T. W. Probably a partner in Collins and Shine.

COUPER, JAMES HAMILTON. Manager and part owner of Hopeton Plantation, adjoining Elizafield.

CRANE, H. A. Savannah grocer, who advertised whisky, flour, cheese, soap, candy, sugar, and other groceries for sale.

CROMLEY, J. Probably connected with Daniel Cromlay, formerly of Charleston, South Carolina, who advertised himself as a "fashionable bootmaker" in Savannah (1853).

CULLINAN, MORTIMER. Merchant of Irish extraction in Darien.

CURTES, DR. Local physician, probably from McIntosh County, since he was once listed as attending Mrs. Thomas Butler King, whose son Mallery Page King married one of the daughters of Hugh Fraser Grant.

DANIELL, DR. Darien physician.

DART, EDGAR CYRUS PARKER. Justice of the inferior court in Glynn County, and attorney.

DAY, WM. F. *See* Monemia Wilson.

DE LAROCHE, [DR.] A. Owner of 1,050 acres on the south side of the Sapelo River, which were advertised for sale in December, 1840.

DE LORME, A. A. Postmaster and merchant in Darien.

DEMERE, JOHN. Planter on St. Simons Island.

DENSLOW & WEBSTER. Savannah merchants, who sold rifles, guns, powder, oil, glass, lead, and agricultural implements.

DENT, GEORGE C. Successful owner of Hofwyl Plantation on the Altamaha River.

DICKSON, JAMES. Possibly connected with firm of Dickson & Hernandez, Savannah confectioners.

DIBBLE, O. J. H. Watch- and clockmaker, Savannah, who in 1839 bought out the stock of D. B. Nichols, Market Square, Savannah.

DONNOLLY, R. B. Operator of general merchandise establishment in Savannah.

DUBIGNON, J. Member of Jekyll Island family. A banker, who served as tax collector of Glynn County in 1845.

DUPREE, [DR.] GEE. Married to Anna Maria Dart, whose family was continuously represented among the public officeholders of Glynn County in the nineteenth century.

DUPREE, LEWIS. Son of Dr. Gee Dupree and Anna Maria Dart.

EASTMAN, M. Landowner in Glynn County, who also sold watches and jewelry in Savannah.

EDEN, THOS. Justice of the Peace and coroner in Glynn County.

ELLIOTT, BISHOP STEPHEN. First Episcopal Bishop of Diocese of Georgia. Consecrated 1840, died 1866.

EVERGLADE, CAPTAIN. Probably refers to the captain of "The Everglade," a coastal steamer for which J. C. Fraser was the agent.

EMMONS, CALVIN. A New York manufacturer of an improved rice-threshing machine, which was introduced in South Carolina in 1831.

FISKE, S. HENRY. Commission merchant, Savannah.

FOLLEN, DR. A. Also spelled Follin. Delegate of Glynn County

Whigs to meet with Whigs of the McIntosh County, 1845.

FORMAN, T. M. *See* Thomas F. Bryan.

FREEBORN, CAPTAIN JAMES. Probably the operator of a coastwise freighter.

FREW, MRS. Dealer in ice cream and confectionery supplies.

GALLOWAY, A. Dyer and renovator, Market Square, Savannah.

GARDNER, [MISS] D. A. Operator of a millinery shop at 159½ Congress Street, Savannah (1859).

GAREY, HETTY. Pastry-cook specialist in Savannah (1849).

GAUDRY, J. B. Savannah merchant, dealer in beef, pork, flour, sugar, and coffee.

GOODBREAD, JOSEPH H. Glynn County tax collector, 1854.

GOULD, HORACE B. St. Simons Island planter, son of James Gould.

GOULD, JAMES. Small planter and contractor on St. Simons Island. Built lighthouse there (1807) and served as its keeper. Was also warden of Christ Church, Fort Frederica.

GOULDING, F. R. Clergyman, physician, and educator, who also wrote stories for young people and tried his hand at inventions. He may have contributed to the invention of the sewing machine. Pastor in Darien after 1853.

GRANT, CHARLES. Younger brother of Hugh Fraser Grant who operated Evelyn Plantation during two periods but was not successful as a planter.

GRANT, [DR.] HARRY ALLEN. Brother of Hugh Fraser Grant, who married considerable wealth in New York City. Financial transactions listed in the documentary section of this study suggest that Harry Allen Grant may have provided Hugh Fraser Grant with considerable sums as loans.

GRANT, H. F., JR. Son of Hugh Fraser Grant.

GRANT, MARY ELIZABETH. Wife of Hugh Fraser Grant.

GRANT, ROBERT. Father of Hugh Fraser Grant and former owner of Elizafield.

GRANT, MRS. SARAH. Mother of Hugh Fraser Grant.

GRIFFIN, G. M. Savannah jeweler.

GROVENSTINE, J. LE. Glynn County planter, who removed to Waynesville as a refugee after the outbreak of war in 1861.

GUYON, WM. H. Also spelled Guion. Agent for carpets and house furnishings.

HABERSHAM, R. & SON. One of the oldest and most famous of the Savannah factorage firms and commission merchants.

HALL, J. M. Brunswick resident, who later in life (1870) ran a saw mill in partnership with Alex Blue of Darien.

HALL, [REV.] WILLIS. Episcopal preacher, who at various times served both St. David's parish, Glynn County, and St. Andrew's at Darien.

HAMILTON & SYMMONS. Savannah dealers in ready-made clothing (1841-45).

HAMMOND, CAPTAIN. Probably the operator of a small coastal freighter serving the Georgia coast.

HARDEE, N. A. & CO. Savannah rice factors.

HARDEN, E. J. Treasurer of Georgia Historical Society.

HAYDEN & GREGG. Silversmiths, Charleston, South Carolina.

HEALD, J. S. Evidently postmaster at some near-by office, probably Darien.

HARRINGTON, G. Operated his own general store in Brunswick, before 1838. In that year he became a member of the firm of Rice, Parker & Co., who were cotton factors and general merchants in Brunswick.

HARRIS, HORACE B. Citizen of Glynn County born on St. Simons Island, who was an attorney in Brunswick.

HAZZARD, [COL.] W. W. Owner of "West Point" Plantation on St. Simons Island; was a brother of Dr. Thomas Hazzard.

HENDRICKSON, G. R. Savannah merchant, who advertised lemon syrup, garden seeds, linseed oil, and paint for sale.

HILLIER, T. A. Proprietor of the City Hotel, Charleston, South Carolina.

HILTON, R. B. & CO. Publishers of the Savannah *Daily Journal and Courier* (1855). Hilton also owned a lumber mill in Belfast.

HOGAN, [MRS.] ELIZABETH HELEN. Sister of Hugh Fraser Grant, who married Dr. Robert Hogan at Elizafield in 1827, and subsequently lived in New York and in other northern regions.

HOGAN & FINLAY. Credit or commercial firm, probably in New York, with which Hugh Fraser Grant's brother-in-law, Robert Hogan, was probably connected. Grant's accounts with this firm in 1844 and 1845 seem to be largely credit and exchange transactions rather than rice or supplies.

HOGAN & MILN. Factors, Charleston, South Carolina.

HOGAN, [DR.] ROBERT. Brother-in-law of Hugh Fraser Grant, who resided in New York. Financial transactions set forth in

Grant's accounts suggest that Robert Hogan either operated or had commercial and credit connections in New York which Grant used on occasion. In 1843 Grant definitely had his Charleston factors, Mitchell and Mure, ship rice to Robert Hogan in New York.

HOLMES, DR. JAMES. Physician and director of bank of Darien, who was elected by the General Association of Bankers as Georgia delegate (1840).

HOOKER, S. A. Savannah merchant, 179 Bay Street, who dealt in gin, coffee, porter, wine, and other provisions. He previously (1837) operated a small merchandizing business in Bethel, near Brunswick.

HOUSTONS, THE MESSIEURS. Glynn County planters, with property located near Buffalo Swamp #2.

HOWARD, [DR.] J. G. Physician, who probably practiced in Savannah.

HUDNALL, H. W. Director of Bank of Darien.

HUGER, THOMAS PINCKNEY. Successful Glynn County planter and distinguished citizen of the state. At one time he purchased Evelyn, a portion of Elizafield Plantation.

INGRAHAM & WEBB. Factors and real estate dealers, Charleston, South Carolina.

JEWETT, SIMEON B. Secretary of Georgia Lumber Company, Lumber City; served as the agent for that company in Darien, and presided over a lumber yard there.

JOHNSTON, JAMES P. Partner in Savannah firm of Scranton and Johnston, who dealt in brandy, gin, etc.

JOHNSTON, J. R. Sometime Glynn County planter, who advertised his plantation for sale in the 1840's, complete with a Sand Hills summer home in Wayne County.

JOHNSTON, OTIS. Savannah factor and merchant, who shipped rice and lumber to West Indies (1838), and also sold shoes for Negroes.

JONES, JOHN L. Possibly the Savannah gunsmith, John T. Jones (1849).

KENDRICK, [MISS] F. Successor to Mrs. Beaulard, Savannah dealer in ladies millinery.

KING, CAPTAIN A. Master of steamer "Matthews," carrying coastwise freight from Savannah to the south.

KING, MALLERY PAGE. Son of T. B. King, a neighboring planter — later to become a son-in-law of Hugh Fraser Grant.

KOLLOCK, [DR.] P. M. Professor of obstetrics and diseases of women and children at Savannah Medical College.

LACKLISON, R. & J. Engineers, contractors, and dealers in heavy machinery, Darien.

LAMB, JOHN. Tax collector of Glynn County.

LAW & BARTOW. Probably commissioners for the Brunswick Canal. This undertaking was routed through Elizafield Plantation, and Hugh Fraser Grant's labor force occasionally was employed in the construction of the canal.

LAWRENCE, JOHN. Planter on St. Simons Island.

LEFFLER, DR. A. Dentist with offices in Savannah in 1859.

LEGARE, O HEAR & CO. Factors and commission merchants, probably in Charleston, South Carolina.

LOCKE & DAVIS. Publishers of the Savannah *Daily Republican.*

LONG, THOMAS TELFAIR. Savannah attorney, who was also a landholder in Glynn County.

LOWRIE ESTATE. *See* S. W. Taylor.

LUCE, CAPTAIN. Probably operator of small freighter serving the Georgia coast.

MACALLISTER, M. H. Savannah attorney.

MCCLESKY & NORTON. Hardware dealers, 148 Congress Street, Savannah (1849).

MCKINLAY, P. Small planter on near-by Sapelo Island.

MABRY, WOODFORD. Attorney; Collector of the Port at Brunswick; later at Darien.

MALLERY, JOHN. Formerly member of Savannah tailoring firm of Price and Mallery, 1837; established his own business in 1839.

MARSHALL & AIKEN. Dealers in table linens and silk umbrellas, Savannah.

MATTHIESSEN, WILLIAM. *See* Poerier and Matthiesen.

MAY, W. H. & CO. Operators of leather shop in Young's Building, Savannah, who sold saddles, bridles, harnesses, and carriage trimmings.

MILLER, A. N. Owner of Eagle Steam Saw Mill in Savannah, who also operated a foundry at Eastern Wharf in that city.

MINIS, A. Savannah merchant, who advertised dry goods, axes, and Spanish seegars for sale.

MITCHELL & COLLINS. Supply house proprietors and agents for Macon Steamboat Line in Darien.

MITCHELL & MURE. Factors, Charleston, South Carolina.

MITCHEL & PEASE. Grocers and supply house, probably in Darien.

MOORE, A. K. Operator of Savannah shop, who specialized in bonnets, lace, sheetings, and shirtings.

MOORE, JAMES W. Tax collector, and proprietor of Oglethorpe House in Brunswick.

MORGAN, JOHN J. Overseer of Elizafield 1848-59. He married Lucy Bills in Glynn County (1844).

MORRELL, J. W. Piano dealer, probably in Savannah.

MOYLAN, EDWARD B. Evidently a resident of Glynn County, since he was listed as a private in the "Brunswick Riflemen" in 1861.

MUMFORD & TISON. Merchants, whose establishment was located at Waynesville. This region was famous as a resort and watering place.

MURE, R. Probably a partner in the factorage house of Mitchell and Mure, Charleston, South Carolina.

MYERS, JAMES. Surveyor of Glynn County.

MYERS, W. H. Evidently a local carriage maker.

NEVITT, LATHROP & ROGERS. Savannah dry-goods merchants, who dealt especially in clothes for Negroes.

NICHOLS, D. B. Proprietor of Savannah establishment, located at the corner of Bryan and Whitaker streets. His advertisements described him as a watchmaker and jeweler, specializing in canes, silver buckles, silver and plated ware, and rings.

NICHOLS, G. S. Savannah clothier, with store at 114 Bryan Street, who advertised ready-made clothing and hats for sale.

OATES, GEORGE. Evidently an agent for the Audubon bird books. He also took subscriptions for the Charleston *Courier*.

ODEN, THOMAS. Possibly a member of the Savannah firm of druggists, Turner and Oden (1849).

Padelford & Co. Also known as Padelford and Fay. Commission merchants and shipping agents, with offices at 104-106 Bay Street, Savannah.

Palmer, Sam'l. Stockholder in the Bank of Darien; executor of estate of W. A. Dunham; and Chairman of Whig Party, McIntosh County, in 1845.

Parkhurst & Adams. Savannah rice merchants.

Parmly, J., Jr. Savannah dentist, a partner in Parmly and Pancoast, 100 Broughton Street.

Pease, T. P. Producer and dealer in "naval stores," who operated a plantation in Darien known as "The Thickets."

Pease & Tarbell. Possibly a Darien firm which distilled both turpentine and spirits.

Pincheon, Stotesbury & Co. Savannah dealers in carpets, oil cloth, sheeting, and ticking. Predecessor firm was Bates and Stotesbury.

Piles, J. D. Deputy sheriff of Glynn County (*1844*); also postmaster in 1850.

Plant, Increase Cook. Cashier of Bank of Brunswick after November 1, 1838.

Poerier & Matthiesen. Possibly a predecessor to the Savannah firm of commission merchants known as Gourdin and Matthison.

Ponce, Antonio. Formerly from St. Augustine, Florida; settled in Savannah where, in 1849, he was manufacturing and selling "seegars."

Postell (John). Deputy Collector of Port of Savannah (1853).

Powell, M. & Co. Ice dealers, with headquarters on South Broad Street, Savannah.

Prentice & Way, John M. Savannah dealers in ship chandlery, cordage, twine, brooms, and buckets (1844).

Price, M. A. Small cattle dealer and livestock raiser, who operated at Sand Hills, Glynn County, the site of the Grant summer home.

Pritchard, R. S. Probably refers to Richard Pritchard, a planter in near-by Cowpens Swamp, Glynn County.

Putmant [Putnam], C. E. Planter or slave dealer from whom J. H. Couper purchased several slaves in 1846.

Ravinel Brother & Co. of Charleston. Famous Charleston producers and dealers in rice.

REED, ELIAS. Coastwise freighter, which called frequently at Elizafield.

REYNOLDS, G. N. & SON. Probably refers to a Savannah tailoring firm.

RICE, PARKER & CO. *See* G. Harrington.

ROBERTS, WILLIAM D. Prominent Whig in Glynn County.

ROBERTSON & BLACKLOCK & CO. Charleston, South Carolina, factors with Alex Robertson, John Blacklock, and Edward N. Thurston as partners.

ROBERTSON & SMITH. Probably Charleston, South Carolina, agents or commercial supply houses connected with the factorage house of Robertson and Thurston.

ROBERTSON & THURSTON. Charleston, South Carolina, factors — successors to Robertson, Blacklock & Co. in which E. N. Thurston was a partner.

RODGERS, J. S. Dealer in dry goods, Savannah (1849).

ROGERS & LADSON. Probably a Savannah dry goods house resulting from the union of J. S. Rogers and the firm of Rokenbaugh and Ladson.

ROKENBAUGH, I. & S. H. Engineers, owners, and operators of Lower Bluff Mill, Darien. May also have sold and repaired milling machinery.

ROKENBAUGH, J. & SON. Probably a successor to I. & S. H. Rokenbaugh.

ROKENBAUGH & LADSON. Savannah dry goods dealers (1855).

ROYAL, [DR.] H. J. Savannah dentist, who specialized in sets of teeth.

SCHLEY, GEORGE. Postmaster at Savannah in 1839, and possibly in subsequent years. Stockholder in central Georgia railroad.

SCRANTON, ALEX. Clerk of Superior Court, Glynn County, and Brunswick merchant.

SHINE, D. Y. Probably a partner in the Darien lumbering firm of Collins & Shine.

SILBER, [MRS.] F. A dressmaker, with headquarters at 25 Whitacker Street, Savannah, (1849).

SKINNER, T. G. Overseer of Elizafield Plantation in 1842; discharged on August 29, 1842.

SMITH, WM. H. & CO. Savannah commission merchants (1859).

SNOW, I. Postmaster in Darien.

SOLOMANS, A. A. Savannah druggist.

SOLOMONS, M. J. & Co. Savannah grocers, with a store at 151 Congress Street, who advertised corn starch, maize, rice flour, syrups, jellies, cocoa seed, brooms, and baskets for sale.

SOUTHERLAND, D. W. McIntosh County planter.

SPAULDING, CHARLES. Son of Thomas Spaulding, a distinguished planter of Sapelo Island.

SPICER, S. Engineer at Cathead Mill, Darien.

STEVENS, CAPTAIN CHARLES. An intriguing character of Danish ancestry who built a boat in England and sailed it to the Georgia coast, where he settled on St. Simons Island. He built his home on the ruins of historic Fort Fredrica and made a living by hauling plantation freight up and down the Georgia coast in his own vessel.

STORER, S. M. Iron and metal dealer, Savannah.

STOTESBERY, HENRY H. Savannah merchant, who sold diapers, doilies, table cloths, muslins, thread, and satinets.

STURTEVANT, MESS. G. Savannah grocers (1849).

STURTEVANT, J. M. Savannah clothing dealer.

SULLIVAN, [DR.] JAMES S. Local physician.

SYLVESTER, E. W. Possibly a member of the Savannah tailoring firm of Sylvester and Back (1849).

TALBOTT, B. Elizafield overseer in 1844-46. Died of "absess of the lungs" October 13, 1846.

TAYLOR, SILAS W. Married Margaret Lowrie; administered Lowrie estate; also served as overseer of the Butler plantations on St. Simons Island known as Hampton or Butler Point.

TEFT, I. Cashier of the State Bank of Georgia, Savannah.

THOMAS, W. B. Savannah real-estate agent and merchant.

THOWBURN & Co. Evidently tree dealers, probably fruit trees.

TROUP, DR. DANIEL HEYWARD BRAILSFORD. Son-in-law of Hugh Fraser Grant, married to Frances Emelia Grant.

TUNNO, J. CHAMPNEY. Neighboring planter, who purchased Champney's Island from H. F. Grant.

TUNNO, W. M. Cotton and rice factor, 97 Bay Street, Savannah; also had offices at North Commercial Wharf in Charleston, South Carolina.

TURNER, T. M. & J. M. Listed as operating a drug store in Monument Square, Savannah, in 1837; advertised lemon syrup, castile soap, and cures for various ailments.

TURNER & JOHNSTON. Operators of a steam sawmill in Darien — dealers in lumber.

VERSTELLE, LUFBURROW, & BUTLER. Dealers in shoes for Negroes and plantation supplies in Savannah (1849).

WALL, LAURENCE W. Savannah resident of undetermined occupation. His name appeared on a voting list of that city in 1853.

WALSH, G. B. Agent for McClesky and Norton, Savannah hardware dealers.

WARNER, W. Savannah carriage maker with shop on West Broad Street.

WALSH, ROBERT & CO. Commission merchants and auctioneers, Brunswick.

WEED, N. B. & H. Dealers in tinplate and hardware in Savannah.

WENDELL, C. Evidently a newspaper agent, who sold a subscription to the Washington *Union* to Hugh Fraser Grant in 1859.

WHITHERS, MORRIS. Evidently a local mason.

WIGGINS, CAPT. Operator of steamboats carrying freight on the Savannah River and along the Georgia coast.

WILLMOTT, T. T. Jeweler and professor of daguerreotype, with offices at 1 Market Square, Savannah.

WILSON, MONEMIA. Probably a neighbor whose property was administered by Hugh Fraser Grant. On several occasions he drew drafts for her in favor of Wm. F. Day.

WILTBERGHER, PETER. Later known under firm name of W. H. Wiltberger & Co., Savannah ice dealers.

WINTON, BURR. Carpenter, housebuilder, and contractor of Brunswick.

WOOD, CLAGHORN & CO. Also listed as Claghorn Wood & Co., Savannah grocers and dealers in ship chandlery.

WRIGHT, MOSES, CHRISTOPHER BURNETT. Glynn County planter, whose property was located across from Hopeton Plantation, on the north bank of the South Branch of the Altamaha River.

YONGE, P. R. & SONS. Darien and Brunswick agents for Ocamulgee Steamboat Co., with main offices in Darien.

# Notes on Sources

The materials for this study were accumulated over the years since 1938. The fortuitous personal acquisition at that time of the basic document, the Elizafield Journal and Account Book of Hugh Fraser Grant, served as the initial stimulus to the project. From that point the trail led through the Library of Congress and the library of the United States Department of Agriculture to various collections of records, manuscripts, newspapers, periodicals, and learned journals in the Carolinas and Georgia. An extended visit to the Altamaha-St. Simons Island-Brunswick area in Georgia turned up valuable data and promising leads. As a result, considerable understanding of Elizafield, its proprietor, and both the techniques and significance of the ante-bellum rice-growing industry in Georgia was acquired and pieced together. The following account of sources is restricted to the more useful materials consulted and omits mention of numerous items which helped to supply a "frame of reference" for the study. The latter were concerned largely with background and incidental intelligence and helped to provide a basis for understanding ante-bellum planter capitalism and the fabric of society in the coastal areas of the South.

A hurried glance at footnote citations will reveal that the James Hamilton Couper records of Hopeton Plantation on the Altamaha River and those of both Charles and Louis Manigault concerning Gowrie Plantation on an island in the Savannah River (together with the Elizafield Journal and Account Book) provided the manuscript foundation for this study. The Couper and Manigault records are preserved in the Southern Historical Collection in the University of North Carolina Library, at Chapel Hill, North Carolina. A portion of the Louis Manigault correspondence, however, is the property of the manuscripts division of the Duke University Library, at Durham, North Carolina. Both of these depositories possess numerous other manuscripts which were invaluable for the project. For example, the manuscript division at the Duke University Library also contains the official records of the Port of Savannah for the years under consideration. Also, in this same depository are located the Godfrey Barnesley papers (1840-56), which supplied considerable insight into the operations of a Savannah rice and cotton merchant whose business activities covered coastal and interior Georgia as well as Mobile and New Orleans. These papers contain an extensive file of the weekly "Prices Current" quotations published by Savannah newspapers. The prices and volume of the flow of the rice trade through that port were gathered from that source for this book.

The Southern Historical Collection, which bids fair to be the greatest single depository of manuscript materials on the antebellum South, made possible the consultation of the Allston-Pringle-Hill papers dealing with South Carolina rice culture. The records of George J. Kollock, Robert Mackey, and William Henry Stiles, all Georgia coastal rice planters, were also examined there. The final large block of manuscripts studied at Chapel Hill was the C. F. Mills papers which included the sales, invoice books, and letter books of a Savannah tycoon who dealt in banking, shipping, and both rice and cotton. These revealed a fascinating picture of a free enterprise entrepreneur shifting funds, merchandise, and crops in the finest Yankee tradition.

The DeRenne papers at the University of Georgia Library at Athens, Georgia, provided a few items, while the Georgia State Department of Archives and History at Atlanta revealed considerable personal and military data on the Hugh Fraser Grant family. The will of Hugh Fraser Grant, which is filed in Chatham County Court House in Savannah, and the property records, preserved in the Glynn County Court House in Brunswick, presented the story of property inheritance and transfers in the plantation area of the Altamaha River region, including those of Elizafield. The special collection on the history of South Carolina agriculture at Clemson Agricultural College, Clemson, South Carolina, was also perused. Data contained in the so-called "Butler Book," which dealt with the affairs of Butler Plantation on the Altamaha River, were made available through the kindness of Mrs. Margaret Davis Cate of Brunswick and Sea Island, Georgia.

The personal papers and notes of the late Professor Ulrich B. Phillips were consulted at Yale University Library. They were not especially valuable for this study since the information on rice culture in them was quite limited. His penciled excerpts from the Manigault papers, which were published in A Documentary History of American Industrial Society (Cleveland, 1910), composed the bulk of the notations on rice. However, a trip to the manuscript division of the Harvard Business School Library was quite profitable, since it turned up three splendid manuscript collections. These were the W. W. Gordon & Co. papers of 500 volumes, which set forth the record of the operations of a Savannah factorage and commission house for the years 1856-1916; numerous volumes of the Tudor family, famous ice dealers who shipped to Southern and West Indian ports; and finally, four volumes of the business records of Larkin and Stackpole (1852-79), Boston importers, exporters, and general merchants who purchased and distributed considerable quantities of Savannah rice.

Newspapers were important sources for various phases of this study, especially for the identification of the persons and firms mentioned by Hugh Fraser Grant in the Elizafield Journal. The Savannah *Daily Georgian* (1840-52), the Savannah *Republican* (1837-54), and the Savannah *Daily Journal and Courier* (1855), were examined in the files of the Georgia Historical Society in Savannah. Savannah City *Directories* for the years 1849, 1859, and 1871 also were checked at the Society's headquarters "Hodgson Hall." In addition, the Brunswick *Advocate* for the year 1837 was made available through the courtesy of Mrs. Margaret Davis Cate of Brunswick and Sea Island, Georgia.

The following bibliographies and government publications were helpful: E. E. Edwards, "A Bibliography of the History of Agriculture in the United States," U.S. Department of Agriculture, Miscellaneous Publication 84 (Washington, 1930); E. E. Edwards, "History of Rice Production in the United States; a Comprehensive List of Annotated References" (MS, U.S. Department of Agriculture, Bureau of Agricultural Economics, Washington, D.C., May 15, 1931, 10 pp. typewritten); E. E. Edwards, "Southern Ante Bellum Agricultural Periodicals in Library of Congress and Department of Agriculture Library" (MS, U.S. Department of Agriculture, Bureau of Agricultural Economics, Washington, D.C., July 22, 1941, 3 pp. typewritten); A. S. Salley, "Bibliography of the Rice Industry in South Carolina," in David Doar, Rice and Rice Planting in the South Carolina Low Country (Charleston, 1936), pp. 54-68; U.S. Department of Agriculture Yearbook (Washington, D.C., 1922, pp.

512-25; Amory Austin, Rice: Its Cultivation, Production, and Distribution in the United States and Foreign Countries (U.S. Department of Agriculture Report Number 6, Washington, D.C., 1893); and House Document 122, 24th Congress, second session (Washington, D.C., December 31, 1836), which is a report on the "Brunswick Canal and Railroad."

Likewise, considerable understanding was derived from a variety of standard reference works and the Proceedings of several learned societies, including: Dictionary of American Biography (20 vols. and index; New York, 1928-37); W. T. Hutchinson, ed., The Marcus W. Jernegan Essays in American Historiography (Chicago, 1937); William S. Irvine, Brunswick and Glynn County, Georgia (Brunswick, 1902); Adiel Sherwood, A Gazetteer of the State of Georgia (Washington, D.C., 1837); George White, Statistics of the State of Georgia (Savannah, 1849); C. S. Wylly, Annals and Statistics of Glynn County, Georgia (Brunswick, 1897); R. F. W. Allston, "Memoir on the Introduction and Cultivation of Rice," Proceedings of the State Agricultural Society of South Carolina (Charleston, 1845), pp. 34-64; and Ulrich B. Phillips, "On the Economics of Slavery, 1815-60," Annual Report of American Historical Association (1912), pp. 150-51, and by the same author, "The Plantation Product of Men," Proceedings of Georgia Historical Association (1918), pp. 12-15.

It would be somewhat unprofitable and also quite difficult to list all the secondary works and printed documents which have contributed data, information, and interpretations to this undertaking. Among the more important volumes were Louis M. Hacker, The Triumph of American Capitalism (New York, 1940), one of whose main theses as set forth in pp. 280-331 of his essay, is illustrated by this study; and three basic studies by Ulrich B. Phillips, American Negro Slavery (New York, 1918), Life and Labor in the Old South (Boston, 1929), and Plantation and Frontier (A Documentary History of American Industrial Society, Vols. I-II; Cleveland, 1910). Closely rivaling these in significance and competence are J. H. Easterby, ed., The South Carolina Rice Plantation, as Revealed in the Papers of Robert F. W. Allston (Chicago, 1945); L. C. Gray, History of Agriculture in the Southern United States to 1860 (Washington, 1933); Francis B. Simkins, The South, Old and New, a History, 1820-1947 (New York, 1947); and Clara Mildred Thompson, Reconstruction in Georgia, Economic, Social, Political, 1865-1872 (New York, 1915).

Other works which proved to be of value were James C. Bonner, "Agricultural Adjustment in Ante-Bellum Georgia," in J. C. Bonner and Lucien E. Roberts, eds., Studies in Georgia History and Government (Athens, 1940) pp. 123-54; Margaret Davis Cate, Our Todays and Yesterdays, a Story of Brunswick and the Coastal Islands (Brunswick, 1926 and 1930); E. B. Copeland, Rice (London, 1924); Loraine M. Cooney, comp., and Hattie C. Rainwater, ed., Garden History of Georgia, 1733-1933 (Atlanta, 1933); E. Merton Coulter, ed., Georgia's Disputed Ruins (Chapel Hill, 1937), and A Short History of Georgia (Chapel Hill, 1933); J. D. B. DeBow, Industrial Resources of the South and West (New Orleans, 1852); Ralph B. Flanders, Plantation Slavery in Georgia (Chapel Hill, 1933); William Harden, History of Savannah and South Georgia (Chicago, 1913); Duncan C. Heyward, Seed from Madagascar (Chapel Hill, 1937); Herbert A. Kellar, ed., Solon Robinson, Pioneer and Agriculturist (2 vols.; Indianapolis, 1936); Frances Anne Kemble, Journal of a Residence on a Georgia Plantation, 1838-39 (New York, 1863); Caroline Couper Lovell, The Golden Isles of Georgia (Boston, 1932); Patrick H. Mell, "Rice Planting in the Agricultural Development of the South," in J. C. Ballagh, ed., The South in the Building of the Nation (Richmond, 1910), V, 169-77; and Frederic L. Olmsted, A Journey in the Seaboard Slave States (New York, 1859).

The nature of this study was such that considerable reliance had to be placed on articles in historical journals and agricultural periodicals. The latter, especially, provided excellent source material, since many of their published items were prepared by or directed towards active rice planters. As would be expected, the *Georgia Historical Quarterly* (Savannah, 1917–) contained many valuable articles concerned with the geography, agriculture, and industry of Savannah and the rice coast. Among the more noteworthy were William M. Brewer, "Some Effects of the Plantation System upon the Ante-Bellum South," XI (September, 1927), 250-73; R. P. Brooks, ed., "Letters of James Hamilton Couper to His Wife," XIV (June, 1930), 150-72; Ralph B. Flanders, "Planters' Problems in Ante-Bellum Georgia," XIV (March, 1930), 17-40; Julia E. Ham, "Old Canoochee-Ogeechee Chronicles," XV (December, 1931), 346-59, XVI

(March, 1932), 47-55, XVI (June, 1932), 146-50, XVI (September, 1932), 232-39, and XVI (December, 1932), 298-31; Charles S. H. Hardee, "Recollections of Old Savannah," XII (June, 1928), 158-76, XII (September, 1928), 255-87, and XII (December, 1928), 353-88; Roland M. Harper, "Development of Agriculture in Lower Georgia from 1850 to 1880," VI (June, 1922), 97-121, "Development of Agriculture in Upper Georgia from 1850 to 1880," VI (March, 1922), 3-27, and "Some Savannah Vital Statistics of a Century Ago," XV (September, 1931), 252-71; Mildred E. Lombard, "Contemporary Opinion of Mrs. Kemble's Journal of a Residence on a Georgia Plantation," XIV (December, 1930), 335-43; Charles H. Olmsted, "Savannah in the '40s," I (September, 1917), 243-52; David M. Potter, Jr., "The Rise of the Plantation System in Georgia," XVI (June, 1932), 114-35; and a series of studies of six Savannah area plantations by the Writers Project of the Works Progress Administration, which were published in each of the numbers of Volumes XXIII and XXIV (1939 and 1940) of the *Quarterly*.

*The Southern Agriculturist and Register of Rural Affairs*, 1st series (Charleston, 1828-39 and 1840), contains many fine articles, letters to the editor, and editorials on the general subject of rice culture in the Carolinas. Some of the Georgia planters, such as James Hamilton Couper of Hopeton Plantation, subscribed to this publication and made careful notes of the information and experienced advice contained in the periodical. A short but illustrative sampling of the wealth of such excellent data and instructions may be found in Anon., "Calculation of Profit on a Rice Mill," II, 444-47; Anon., "The Winter Flowing of Rice Lands," I, 531-34; City Rustic, "On the Pounding of Rice," I, 351-52; James C. Darby, "On the Embanking and Preparation of Marsh Land, for the Cultivation of Rice," II, 23-28, and "On Planting and Managing a Rice-Crop," II, 247-54; Paul Hamilton, "Directions for the Water Culture of Rice," IV, 10-12; Wm. B. M——— and Jordan Myrick, "On the Culture of Rice," IV, 288-92; Hugh Rose, "On Open Rice-Planting," II, 370-71; and William Washington and Hugh Rose, "Queries and Answers on the Culture of Rice," I, 166-70, 215-23, and 268-70.

The new series of this excellent journal was launched in 1841 under the title of *Southern Agriculturist and Horticulturist* and continued publication through 1846. This series followed the same general pattern as the earlier issues and was under the supervision of the same editor (J. D. Legare) for at least a portion of the period. The articles on rice, however, had a tendency to run much longer and also to be of considerably more significance than those in the first series. Several reports, including some by Governor R. F. W. Allston to the Agricultural Society of South Carolina, were printed in this journal during these years. Some of the more important items were Robert F. W. Allston, "Report of the Committee on Cultivation of Rice to the Agricultural Society of South Carolina," III (September, 1843), 241-46; Samuel A. Cartwright, "Cultivation of Rice," III (September, 1843), 333-37; J. D. Legare, "Synopsis of the Culture of Rice—on Black River," I (February, 1841), 80-81; Thomas Pinckney, "On the Use of Fascines in Breaks or Creeks," I (July, 1841), 346-52; Report of Committee of Agricultural Society of South Carolina on "Expenses of Preparing Rice for Market," III (December, 1843), 456-58; and J. Lawrence Smith, "The Effect of Drought Upon the Rice Lands," V (November, 1845), 425-26.

The enterprising editor of *DeBow's Review* (New Orleans) deemed it desirable to republish several of the longer studies of Governor R. F. W. Allston on the status of rice-growing and other seacoast crops in the South in I (April, 1846), 320-56; IV (December, 1847), 502-11; XVI (June, 1854), 589-615. The last mentioned was one of the more famous of Allston's essays and was partially reprinted in Ulrich B. Phillips, Plantation and Frontier (Cleveland, 1910), I, 259-65.

*Agricultural History* (Washington, 1927—), the publication of the Agricultural History Society, is the sole American learned journal attempting to set forth the historical development of American agriculture in particular and throughout the world in general. Possibly because of the broad scope of its extended coverage rice, rice plantations, and the rice-growing industry along the South Atlantic coastal region of the United States are not represented by many articles. Several, however, do throw some light on the conditions, practices, and problems in the growing of rice in that area before 1860, including L. C. Gray, "Economic Efficiency and Competitive Advantages of Slavery under the Plantation System," IV (April, 1930), 32-41; Albert V. House, Jr., "The Management of a Rice Plantation in Georgia 1834-1861, as Revealed in the Journal of Hugh Fraser Grant," XIII (October, 1939), 208-17; Albert V. House, Jr., ed., "Charles

Manigault's Essay on the Open Planting of Rice," XVI (October, 1942), 184-93; Ulrich B. Phillips, "The Historic Civilization of the South," XII (April, 1938), 142-50; Willard Range, "The Agricultural Revolution in Royal Georgia," XXI (October, 1947), 250-55; Robert W. Smith, "Was Slavery Unprofitable in the Ante-Bellum South?" XX (January, 1946), 62-64; and Edgar T. Thompson, "The Climactic Theory of the Plantation," XV (January, 1941), 49-60.

*The Journal of Southern History* (Lexington, Kentucky, 1935–) also included a few informative items, including J. H. Easterby, "The South Carolina Rice Factor as Revealed in the Papers of Robert F. W. Allston," VII (May, 1941), 160-72; Albert V. House, Jr., ed., "Deterioration of a Georgia Rice Plantation during Four Years of Civil War," IX (February, 1943), 98-113; R. E. Russell, "The General Effects of Slavery upon Southern Economic Progress," IV (February, 1938), 34-54; and J. Carlyle Sitterson, "Financing and Marketing the Sugar Crop of the Old South," X (May, 1944), 188-99. The early files of the *American Historical Review* (Washington, 1895–) printed two very stimulating articles by Alfred H. Stone entitled, "Some Problems in Southern History," XIII (July, 1908), 779-97, and "The Cotton Factorage System of the Southern States," XX (April, 1915), 557-65. In this same journal there also appeared two of the most distinguished and relevant essays of Ulrich B. Phillips, "Plantations with Slave Labor and Free," XXX (July, 1925), 738-53, which was reprinted in *Agricultural History*, XII (January, 1938), 77-95, and "The Central Theme of Southern History," XXXIV (October, 1928), 30-43. Finally, reference should be made to Dorothy Seay Magoffin, "A Georgia Planter and His Plantations 1837-1861," *North Carolina Historical Review*, XV (October, 1938), 354-77; Arthur H. Cole, "The American Rice-Growing Industry," *Quarterly Journal of Economics*, XLI (August, 1927), 595-643; and Ulrich B. Phillips, "The Economics of the Plantation," *South Atlantic Quarterly*, II (July, 1903), 231-36.

# INDEX

ALTAMAHA RICE FIELDS
Elizafield, Evelyn and Grantly Plantations
ALTAMAHA RIVER
HEAVILY WOODED
Old Soldier Creek
GAMBERS ISLAND
Minnow Creek
SOUTH BRANCH
Couper River
Hammersmith Creek
Honeygall Creek
WOODED